Food & Wine
MAGAZINE'S
FAVORITE DESSERTS

Food & Wine
MAGAZINE'S
FAVORITE DESSERTS

MORE THAN 150 DELECTABLE RECIPES FROM AMERICA'S FASTEST-GROWING FOOD MAGAZINE

American Express Publishing Corporation
New York

FOOD & WINE MAGAZINE
EDITOR IN CHIEF: Dana Cowin
FOOD EDITOR: Tina Ujlaki
CREATIVE DIRECTOR: Stephen Scoble

FOOD & WINE BOOKS
EDITOR IN CHIEF: Judith Hill
ART DIRECTOR: Nina Scerbo
MANAGING EDITOR: Terri Mauro
EDITORIAL ASSISTANT: Evette Manners
COPY EDITOR: Barbara A. Mateer
ART ASSISTANT: Leslie Andersen
PRODUCTION MANAGER: Yvette Williams-Braxton

Vice President, Consumer Marketing: Mark V. Stanich
Vice President, Books and Information Services: John Stoops
Marketing Director: Tom Reynolds
Operations Manager: Doreen Camardi
Business Manager: Joanne Ragazzo

PACKAGED BY COLEEN O'SHEA LITERARY ENTERPRISES
DESIGNED BY: Barbara Cohen Aronica
EDITED BY: Stephanie Lyness
COPYEDITED BY: Stacy Kamisar

Photo credits
(FRONT COVER PHOTO) Michael McLaughlin
(BACK COVER PHOTOS) Elizabeth Watt, Chocolate Zabiglione Trifle; Mark Thomas, Peach Pouch Pie with Berries;
Carin and David Riley, Lemon Flans; Bill Bettencourt, Almond and Strawberry Tart; Ellen Silverman, PB & Js;
Alan Richardson, Mom's Chocolate Cake.

Recipes pictured on cover and interior
(FRONT) Ginger Star Shortcakes with Summer Berries (recipe page 201)
(BACK) Top left: Chocolate Zabiglione Trifle (recipe page 277); Top center: Peach Pouch Pie with Berries (recipe page 183);
Middle left: Lemon Flans (recipe page 231); Middle center: Almond Strawberry Tart (recipe page 141);
Bottom left: PB & Js (recipe page 126); Bottom right: Mom's Chocolate Cake (recipe page 13);
(RECIPE PICTURED ON PAGE 2) Peach Pouch Pie with Berries (recipe page 183)

AMERICAN EXPRESS PUBLISHING CORPORATION
©1998 American Express Publishing Corporation

LIBRARY OF CONGRESS CATALOGING-IN-PUBLICATION DATA
Food & wine's favorite desserts: more that 150 recipes from America's fastest-growing food magazine.
p.   cm.
Includes index.
ISBN 0-916103-50-1
1. Desserts   I. Food & wine (New York, N.Y.)
TX773.F64   1998
841.8'6—dc21   98-30900
CIP

Published by American Express Publishing Corporation
1120 Avenue of the Americas, New York, New York 10036

Manufactured in the United States of America

CONTENTS

Fondue au Chocolat, recipe page 285

Heath Bar Brownies and Walnut Passion, recipes pages 83 and 85

INTRODUCTION

It takes a lot to get either of us away from our desks. The piles of phone messages, the unread manuscripts, and the ever-alluring e-mail all conspire to keep us in our chairs.

But one thing makes both of us get up and go: The scent of a pie, a cake, or cookies fresh from the oven. Such seductive smells are guaranteed to draw us to the FOOD & WINE test kitchen, which is just a waft away.

Our desserts of the past several years, collected in this special volume, have been an olfactory delight—and, of course, a gustatory one too. From the selection of recipes here, you'll see that we are omnivores when it comes to sweets. The collection includes the most delicious incarnation of every kind of dessert imaginable: Homey pies and haute tarts, light nothings and decadent confections, five-minute fixes and five-hour projects, seasonal indulgences and all-weather treats.

This volume comprises a virtual greatest-hits collection from some of the best-known dessert authorities (Maida Heatter, Alice Medrich) and restaurant pastry chefs (Lindsey Shere of Chez Panisse in California, Jacques Torres of Le Cirque 2000 in New York). Satisfaction is guaranteed for every sort of sweet tooth and every level of expertise.

You can be sure that when the aroma of any of these desserts fills your house, folks will come running—and will walk away happy.

Dana Cowin

Editor in Chief
FOOD & WINE Magazine

Judith Hill

Editor in Chief
FOOD & WINE Books

Pears Poached in White Wine with Star Anise, recipe page 243

Food & Wine

MAGAZINE'S

FAVORITE DESSERTS

chapter 1
CAKES

Mom's Chocolate Cake

MOM'S CHOCOLATE CAKE

This is a real old-fashioned American chocolate layer cake. It's very moist, very chocolatey, a snap to make, and best baked the day before serving. FOOD & WINE test kitchen associate director Marcia Kiesel acquired the recipe from her friend, Joyce Cole, who got it from her mother.

MAKES ONE 8-INCH CAKE

CHOCOLATE CAKE:

2 cups flour

2 teaspoons baking powder

2 teaspoons baking soda

1 teaspoon salt

2 cups sugar

2 cups water

4 ounces unsweetened chocolate

6 tablespoons unsalted butter

1 teaspoon vanilla extract

2 eggs, lightly beaten

CHOCOLATE FROSTING:

1⅓ cups heavy cream

1½ cups sugar

6 ounces unsweetened chocolate

¼ pound plus 2 tablespoons unsalted butter

1½ teaspoons vanilla extract

Pinch salt

1. Heat the oven to 350°. For the cake, butter and flour two 8-by-1½-inch round cake pans. Cover the bottoms with waxed paper.

2. In a medium bowl, sift together the flour, baking powder, baking soda, and salt; set aside.

3. In a medium saucepan, combine the sugar with the water. Bring to a boil over high heat. Stir until the sugar dissolves and pour into a large bowl. Add the chocolate and butter and let sit, stirring occasionally, until melted and slightly cooled. Stir in the vanilla.

4. Beat the eggs into the chocolate mixture with an electric mixer at medium speed until combined. Add all of the dry ingredients at once and beat at medium speed until smooth.

5. Pour the batter into the prepared pans and bake until a toothpick stuck in the center comes out clean, about 25 minutes. Cool the cakes in their pans for about 25 minutes, then invert onto a rack to cool completely. ➤

6. For the frosting, in a medium saucepan, bring the cream and sugar to a boil over moderately high heat. Reduce the heat to low and simmer, stirring occasionally, until the liquid reduces slightly, about 6 minutes.

7. Pour the mixture into a medium bowl and add the chocolate, butter, vanilla, and salt. Let stand, stirring occasionally, until the chocolate and butter are melted.

8. Set the bowl in a larger bowl of ice water. Using a hand-held electric mixer, beat the frosting on medium speed, scraping the sides occasionally with a rubber spatula, until thick and glossy, about 5 minutes.

9. Set one cake, right-side up, on a serving platter. Using a metal spatula, spread one-third of the chocolate frosting evenly over the cake. Top with the second cake and frost the top and sides with the remaining frosting.

—Marcia Kiesel

FIFTEEN MINUTE MAGIC

In this rich cake, a flavorful blend of amaretti cookies and blanched almonds replaces the usual flour. Made in a food processor, the batter takes no more than fifteen minutes to put together. Serve the cake with whipped cream or vanilla ice cream and a Tawny Porto, such as the Sandeman 20 Year Old, or an Italian vin santo, such as the 1989 Badia a Coltibuono.

MAKES ONE 8-INCH CAKE

- 3 ounces bittersweet chocolate, chopped
- 1 ounce unsweetened chocolate, chopped
- 6 large double amaretti cookies
- ¾ cup blanched, slivered almonds
- ¼ pound unsalted butter
- ½ cup granulated sugar
- 3 large eggs, at room temperature
- 1 teaspoon each confectioners' sugar and unsweetened cocoa, for dusting

1. Heat the oven to 350°. Butter an 8-inch round cake pan. Cover the bottom with waxed paper and butter the paper. Dust the pan with flour and tap out the excess. Melt the chocolates together in a bowl, either over a pot of simmering water or in a microwave oven.

2. In a food processor, pulse the amaretti cookies with the almonds until ground evenly. Place on a sheet of waxed paper.

3. Add the butter, granulated sugar, and eggs to the processor and cream until satiny smooth, scraping down the sides as necessary, about 3 minutes. Add the amaretti mixture and the melted chocolate and pulse until blended.

4. Scrape the batter into the prepared pan. Bake in the middle of the oven until the cake domes somewhat and the top is dry and slightly cracked, 25 to 30 minutes. Let cool on a rack for 10 minutes. Run a blunt knife between the cake and pan and unmold the cake. Peel off the waxed paper and let the cake cool right-side up on the rack.

5. Dust the top of the cake with the confectioners' sugar and cocoa. Serve at room temperature.

—DORIE GREENSPAN

MAKE IT AHEAD

The cake can be made ahead, wrapped airtight, and kept at room temperature for three days, or it may be frozen for up to one month. Don't dust with the confectioners' sugar and cocoa until just before serving.

CHOCOLATE CLOUD CAKE

This elegant, two-layer chocolate cake is made up of a tender chocolate cake, lightened with beaten egg whites and frosted with a rich chocolate ganache.

MAKES ONE 9-INCH CAKE

CHOCOLATE CAKE:

- 2 cups cake flour
- 1 teaspoon baking soda
- 1 teaspoon baking powder
- ½ teaspoon salt
- 1 cup light-brown sugar
- 1 cup granulated sugar
- 3 ounces unsweetened chocolate, chopped
- ½ cup water
- ¼ pound unsalted butter, at room temperature
- 3 large eggs, separated, at room temperature
- ¾ cup milk, at room temperature
- 1 teaspoon vanilla extract

WHIPPED GANACHE:

- 8 ounces bittersweet chocolate, chopped
- 2 cups heavy cream
- 1 teaspoon vanilla extract

- 2 ounces bittersweet chocolate, coarsely grated or shaved, for decorating

1. Heat the oven to 350°. For the cake, cover the bottoms of two 9-by-2-inch round cake pans with waxed paper and butter the waxed paper.

2. In a large bowl, sift together the flour, baking soda, baking powder, and salt. In a medium saucepan, combine the brown sugar, granulated sugar, unsweetened chocolate, and water, and cook over moderately low heat, stirring, until smooth. Let cool slightly, while stirring occasionally.

3. In a large bowl, using an electric mixer, beat the butter and egg yolks until blended. Gradually beat in the chocolate mixture. Beat in the dry ingredients in two batches, alternating with the milk, until smooth. Beat in the vanilla. (The batter will be rather thin.)

4. In a medium bowl, using clean beaters, beat the egg whites until barely firm. Stir one-third of the whites into the batter. Fold in the remaining whites until incorporated.

5. Scrape the batter into the two prepared pans. Bake the cakes in the bottom third of the oven until a toothpick stuck in the center comes out clean, 25 to 30 minutes. Let the cakes cool in the pans

on a rack for 15 minutes, then remove from the pans and place right-side up on racks to cool completely.

6. For the ganache, in a saucepan, melt half of the bittersweet chocolate in the heavy cream over moderately low heat, stirring. Remove from the heat and stir in the vanilla and remaining chocolate until smooth. Scrape the ganache into a bowl and refrigerate until chilled, at least 3 hours or overnight.

7. Using an electric mixer, briefly beat the ganache until it is thick enough to hold its shape. Do not overbeat or the ganache will become grainy; if it does, melt it again over low heat, chill, and beat it once more.

8. Peel the paper from the cake layers. Place one layer right-side up on a cake platter and spread one scant cup of the whipped ganache on top. Place the second cake layer upside down on top of the filling. Spread the sides and top of the cake evenly with the remaining whipped ganache. If desired, reserve about ½ cup of the ganache for decorating as follows: Using a pastry bag fitted with a star tip, pipe simple stars or a scallop trim around the top or the base of the cake.

9. Sprinkle the grated chocolate over the top of the cake. To serve, slice gently with a serrated cake knife.

—TRACEY SEAMAN

MAKE IT AHEAD

The unfrosted cake layers will keep, wrapped in plastic, for one day at room temperature. Once frosted, the cake will keep one day in the refrigerator.

MANDARIN CHOCOLATE CAKE

This moist layer cake is decorated with modeling chocolate, which resembles a pliable Tootsie Roll. The cake tastes wonderful with a small glass of Grand Marnier—or just a cup of espresso.

MAKES ONE 8-INCH CAKE

CAKE:

- 2 cups flour
- 1 teaspoon baking soda
- Pinch salt
- ½ pound unsalted butter, at room temperature
- 5 ounces unsweetened baking chocolate, chopped
- 1¾ cups hot, strong-brewed coffee
- ¼ cup orange liqueur
- 2 cups sugar
- 2 large eggs
- 1 teaspoon vanilla extract

CHOCOLATE GANACHE:

- 24 ounces bittersweet or semisweet chocolate, chopped
- 2 cups heavy cream

Modeling Chocolate, next page

1. Heat the oven to 275°. For the cake, butter two 8-inch round cake pans. Cover the bottoms with two rounds of waxed paper and butter the paper. Dust the pans with flour and tap out the excess.

2. In a bowl, whisk together the flour, baking soda, and salt. In a large bowl, combine the butter, unsweetened baking chocolate, hot coffee, and liqueur; stir occasionally until the chocolate and butter melt. Stir in the sugar until dissolved and the mixture is completely cool. Add the flour mixture in two batches, whisking between additions. Whisk in the eggs and vanilla. Divide the batter evenly between the prepared pans and bake in the middle of the oven until a toothpick stuck in the center of the cakes comes out clean, about 1¼ hours. Let the cakes cool completely in the pans on a rack. Refrigerate for at least 6 hours or overnight.

3. For the ganache, put the chocolate in a large heatproof bowl. In a medium saucepan, bring the cream just to a boil over low heat. Pour the cream over the chocolate, cover, and let stand for 5 minutes. Whisk the ganache gently until silky and smooth.

4. Put 1½ cups of the ganache into a medium bowl; reserve the remaining ganache to glaze the cake. Set the bowl over ice and whisk the ganache gently until

it becomes thick and spreadable enough to act as a filling.

5. To unmold the cakes, set one pan at a time over a burner on low heat for 10 seconds. Run a blunt knife around the cakes to loosen it; invert onto a rack. Remove the paper. Split each cake in half horizontally to make four layers.

6. Place one cake layer on a stiff cardboard round on a wire rack and spread the layer with ½ cup of the ganache filling. Repeat with the remaining cake layers and ganache, ending with a plain cake layer. Pour the reserved ganache glaze over the cake, spreading it around the top and sides with a metal spatula. Let the glaze drip for 2 to 3 minutes. Using two spatulas, remove the cake to a plate. Decorate with the modeling chocolate and refrigerate briefly to set the glaze.

—COLETTE PETERS

MODELING CHOCOLATE

The modeling chocolate may be refrigerated, wrapped in plastic, for up to one month.

MAKES ABOUT 1 CUP

8 ounces semisweet chocolate chips
¼ cup plus 1 tablespoon light corn syrup

1. Melt the chocolate in a double boiler, stirring occasionally, until it is smooth. Then stir in the corn syrup; the chocolate will stiffen almost immediately. Stir until completely combined. Put the chocolate in a sturdy plastic bag and refrigerate until firm.

2. Work the chocolate with your hands until pliable. Hand-shape into flowers, braids, or ropes. Or pat the chocolate into a disk and roll it out to the desired thickness by hand, or in a manual pasta machine, then use it to make ribbons or for cutting out shapes.

WHAT IS CHOCOLATE?

It's the food of the gods—at least that's the translation of the ancient Greek word for the genus of cacao, *Theobroma,* from which chocolate is derived. It comes in varieties ranging from so-bitter-one-taste-makes-you-shiver to so-sweet-it's-cloying, and in colors that range from mahogany to ivory.

• UNSWEETENED (baking) CHOCO-LATE is the most basic, just chocolate liquor and cocoa butter.

• BITTERSWEET and SEMISWEET CHOCOLATE are made by varying the amount of cocoa butter, sugar, vanilla (or vanillin), and lecithin. While one manufacturer's bittersweet may be another's semisweet, both contain at least 35 percent chocolate liquor by weight; that's the law in the United States.

• SWEET CHOCOLATE, a designation that is often used by domestic chocolate producers, indicates at least 15 percent chocolate liquor and usually some sweeteners in addition to sugar.

• MILK CHOCOLATE does indeed contain milk—although usually the powdered kind—and at least 10 percent chocolate liquor.

• WHITE CHOCOLATE is, quite literally, a chocolate of a different color—and composition. It's iffy right down to its name; yes, it's white, but it's really not chocolate. In most cases, what's called "white chocolate" is really a compound based on vegetable fat rather than the cocoa butter that makes real chocolate so luxurious. If white chocolate doesn't contain cocoa butter (many European brands do), it should be labeled white confectionery coating or summer coating—and used only for decorations.

CHOCOLATE ANGEL FOOD CAKE WITH MARSHMALLOW FROSTING

Except for a minuscule amount of fat in the cocoa powder in the cake and in the chocolate shavings on top, this is a totally fat-free dessert. An extra-thick layer of fluffy marshmallow frosting is the perfect topping for this light yet rich-tasting cake.

MAKES ONE ANGEL FOOD CAKE

ANGEL FOOD CAKE:

1 cup superfine sugar

½ cup unsweetened cocoa powder

⅓ cup cake flour

¼ teaspoon salt

8 large egg whites, at room temperature

½ teaspoon cream of tartar

MARSHMALLOW FROSTING:

3 large egg whites, at room temperature

¾ cup sugar

⅓ cup water

¼ teaspoon cream of tartar

1 teaspoon vanilla extract

Chocolate shavings, for decorating

1. Heat the oven to 350°. For the cake, sift ⅔ cup of the superfine sugar onto a piece of waxed paper or parchment and set aside. Sift the remaining ⅓ cup superfine sugar with the cocoa powder, flour, and salt and set aside.

2. In the large bowl of a standing electric mixer, beat the egg whites at medium speed until foamy. Add the cream of tartar and continue beating until the foam is white and holds the lines from the beater. Increase the speed to medium-high and continue beating the egg whites, adding the sifted superfine sugar 1 tablespoon at a time, until they hold soft peaks when the beaters are lifted.

3. Remove the bowl from the mixer. Sift and fold the dry ingredients into the beaten egg whites with a large rubber spatula. Pour the batter into a 10-cup angel food cake pan or Bundt pan and smooth the top. Gently bang the pan once on your work surface to release any large air pockets.

4. Bake the cake in the bottom third of the oven until a toothpick stuck in the center of the cake comes out clean, about 35 minutes. Invert the cake pan over a narrow-necked bottle and let cool completely in the pan, about 1 hour.

5. For the frosting, put the egg whites in the bowl of a standing mixer. In a small

heavy saucepan, combine the sugar and water. Bring to a boil over moderately high heat, brushing the inside of the saucepan occasionally with a wet pastry brush.

6. When the sugar syrup comes to a boil, begin beating the egg whites at medium-high speed. When they become foamy, add the cream of tartar. Beat at medium speed until the egg whites hold stiff peaks when the beaters are lifted.

7. Insert a candy thermometer into the sugar syrup and cook until it reaches 242°. Remove from the heat. With the mixer still at medium-high speed, beat the sugar syrup into the egg whites in a slow stream until completely incorporated. Increase the speed to high and beat for 5 minutes, scraping the sides of the bowl once with a rubber spatula. Add the vanilla and beat for 1 more minute. The icing will still be a little warm.

8. Run a thin, flexible metal spatula or knife between the cake and the sides and center tube of the pan to loosen (you may need to jiggle the pan to completely release the cake). Invert the cake onto a cardboard cake circle or onto a serving platter.

9. Using a metal icing spatula, spread a thin layer of frosting over the entire cake, including the inside of the center opening, to secure the crumbs. Then coat the cake with the remaining frosting. Decorate the top of the cake with the chocolate shavings. To serve, slice with a serrated knife or an angel food comb.

—PEGGY CULLEN

SUGAR SYRUPS

Boiling a sugar syrup—a mix of sugar and water—is the first step in making most confections. As the sugar cooks, it reaches different stages that correspond to various uses. To decide if the syrup has reached the right stage, use a candy thermometer, or drop a teaspoon of the syrup into ice water and knead it with your fingers (until the hard-crack stage, when the syrup becomes too hot to test by hand.)

THREAD (230° to 234° F)
    Makes a limp, thin thread.
SOFT BALL (235° to 242° F)
    Makes a soft, sticky ball.
FIRM BALL (244° to 248° F)
    Makes a firm, flexible ball.
HARD BALL (250° to 266° F)
    Makes a stiff, sticky ball.
SOFT CRACK (270° to 290° F)
    Separates into firm strands.
HARD CRACK (300° to 310° F)
    Separates into hard, brittle pieces.
CARAMEL (320° to 375° F)
    Changes color from light amber
    to dark brown.

—CAROLE BLOOM

Chocolate Buttermilk Cake with Blackberry Meringue

Filled with sweet, billowing blackberry meringue, this rich-tasting chocolate cake is a stunning dessert. If you prefer, you can make a plain meringue without the preserves or berries and garnish the cake with whatever fruit you like. This velvety chocolate cake begs for a sweet, spritzy wine, such as the 1996 Linden Vineyards Late Harvest Vidal.

MAKES ONE 9-INCH CAKE

Chocolate Cake:

- 3 cups flour
- 2 cups granulated sugar
- ¾ cup unsweetened Dutch-process cocoa powder
- 2 teaspoons baking soda
- 1 teaspoon salt
- 2½ cups fresh or thawed frozen blackberries,
- 1 cup low-fat (1.5%) buttermilk
- ⅔ cup vegetable oil
- 2 tablespoons distilled white vinegar
- 2 teaspoons vanilla extract

Blackberry Filling and Meringue:

- ¾ cup egg whites (about 6)
- 1½ cups granulated sugar
- ½ teaspoon cream of tartar
- 1½ cup seedless blackberry preserves, at room temperature

- 1 pint fresh or thawed blackberries plus extra for garnish
- 2 tablespoons confectioners' sugar, for dusting

1. Heat the oven to 350°. For the cake, coat two 9-by-2-inch round cake pans with vegetable-oil cooking spray. Cover the bottoms with parchment paper, then lightly spray the paper. In a large bowl, sift together the flour, granulated sugar, cocoa, baking soda, and salt.

2. Pass the blackberries through a fine strainer set over a bowl; you should have 1 cup of puree. Whisk in the buttermilk, oil, vinegar, and vanilla. Pour the blackberry mixture into the dry ingredients and blend. Divide the batter evenly between the prepared pans and bake until the cakes pull away from the sides and the tops spring back when pressed, about 40 minutes. Let cool on a rack for 10 minutes, then unmold and cool completely.

3. For the filling, in a large heatproof bowl, whisk the egg whites with the granulated sugar and cream of tartar. Set the bowl over a saucepan filled with about an inch of simmering water and whisk until the sugar dissolves and the whites are hot to the touch, about 5 minutes. Transfer to a standing mixer and beat at high speed until

completely cool, about 15 minutes. Stir the preserves until smooth and fold gently into the meringue.

4. Using a serrated knife, split the cakes in half horizontally. Stir the preserves until smooth, then spread thinly on three of the cut cake layers. Set one of the layers on a large plate, preserves-side up. Spread one-third of the meringue on top and press one-third of the blackberries into the meringue. Layer the cake, repeating with the two cake layers, preserves-side up, and the remaining meringue and blackberries. Top with the final cake layer and let stand at room temperature for 1, or up to 3, hours. Just before serving, sift the confectioners' sugar over the top of the cake and garnish with the additional blackberries.

—KRISTINE M. SMITH

MAKE IT AHEAD

The cake layers can be made ahead. Wrap them in plastic and set them aside for up to one day at room temperature. Then fill and layer the cake.

GERMAN CHOCOLATE CAKE

If you are not comfortable using a pastry bag, simply spread half of the ganache on the second cake layer and the other half around the sides of the cake.

MAKES ONE 8-INCH CAKE

CHOCOLATE CAKE:

- 1 cup sugar
- ¾ cup flour
- ½ cup unsweetened cocoa powder, preferably Dutch process
- 1 teaspoon baking soda
- ½ teaspoon baking powder
  Pinch salt
- 2 large eggs
- ½ cup cold, strong-brewed coffee
- ½ cup buttermilk
- ½ teaspoon vanilla extract
- 4 tablespoons unsalted butter, melted

NUT FILLING:

- 2 large egg yolks
- ¾ cup sugar
- ¾ cup evaporated whole milk
- 3 tablespoons unsalted butter, cut into small pieces
- 1 cup unsweetened shredded coconut*
- 1 cup chopped pecans
- ¾ teaspoon vanilla extract

GANACHE:

- 1 cup heavy cream
- ½ pound semisweet chocolate, chopped

*Available at specialty-food stores and health-food stores.

1. Heat the oven to 350°. For the cake, butter an 8-by-2-inch round cake pan and cover the bottom with parchment paper. In a bowl, sift together the sugar, flour, cocoa, baking soda, baking powder, and salt. In another bowl, whisk together the eggs, coffee, buttermilk, and vanilla.

2. Beat the coffee mixture into the dry ingredients in two batches with an electric mixer at low speed. Beat in the butter. Pour the batter into the prepared pan and bake until a toothpick stuck in the center comes out clean, about 50 minutes. Let the cake cool in the pan.

3. For the nut filling, in a heavy, medium saucepan, whisk together the egg yolks and sugar. Whisk in the evaporated milk, then the butter. Cook over moderate heat, stirring constantly, until the mixture thickens and coats a spoon lightly, about 10 minutes; do not let it boil. Remove from the heat and stir in the coconut, pecans, and vanilla. Pour the filling into a bowl and let cool completely.

4. For the ganache, in a small saucepan, bring the cream to a boil over moderately high heat. Remove from the heat and stir in the chocolate. Let stand for 1 minute, then whisk until smooth. Transfer the ganache to a bowl and refrigerate, stirring

occasionally, until chilled and thickened, about 2 hours.

5. Invert the cake onto a work surface and peel off the paper. Using a serrated knife, slice the cake horizontally into three even layers. Set one layer on a large plate and spread half of the nut filling on top. Add the second cake layer and cover with a ¼-inch-thick layer of ganache. Set the third cake layer on top and cover with the remaining nut filling. Spread half of the remaining ganache on the sides of the cake. Transfer the rest of the ganache to a pastry bag fitted with a medium star tip. Pipe a border of rosettes around the top of the cake and serve.

—MICHELLE AND BILL BRACKEN

MAKE IT AHEAD

The unfrosted cake will keep, wrapped in plastic, one day at room temperature. The ganache and the nut filling will each keep one day in the refrigerator. If the cold ganache is too thick to spread, stir it briefly.

SLICING THE LAYERS

Slicing the cake into even layers is a little tricky. For professional-looking results, put the cake on a cardboard cake round, then on a cake-decorating turntable. With a serrated cake knife, using an even sawing motion, slice the cake into layers; turn it as you proceed. Before you remove the top layer, place toothpicks in a vertical line down the side of the cake, one in each layer, so you will be able to realign the layers after you have spread the filling on them.

THE NEW CHOCOLATE DECADENCE

The most popular chocolate dessert I ever sold at my Cocolat shops is called Chocolate Decadence, which is made with only one tablespoon of flour and a full pound of chocolate. If you yearn for a creamy truffle-like cake—but with half the calories and a quarter of the fat per serving—salvation is here. For an extra splurge (and two more grams of fat per tablespoon), try a slice with a dollop of whipped cream. Or, serve with a sauce made of unsweetened frozen raspberries pureed with sugar, to taste. Allow enough time to refrigerate the cake at least one day before serving, to let it firm up.

MAKES ONE 8-INCH CAKE

 5 ounces bittersweet or semisweet chocolate, chopped

 1 large egg, at room temperature

 1 large egg yolk, at room temperature

 1 teaspoon vanilla extract

 ½ cup plus 1½ teaspoons unsweetened Dutch-process cocoa powder

 ⅔ cup plus ¼ cup sugar

 2 tablespoons flour

 ¾ cup low-fat (1%) milk

 2 large egg whites

 ⅛ teaspoon cream of tartar

1. Heat the oven to 350°. Spray the sides of an 8-by-2-inch round cake pan with vegetable-oil cooking spray. Cover the bottom with parchment or waxed paper.

2. Place the chocolate in a large bowl. In a small bowl, lightly beat the whole egg, egg yolk, and vanilla.

3. In a heavy, medium saucepan, combine the cocoa with the ⅔ cup sugar and the flour. Gradually whisk in enough of the milk to form a smooth paste. Then whisk in the remaining milk. Bring to a simmer over moderate heat, stirring constantly with a wooden spoon. Simmer very gently, stirring constantly, for 1½ minutes. Pour the hot cocoa mixture over the chocolate. Let sit for 30 seconds, then whisk until completely smooth. Whisk in the egg mixture.

4. Using an electric mixer, beat the egg whites until foamy. Add the cream of tartar and beat until soft peaks form when the beaters are lifted. Continue beating the egg whites, adding the remaining ¼ cup sugar gradually, until they hold firm peaks when the beaters are lifted.

5. Using a large rubber spatula, fold one-quarter of the beaten egg whites into the chocolate mixture. Fold in the remaining whites.

6. Scrape the batter into the prepared pan and smooth the top. Set the cake pan into a large baking pan and place in the lower part of the oven. Pour enough boiling

water into the baking pan to reach halfway up the sides of the cake pan. Bake until the cake springs back when pressed gently, about 30 minutes. (The cake will still be quite wet inside, but it will firm up as it sits.) Remove the cake pan from the water bath and cool completely. Cover with plastic wrap and refrigerate overnight.

7. To serve, run a thin, sharp knife around the edge of the pan to loosen the cake. Invert the cake on a plate covered with waxed paper. Peel off the parchment or waxed paper and turn the cake right-side up on a serving plate. Slice the cake with a thin, sharp knife, dipping it in hot water and wiping it dry between slices.

—ALICE MEDRICH

MAKE IT AHEAD

The cake will keep in the refrigerator for up to two days, or in the freezer for up to two months. If you refrigerate it, leave the cake in the pan. If you freeze it, unmold the cake first and wrap it well.

BOARDWALK BUTTERCRUNCH CAKE

This candy-studded cake is for those people who are happiest with something crunchy and sweet.

MAKES ONE 9-INCH CAKE

BUTTER CAKE:

½ pound unsalted butter, at room temperature

1 cup superfine sugar

3 large eggs, at room temperature

1½ cups flour

2 teaspoons baking powder

½ teaspoon salt

¼ cup plus 2 tablespoons milk, at room temperature

1 teaspoon vanilla extract

CARAMEL PASTRY CREAM:

¾ cup sugar

¼ teaspoon lemon juice

¼ cup heavy cream

1¾ cups milk

1 vanilla bean, split lengthwise

6 egg yolks

⅓ cup cornstarch

¾ cup heavy cream

6 ounces bittersweet chocolate, chopped

Pecan Buttercrunch, page 33

1. Heat the oven to 350°. For the cake, butter and flour a 9-by-2-inch round cake pan.

2. In a medium bowl, using an electric mixer, beat the butter until fluffy. Beat in the sugar until light and fluffy. Add the eggs, one at a time, beating well after each addition.

3. In a medium bowl, combine the flour, baking powder, and salt. Sift one-third of the dry ingredients into the butter mixture and beat until blended. Beat in half of the milk and vanilla. Repeat with another third of the dry ingredients and the remaining milk and vanilla. Add the remaining dry ingredients and mix to blend well.

4. Scrape the batter into the prepared pan, spreading it slightly higher around the edges. Bake until a toothpick stuck in the center comes out clean, 40 to 45 minutes. Remove the cake from the pan immediately and let it cool completely, right-side up.

5. Trim the crusty top of the cooled cake to even it. Using a serrated knife, slice the cake horizontally into three even

layers. Reserve the bottom layer to use as the top.

6. For the pastry cream, put ½ cup plus 2 tablespoons of the sugar into a medium nonreactive saucepan. Add the lemon juice and blend it evenly into the sugar. Cook over moderate heat, stirring, until the sugar melts and turns deep amber, 6 to 8 minutes.

7. Remove the sugar mixture from the heat and slowly stir in the cream and milk. Scrape the seeds from the vanilla bean into the milk mixture and add the pod of the bean. Return to moderate heat and cook, stirring occasionally, until the mixture just reaches a boil. If the sugar is not completely dissolved, reduce the heat and continue to cook, stirring, until all of the sugar is melted. Remove the caramel milk from the heat and strain.

8. In a heavy medium saucepan, beat the egg yolks and the remaining 2 tablespoons sugar until light and slightly thickened. Sift in the cornstarch and whisk to combine.

9. Whisk the hot caramel milk into the egg yolks until smooth. Bring to a boil over moderately high heat, whisking constantly, until the pastry cream is thick, about 1 minute. Scrape into a bowl and press plastic wrap onto the surface. Refrigerate until cool, about 2 hours.

10. In a medium bowl, beat ¼ cup of the heavy cream just until it holds firm peaks when the beaters are lifted. Whisk the caramel pastry cream until smooth and fold in the whipped cream. Fold in 1⅔ cups of the pecan buttercrunch (use the largest pieces of candy).

11. Place the first cake layer on an inverted cake pan and cover with 1½ cups of the buttercrunch filling. Place the second cake layer on top and cover with the remaining filling. Top with the bottom cake layer, bottom-side up, to create a smooth, flat surface. Smooth any filling around the sides, then refrigerate the cake on the pan until the filling is firm, about 30 minutes.

12. In a small heavy saucepan, scald the remaining ½ cup heavy cream and remove it from the heat. Add the chocolate and stir until melted and smooth, then set it aside to cool. (The glaze should be pourable but not too warm.)

13. Pour the cooled chocolate glaze over the cake, smoothing the top and sides with a spatula. Use any drippings to touch up bare spots. Press the remaining buttercrunch onto the sides of the cake and the rim of the top. Refrigerate the cake on the pan until the chocolate is set, about 30 minutes. Transfer the cake to a platter and serve.

—PEGGY CULLEN

Pecan Buttercrunch

MAKES ABOUT 2¾ CUPS

1¼ cups sugar

½ teaspoon lemon juice

4 tablespoons unsalted butter

1½ cups pecan halves

1. Oil a large cookie sheet and metal spatula. Place the sugar in a heavy medium saucepan. Add the lemon juice and blend it into the sugar.

2. Add the butter and cook over moderately high heat, stirring until the sugar melts and becomes a deep amber color, about 10 minutes. Remove from the heat and stir in the pecans.

3. Pour the mixture out onto the prepared cooked sheet immediately. Using the oiled spatula, turn the sugar over onto itself until it stops spreading. Press the buttercrunch flat and set aside at room temperature to cool, about 15 minutes.

4. Chop the buttercrunch into 1-inch pieces. Place one-third of the buttercrunch in a food processor and chop into ½-inch pieces. Repeat with the remaining buttercrunch, adding it to the processor in two batches. Any large pieces can be cut with a knife.

VANILLA SOUR-CREAM BUNDT CAKE

A velvety yet moist crumb, fine buttery flavor, and excellent keeping properties make this Bundt cake a hit. It is delicious plain or with whipped cream. It also goes well with fruit or ice cream.

MAKES ONE BUNDT CAKE

 3 cups cake flour

1⅔ cups granulated sugar

2½ teaspoons baking powder

 ¾ teaspoon salt

 ½ cup sour cream

 ⅓ cup milk

 3 large whole eggs

 2 large egg yolks

 1 tablespoon vanilla extract

10 ounces unsalted butter, at room temperature

Confectioners' sugar, for dusting

1. Heat the oven to 350°. Butter and flour a 12-cup Bundt pan or tube pan. Tap out any excess flour.

2. Sift the cake flour, granulated sugar, baking powder, and salt into the bowl of a standing electric mixer.

3. In a medium bowl, using a fork, beat together the sour cream, milk, whole eggs, egg yolks, and vanilla until very well blended and smooth.

4. Add the butter and half of the egg mixture to the dry ingredients. Beat at low speed just until thoroughly incorporated. Increase the speed to high and beat the mixture for 1 minute; do not overmix. Add the remaining egg mixture and beat at medium-high speed until the batter is fluffy and smooth, about 1 minute longer.

5. Scrape the batter into the prepared Bundt pan. Tap the pan on the counter several times to remove any air bubbles. Bake the cake in the middle of the oven until a toothpick stuck in the thickest part comes out clean, 50 to 60 minutes. Let cool completely in the pan.

6. Run a thin knife around the pan edges to loosen the cake, then invert it onto a serving plate. Using a small strainer, sift the confectioners' sugar over the cake.

—NANCY BAGGET

MAKE IT AHEAD

The cake will keep, covered, for up to five days at room temperature, or up to two weeks wrapped airtight and frozen.

HAZELNUT-DACQUOISE FAN CAKE

In this dramatic-looking dessert, crisp disks of hazelnut meringue alternate with sponge cake, vanilla-flavored strawberries, and whipped cream.

MAKES ONE 9-INCH CAKE

SPONGE CAKE:

⅔   cup cake flour

¾   teaspoon baking powder

¼   teaspoon salt

2   large eggs

4   large egg yolks

¾   cup granulated sugar

1   teaspoon vanilla extract

1½   tablespoons unsalted butter

3   tablespoons milk

HAZELNUT DACQUOISE:

⅔   cup hazelnuts

½   cup confectioners' sugar

1   tablespoon cornstarch

4   large egg whites

¼   teaspoon cream of tartar

¾   cup superfine sugar

About 2½ pints strawberries

2   tablespoons superfine sugar

1½   teaspoons vanilla extract

2   cups heavy cream

¼   cup confectioners' sugar

1. Heat the oven to 350°. For the sponge cake, butter and flour a 9-by-2-inch round cake pan. In a small bowl, sift together the flour, baking powder, and salt. Whisk to combine.

2. In the bowl of a standing electric mixer, whisk together the eggs, egg yolks, and granulated sugar. Set the bowl over a saucepan of barely simmering water; don't let the bottom of the bowl touch the water. Whisk vigorously until the mixture is warm to the touch. Return the bowl to the mixer. Beat at medium-high speed for 2 minutes. Add the vanilla and continue beating until the mixture is the consistency of whipped cream, 2 to 3 minutes longer.

3. Meanwhile, in a small saucepan, melt the butter in the milk. (Do not boil.) Remove from the heat and whisk.

4. Sift one-third of the dry ingredients over the whipped eggs and gently fold. Repeat this procedure twice. Pour the warm milk mixture into the batter in a slow stream and continue folding until just incorporated.

5. Scrape the batter into the prepared pan and bake until a toothpick stuck in the center of the cake comes out clean, about 30 minutes. Cool in the pan for 2 minutes, then turn the cake out to cool completely. ➤

6. For the hazelnut dacquoise, heat the oven to 425°. Spread the hazelnuts on a baking sheet and toast in the oven until fragrant, about 8 minutes. Wrap the hot nuts in a kitchen towel and rub vigorously to remove most of the skins. Let the nuts cool completely. Lower the oven temperature to 225°.

7. Line two large cookie sheets with parchment paper. Using the bottom of the 9-inch cake pan as a guide, trace two circles on one sheet of parchment paper and a third on the other.

8. In a food processor, grind the hazelnuts finely with the confectioners' sugar and cornstarch.

9. Put the egg whites in the large bowl of the standing electric mixer and set it over a saucepan filled with about an inch of simmering water. Whisk the egg whites vigorously until warm to the touch; don't stop for even a few seconds or the whites will cook. Then beat the egg whites with the mixer at high speed until foamy. Add the cream of tartar and beat until soft peaks form when the beaters are lifted. Continue beating the egg whites, adding the superfine sugar 1 tablespoon at a time and beating for 10 seconds between each addition, until they hold firm peaks when the beaters are lifted and the meringue is stiff and glossy. Using a large rubber spatula, fold the nut mixture gently into the meringue.

10. Scoop the meringue into a pastry bag fitted with a #5 open star tip (about ½

inch). Pipe a ring of meringue on one of the outlined circles on the cookie sheets, about ¼-inch in from the perimeter. Then, starting in the center of the circle, pipe a continuous spiral to meet the outer ring Fill in any holes with more meringue. Repeat to fill in the other two circles. Bake the meringues until dry and firm, about 2 hours.

11. Set aside eight perfect strawberries. Slice all the remaining berries ¼-inch thick. Toss the berries in a bowl with the superfine sugar and vanilla. Set aside, stirring occasionally.

12. In a small, chilled bowl, whip the cream and confectioners sugar until slightly firmer than soft peaks. Refrigerate until ready to use.

13. No more than 3 hours before serving, assemble the cake. Split the sponge cake into two even layers and invert the top layer onto a 9-inch cardboard cake round or serving platter.

14. Drain the strawberries, reserving the juice. Using a pastry brush, dab half of the strawberry juice on the cake layer. Distribute evenly half of the sliced strawberries on the cake and spread 1 heaping cup of the whipped cream on top. Place a dacquoise disk over the whipped cream and spread with an additional ½ cup of the whipped cream. Repeat the layering with the second cake layer, the remaining strawberry juice and strawberries, another heaping cup of whipped cream, and a second dacquoise disk.

15. Using a serrated knife, quarter the remaining dacquoise disk, then cut each quarter in half to get eight wedges. If a wedge breaks, just glue it with a little whipped cream. Whisk the remaining whipped cream until it's stiff, then transfer it to a pastry bag fitted with the #5 star tip. Pipe eight evenly spaced rosettes of whipped cream about ½ inch from the edge of the cake. Lay a reserved strawberry on each rosette and lean a wedge of the dacquoise against each berry, with the point toward the center of the cake. To serve, slice with a serrated knife.

—Peggy Cullen

Make It Ahead

The sponge cake will keep at room temperature, wrapped in plastic, for one day. If the weather is dry, the dacquoise will keep in a cool, dry place, unwrapped, for one day.

Basic Meringue Types

For all of the following meringues, the basic proportion of sugar to egg whites is two to one by weight (one-quarter cup of sugar for each egg white). This can be reduced to as little as one to one for a thinner mixture, for topping a pie, for example.

• Simple or Cold Meringue is used in angel food cake, macaroons, and delicate baked meringue shells to hold fruit, whipped cream, and ice cream. For a simple meringue, beat egg whites until they reach the soft-peak stage, then gradually add the sugar and beat until the whites are stiff and glossy but not dry. Since this meringue isn't cooked, use superfine sugar; it dissolves more easily than granulated.

• Cooked or Warm Meringue is good for pie toppings, baked Alaska, dacquoise layers, icings, and dried meringue baskets. Heat the sugar and unbeaten egg whites together until they are warm to the touch and the sugar dissolves, then beat on high speed until the meringue is stiff, glossy, and cool. Granulated sugar is fine for cooked meringue, since heating the sugar will dissolve it.

• Italian or Boiled Meringue is the sturdiest one of all. It is used for unbaked foods, such as marshmallows, icings and buttercreams: Heat a sugar syrup to either the soft- or firm-ball stage (see box on page 23), pour it into partially beaten egg whites and beat until the whites are stiff and cool. Use granulated sugar when making these meringues.

ALMOND CAKE WITH CITRUS SYRUP

Warm, lemony syrup is poured over this Spanish cake, making it moist and fragrant. The recipe is an adaptation of an almond-and-orange Passover cake from *The Book of Jewish Food* (Knopf) by Claudia Roden.

MAKES ONE 9-INCH CAKE

ALMOND CAKE:

2 tablespoons matzo meal

1 cup sugar

1 cup ground almonds

½ cup finely chopped almonds

   Finely grated zest of 1 large lemon

8 large eggs, separated

CITRUS SYRUP:

⅓ cup sugar

¼ cup lemon juice

   Finely grated zest of 1 large lemon

½ cup water

Confectioners' sugar, for dusting (optional)

1. Heat the oven to 325°. For the cake, oil the bottom and sides of a 9-by-3-inch springform pan. Cover the bottom with parchment paper and oil the paper. Coat the bottom and sides evenly with the matzo meal and tap out the excess. Refrigerate the pan.

2. In a large bowl, using a wooden spoon, mix together the sugar, almonds, lemon zest, and egg yolks.

3. In a large bowl, preferably copper, whisk the egg whites until they hold firm peaks when the beaters are lifted. Stir one quarter of the whites into the almond mixture to lighten it. Using a large rubber spatula, gently fold in the remaining whites in three additions.

4. Pour the mixture into the prepared pan. Bake on the lowest shelf of the oven until a toothpick stuck in the center comes out clean, about 1 hour. Let cool 10 minutes. Run a knife around the cake edge, remove the pan side, and invert onto a wire rack. Peel off the parchment and let cool.

5. For the citrus syrup, in a small stainless-steel saucepan, combine the sugar, lemon juice, zest, and water. Bring to a boil over moderate heat, stirring to dissolve the sugar. Simmer over moderately low heat for 2 minutes. Remove from the heat and let the syrup steep 15 minutes.

6. Reheat and strain the syrup. Transfer the cake to a plate and prick all over with a fork. Pour the syrup evenly over the cake and set aside at room temperature for at least 3 hours, or overnight. Sift confectioners' sugar over the cake, if using, and serve.

—PETER HOFFMAN

HAZELNUT POUND CAKE

This buttery pound cake calls for whole wheat pastry flour, which adds the nuttiness of whole wheat but keeps the texture of the cake tender. This pound cake is great by itself for breakfast or topped with a scoop of coffee ice cream for dessert. Let the cake cool completely to allow the flavors to mellow.

MAKES ONE 10-INCH CAKE

1¾ cups hazelnuts

½ pound plus 1 tablespoon unsalted butter, at room temperature

1 cup sugar

⅓ cup plus 3 tablespoons pure maple syrup, at room temperature

4 large eggs, at room temperature

1½ teaspoons vanilla extract

1 cup unbleached all-purpose flour

1 cup whole wheat pastry flour*

2½ teaspoons baking powder

½ teaspoon salt

⅓ cup buttermilk or plain yogurt

*Available at health-food stores.

1. Heat the oven to 350°. Butter a 10-by-2½-inch springform pan. Spread the hazelnuts on a large baking sheet and toast in the oven until the skins are blistered, about 10 minutes. Wrap the nuts in a towel and rub them vigorously to remove most of the skins. Let them cool completely. Finely chop ¼ cup of the nuts. Place the remaining nuts in a food processor and pulse until finely ground.

2. In a large bowl, using an electric mixer, beat the ½ pound of butter at high speed until creamy. Gradually beat in the sugar and the ⅓ cup maple syrup until fluffy. Beat in the eggs one at a time, then beat in the vanilla. The mixture will appear slightly curdled.

3. In a medium bowl, sift together the unbleached and whole wheat flours, baking powder, and salt. Gently stir half of the flour mixture into the batter. Stir in the buttermilk, then stir in the remaining dry ingredients. Using a rubber spatula, fold in the ground nuts.

4. Scrape the batter into the prepared pan and smooth the surface. Bake in the middle of the oven until a toothpick stuck in the center of the cake comes out clean, about 1 hour. Cool completely in the pan. Remove the sides of the springform pan.

5. In a small saucepan, combine the remaining 1 tablespoon butter and the 3 tablespoons maple syrup and bring to a boil over moderately high heat. Remove from the heat, and swirl the pan to mix. Spoon the glaze evenly over the cooled cake and sprinkle the chopped hazelnuts on top.

—KEN HAEDRICH

LEMON POUND CAKE WITH BERRIES IN LEMON POMEGRANATE SYRUP

This moist, lemony pound cake, also good on its own, can be made in five 9-by-4½-by-2-inch loaf pans rather than the six disposable pans used in Step 1. You can substitute cranberry juice for the pomegranate juice in the syrup, but it lacks the latter's tangy, intense flavor. You can also use any combination of fresh berries to replace those specified here; you should have about twelve pints. This makes a wonderful finish to a large party.

MAKES 50 SLICES

14 ounces unsalted butter, at room temperature

5 cups granulated sugar

10 large eggs, lightly beaten

3 tablespoons finely grated lemon zest

7½ cups sifted flour

1¼ teaspoons baking powder

1¼ teaspoons baking soda

1¾ teaspoons salt

3 cups plus 2 tablespoons buttermilk

1½ tablespoons vanilla extract

5 cups heavy cream

¼ cup plus 3 tablespoons confectioners' sugar

¼ cup brandy or rum

10 pints hulled strawberries, halved if large

1½ pints raspberries

Pomegranate Syrup, next page

1. Heat the oven to 325°. Butter and flour six 8-by-4-by-2 ¼-inch disposable foil loaf pans.

2. In a large bowl, using an electric mixer, cream the butter and granulated sugar on medium speed until light and fluffy. Mix in the eggs on low speed until blended. Add the lemon zest (the mixture may look curdled).

3. In a medium bowl, sift together the flour, baking powder, baking soda, and salt. In another medium bowl, combine the buttermilk and vanilla. On low speed, beat the dry ingredients into the butter mixture, alternating with the buttermilk, beginning and ending with the dry ingredients; mix until just combined. Scrape the batter into the prepared loaf pans and smooth the tops.

4. Bake the pound cakes in the upper and lower thirds of the oven, switching the pans halfway through baking, until the tops are golden and a toothpick stuck in the center of the cake comes out clean, about 50 minutes. Let the cakes cool in the pans for 5 minutes, then remove them from the pans and let cool completely. ➤

5. No more than 1 hour before serving, beat the heavy cream to soft peaks. Add the confectioners' sugar and brandy and continue beating until firm. Put the whipped cream in a large serving bowl. In another large serving bowl, toss the strawberries and raspberries with the pomegranate syrup. Slice the cakes and serve the cream and berries alongside.

—GRACE PARISI

POMEGRANATE SYRUP

4 cups pomegranate juice*

¼ cup grenadine (optional)

2 cups sugar

Zest of ½ medium orange, cut into thick strips

*Available at health-food stores and Middle Eastern markets.

In a medium nonreactive saucepan, combine the pomegranate juice, grenadine, if using, sugar, and orange zest. Bring to a boil over moderately high heat, stirring, just until the sugar dissolves. Reduce the heat to moderately low and simmer until reduced to 2 cups, about 35 minutes. Discard the orange zest and let the pomegranate syrup cool completely.

HUNGARIAN COFFEE CAKE

Chocolate, cinnamon, walnuts, and prunes swirl through this moist sour-cream cake. The coffee cake will keep, wrapped and refrigerated, for up to five days.

MAKES ONE 10-INCH BUNDT CAKE

½ pound unsalted butter

1 tablespoon finely grated orange zest

2 cups sugar

2 teaspoons vanilla extract

¼ teaspoon salt

2 cups sour cream

3 large eggs

1½ teaspoons baking soda

1 teaspoon baking powder

3 cups flour

½ cup prune puree*

1 tablespoon cinnamon

2 tablespoons cocoa powder

½ cup chopped walnuts

*Prune puree, also known as prune pastry filling or lekvar, is available at most supermarkets.

1. Heat the oven to 350°. Butter a heavy nonstick 10-inch Bundt pan. In a large saucepan, melt the butter over moderate heat, adding the orange zest halfway through. Remove from the heat.

2. Using a wooden spoon, stir in the sugar, vanilla, salt, sour cream, and eggs until smooth. Add the baking soda and baking powder in pinches, breaking up any lumps with your fingers, and mix. Vigorously mix in the flour. Spoon the prune puree over the batter and sprinkle the cinnamon, cocoa, and walnuts evenly on top. Swirl in these ingredients.

3. Pour the batter into the prepared pan and bake until a toothpick stuck in the center comes out with a crumb or two clinging to it, 50 to 55 minutes. Let the cake cool in its pan on a rack for 10 minutes. Then invert the cake onto the rack and allow it to cool completely.

—ANDREW SCHLOSS

PUMPKIN-SEED CUPCAKES

This batter can be baked in an 8-inch round cake pan as an impressive dessert.

MAKES 12 CUPCAKES

CUPCAKES:

1	cup raw pumpkin seeds
1	cup raw sunflower seeds
1⅔	cups flour
1½	teaspoons ground ginger
1	teaspoon cinnamon
¾	teaspoon salt
½	teaspoon baking soda
½	teaspoon baking powder
½	teaspoon nutmeg
¼	teaspoon ground cloves
1½	cups sugar
½	cup vegetable oil
2	large eggs, lightly beaten
1	scant cup canned pumpkin puree
⅓	cup warm water

CREAM CHEESE FROSTING:

6	ounces cream cheese, at room temperature
6	tablespoons unsalted butter, at room temperature
¾	cup confectioners' sugar
1	teaspoon vanilla extract

1. Heat the oven to 350°. For the cupcakes, toast the pumpkin and sunflower seeds on a large rimmed baking sheet, stirring once or twice, until light golden, about 12 minutes. Let cool, then put them into a small bowl.

2. Butter a 12-cup muffin tin. In a medium bowl, sift together the flour, ginger, cinnamon, salt, baking soda, baking powder, nutmeg, and cloves. Whisk to combine. In another medium bowl, using an electric mixer, beat the sugar with the oil. Add the eggs and beat at high speed until the mixture lightens in color. Reduce the speed to low and beat in the pumpkin puree and water.

3. Whisk the pumpkin mixture into the dry ingredients, scraping the bottom of the bowl to incorporate the flour. Spoon the batter into the prepared muffin cups and bake until a toothpick stuck in the center comes out clean, about 25 minutes. Let the cupcakes cool in the pan for 10 minutes, then turn them out onto a rack to cool completely.

4. For the frosting, beat the cream cheese with the butter until smooth. Beat in the sugar and vanilla.

5. Spread the frosting on the cupcakes with a small metal spatula or a knife. Roll the cupcakes in the toasted seeds to coat the top and then serve.

—PEGGY CULLEN

Maple Spice Cake with Caramel Cream

The spices in this cake are reminiscent of apple pie and mulled cider. If you want a final flourish, serve the cake with sliced, peeled apples sautéed in a little butter with lemon juice and cinnamon sugar.

MAKES ONE 8-INCH CAKE

SPICE CAKE:

¼ pound unsalted butter, at room temperature

1⅓ cups light-brown sugar

2 large eggs, at room temperature

⅓ cup pure maple syrup

2½ cups cake flour

1½ teaspoons cinnamon

1 teaspoon baking powder

1 teaspoon baking soda

1 teaspoon ground allspice

¾ teaspoon ground ginger

½ teaspoon salt

1 cup buttermilk

CARAMEL CREAM:

⅔ cup granulated sugar

3 tablespoons water

2½ cups heavy cream

2 tablespoons confectioners' sugar

1. Heat the oven to 350°. For the cake, cover the bottoms of two 8-by-2-inch round cake pans with waxed paper and butter the waxed paper.

2. In a large bowl, using an electric mixer, cream the butter with the brown sugar until fluffy. Add the eggs one at a time, beating well after each addition. Beat in the maple syrup.

3. In a medium bowl, whisk the flour with the cinnamon, baking powder, baking soda, allspice, ginger, and salt. Mix the dry ingredients into the batter in three additions, alternating with the buttermilk.

4. Scrape the batter into the prepared cake pans and smooth the top. Bake the cakes in the bottom third of the oven until a toothpick stuck in the center of the cake comes out clean, about 35 minutes. Let the cakes cool for 15 minutes, then remove the cakes from the pans, peel off the waxed paper, and let cool completely, right-side up.

5. For the caramel cream, in a medium saucepan, combine the sugar and water. Bring the mixture to a boil over moderately high heat and boil (brushing down the sides of the pan with a pastry brush dipped in water to dissolve any sugar crystals) until the sugar turns a rich, tea-like brown,

about 5 minutes. Remove from the heat and carefully pour in ½ cup of the heavy cream; stand back to avoid spatters. Stir with a wooden spoon until blended and smooth. Let cool completely.

6. Beat the remaining 2 cups heavy cream with the confectioners' sugar until firm. Fold ½ cup of the caramel into the whipped cream in two additions, and reserve the remaining caramel.

7. Place one cake layer right-side up on a cake platter. Spread 1 cup of the caramel cream on top. Cover with the second cake layer, bottom-side up. Spread the sides and top of the cake with the remaining caramel cream. Drizzle the reserved caramel in zigzags over the top of the cake. To serve, slice gently with a serrated cake knife.

—TRACEY SEAMAN

MAKE IT AHEAD

The unfrosted cakes will keep at room temperature, wrapped in plastic, for one day. The caramel cream will keep, at room temperature, for up to four hours. Or, refrigerate the frosted cake for up to three hours.

FROSTING THE CAKE

To make frosting the cake extra-easy, spoon the frosting into a pastry bag fitted with a wide star or plain tip. Pipe the frosting in zigzags around the sides of the cake. Then pipe a spiral on top of the cake, beginning at the edge. Using an icing spatula, spread the frosting on the sides as you turn the cake. Then, holding the spatula at a slight angle, smooth the top from the edge to the center.

GINGERED APPLE CAKE

This tender apple cake is best served the same day it is made.

MAKES 6 SERVINGS

3 tart apples, such as Granny Smith, Winesap, or Baldwin (about 1½ pounds)

¾ cup dry white wine

⅓ cup plus 2½ tablespoons sugar

Zest of 1 lemon

1 tablespoon finely chopped fresh ginger

½ cup flour, sifted

⅓ teaspoon baking powder

3 large eggs, separated

1½ cups heavy cream, 1 cup chilled

1 tablespoon unsalted butter, melted

2 teaspoons Calvados or other apple brandy

1. Heat the oven to 375°. Set a shallow baking pan on the lowest shelf of the oven and fill it with water. Butter the bottom and sides of an 8-by-2-inch baking dish, preferably glass. Peel, halve, and core the apples.

2. In a large nonreactive saucepan, simmer the wine, the ⅓ cup sugar, the lemon zest, and the ginger for 5 minutes. Add the apples, cover, and poach over moderate heat, turning once, until tender, about 10 minutes. Remove from the heat. Using a slotted spoon, place the apples, cut sides down, in the baking dish. Place the saucepan over low heat and cook the poaching liquid until slightly reduced, about 4 minutes. Pour the liquid over the apples.

3. In a small bowl, sift the flour with the baking powder. In a medium bowl, beat the egg yolks with 1 tablespoon sugar until thickened and light colored. Stir in ½ cup of the heavy cream and the melted butter. Stir in the flour mixture.

4. In a clean bowl, beat the egg whites until foamy. Continue beating the egg whites, adding 1 tablespoon sugar, until they hold firm peaks when the beaters are lifted. Fold a little of the egg yolk mixture into the whites, then fold the whites into the remaining yolk mixture and blend until there are no streaks of white left. Pour the batter over the apples.

5. Bake the apple cake in the middle of the oven until golden brown, about 25 minutes. Meanwhile, in a large bowl, whip the remaining 1 cup cream, the remaining ½ tablespoon sugar, and the Calvados until the cream holds soft peaks. Refrigerate the whipped cream until ready to serve. Transfer the apple cake to a rack to let it cool slightly.

6. Serve the cake warm with the whipped cream.

—ANN AMERNICK

St. Louis Orange Ring Cake

Sue Crouse sent this cake recipe from Warren, Ohio. She wrote, "My grand-mother would never give this recipe to anyone—she said that it came from St. Louis." It is wonderful.

MAKES ONE BUNDT CAKE

1¾ cups sifted flour

1 teaspoon baking powder

1 teaspoon baking soda

½ pound unsalted butter, at room temperature

1½ cups sugar

2½ teaspoons finely grated orange zest

3 eggs, separated, at room temperature

1 cup plain yogurt

1½ teaspoons vanilla extract

Pinch salt

½ cup orange juice

3 tablespoons lemon juice

1. Heat the oven to 325°. Butter and flour a 12-cup Bundt, kugelhopf, or tube pan and tap out any excess.

2. In a medium bowl, sift the flour with the baking powder and baking soda three times to be sure it is fully mixed and set aside.

3. In a large bowl, using an electric mixer, beat the butter until very light and fluffy. Beat in 1 cup of the sugar and the orange zest; beat until very light and fluffy, about 8 minutes. Add the egg yolks, beating until fully incorporated, then add the yogurt and vanilla. Continue beating until very light and fluffy, about 2 minutes. Using a wooden spoon, gently stir in the sifted dry ingredients until blended.

4. In a large bowl, beat the egg whites with the salt until they hold firm peaks when the beaters are lifted. Using a large spatula, fold the whites into the batter until just blended. Scrape the batter into the prepared pan and smooth the top.

5. Bake the cake until a toothpick stuck in the center comes out clean, about 1 hour. Let cool in the pan for about 10 minutes.

6. Meanwhile, in a small nonreactive saucepan, combine the orange juice, lemon juice, and the remaining ½ cup sugar. Bring to a boil over moderate heat, stirring. Reduce the heat to moderately low and simmer gently until the syrup has reduced to about ½ cup, 8 to 10 minutes.

7. Run a thin, sharp knife around the inside rim of the pan to loosen the cake and invert the cake onto a serving plate. Brush the hot syrup over the entire cake. Serve the cake warm, or at room temperature.

—Richard Sax

ORANGE CHIFFON CAKE WITH RHUBARB JAM

This airy orange-infused dessert has the texture of a rich chiffon cake.

MAKES ONE 10-INCH CAKE

RHUBARB JAM:

½ cup sugar

¼ cup orange juice

1 pound rhubarb, trimmed and thickly sliced

2 teaspoons finely grated orange zest

CHIFFON CAKE:

1½ cups cake flour

1 tablespoon baking powder

Pinch salt

6 large eggs at room temperature, separated

1¾ cups sugar

2 tablespoons finely grated orange zest

½ cup vegetable oil

½ cup orange juice

Pinch cream of tartar

1. For the jam, in a heavy saucepan, bring the sugar and orange juice to a boil over moderately high heat, stirring. Add three-quarters of the rhubarb and the orange zest and simmer, stirring, until the rhubarb is softened and slightly thickened, about 5 minutes. Add the remaining rhubarb and cook until just tender, about 2 minutes. Let the jam cool.

2. Heat the oven to 375°. For the cake, in a bowl, sift together the flour, baking powder, and salt. In a large bowl, beat the egg yolks with 1½ cups of the sugar and the orange zest on high speed until light and fluffy, about 3 minutes. Gradually beat in the oil. Working in batches, alternately fold in the flour mixture and the orange juice, beginning and ending with the flour mixture.

3. In a large bowl, beat the egg whites with the cream of tartar until very soft peaks form. Continue beating the egg whites, adding the remaining ¼ cup of sugar gradually, until they hold firm peaks when the beaters are lifted. Fold one-third of the whites into the cake batter until incorporated, then fold in the remaining whites until just blended.

4. Scrape the batter into a 10-inch tube pan with a removable bottom and smooth the top. Bang the pan once lightly on your work surface to force any air bubbles out of the batter. Bake the cake in the bottom third of the oven until the top springs back when pressed lightly, about 30 minutes. Invert the cake pan onto a jar and let cool in the pan.

5. Run a thin, metal knife between the cake and the sides of the pan to loosen. Invert the cake onto a cake plate and serve with the rhubarb jam.

—JOSEPH KELLER

ORANGE LAYER CAKE WITH ORANGE BUTTERCREAM FROSTING

If you don't have time to make this multilayered cake all at once, make the orange buttercream and the cake layers in advance separately. The buttercream in this recipe is made with egg whites and has a lighter taste and texture than the classic French buttercream made with egg yolks. Candied orange slices are an appealing sweet-tart accompaniment to the cake. Any leftover slices and syrup can be refrigerated and served later over ice cream. If you don't have time to make the candied orange slices, just serve the cake with vanilla ice cream.

MAKES ONE 9-INCH CAKE

CAKE:

3	cups flour
1	tablespoon baking powder
¾	teaspoon salt
12	tablespoons unsalted butter, at room temperature
2	cups sugar
4	large eggs, at room temperature
2	teaspoons orange extract
1	tablespoon plus 1 teaspoon minced orange zest
1½	cups milk

ORANGE BUTTERCREAM FROSTING:

1	cup plus 2 tablespoons sugar
⅓	cup water
4	large egg whites, at room temperature
¼	teaspoon cream of tartar
¾	pound unsalted butter, at room temperature
3	tablespoons orange liqueur

Candied Orange Slices, page 57

1. Heat the oven to 350°. For the cake, butter and flour two 9-by-1½-inch round cake pans. In a medium bowl, whisk the flour with the baking powder and salt.

2. In a large bowl, using an electric mixer, beat the butter and sugar at medium speed until light and fluffy, 8 to 10 minutes. Beat in the eggs 1 at a time, stopping to scrape the bowl with a rubber spatula after each addition. Then beat in the orange extract and orange zest. Beat in the dry ingredients at low speed, alternately with the milk in three batches. Scrape the bowl frequently.

3. Pour the batter into the prepared pans and smooth the tops. (The pans will be almost three-quarters full.) Bake in the lower part of the oven until a toothpick stuck in the center of the cakes comes out clean, 35 to 40 minutes.

4. Let the cakes cool in the pans on a rack for 10 minutes. Run a thin, sharp

knife around the edge of the pans and invert the cakes onto the rack. Turn the cakes right-side up and allow the cakes to cool completely.

5. For the frosting, in a small heavy saucepan, combine the 1 cup sugar and the water. Bring to a boil over moderate heat and boil (brushing the inside of the saucepan occasionally with a pastry brush dipped in cold water to dissolve any sugar crystals) until the syrup reaches the softball stage, about 10 minutes. A candy thermometer should register 238°.

6. Meanwhile, in a large bowl, beat the egg whites until foamy. Add the cream of tartar and beat until the whites hold soft peaks. Continue beating the egg whites, adding the remaining 2 tablespoons sugar gradually, until they hold firm peaks when the beaters are lifted.

7. Reduce the speed to medium-low and beat in the hot sugar syrup in a thin, steady stream; be careful to avoid splatters. Beat until the whites are thick and completely cool to the touch, 8 to 10 minutes.

8. Increase the speed to medium. Add the butter, 1 tablespoon at a time, and beat until the buttercream is completely smooth, thick, and spreadable, about 5 minutes. If the mixture looks curdled at any time, increase the speed to high and beat until completely smooth, then reduce the speed to medium and beat in

the remaining butter. Just before using, beat in the orange liqueur.

9. Using a serrated knife, trim the top of each cooled cake to make it level. Halve each cake horizontally. Place one top layer on a serving platter. Using a metal icing spatula, spread a scant ½ cup of the buttercream over the cake. Cover with a bottom layer and another scant ½ cup of buttercream. Repeat the layering with the second bottom layer and top layer and a scant ½ cup buttercream between them. Frost the top and sides of the cake with the rest of the buttercream. Let sit at room temperature for 1 to 2 hours before serving.

10. Slice the cake and place two or three of the candied orange slices, along with a spoonful of the reserved orange syrup, next to each serving.

—JUDITH SUTTON

CANDIED ORANGE SLICES

MAKES 36 TO 40 SLICES

3 large navel oranges

3 cups sugar

3 cups water

1. Using a very sharp knife, slice the unpeeled oranges crosswise $\frac{1}{8}$-inch thick (you should have 36 to 40 slices).

2. In a wide 6-quart nonreactive saucepan, bring the sugar and the water to a simmer, stirring until the sugar dissolves. Simmer for 5 minutes. Add the orange slices and simmer gently over low heat, occasionally spooning some of the syrup over the slices, until the orange peel is very tender and the white pith is almost translucent, about 2 hours. Do not overcook the oranges or the centers will fall apart. Using tongs, carefully transfer the orange slices in single layers to baking sheets lined with waxed paper or parchment to drain and cool. Reserve the orange syrup for finishing the cake or another use.

MAKE IT AHEAD

All of the elements of the cake can be made ahead. The cooled, unfrosted cakes will keep at room temperature, well wrapped, for up to two days. The buttercream can be covered and kept at room temperature for up to four hours or refrigerated for up to five days. If it has been refrigerated, bring it to room temperature and then beat with an electric mixer until smooth. The orange slices and syrup can be prepared up to three days ahead; cover and refrigerate them separately.

The frosted cake (without the orange slices) will keep, covered and refrigerated, for up to three days. Bring it to room temperature before serving.

DIRTY BANANA CAKE

This rich cake was inspired by the Dirty Banana, a blender drink I enjoyed more than once during a college break. It combines the creamy sweetness of bananas with coffee's slightly bitter taste. When preparing it, allow enough time for the filling to chill.

MAKES ONE 9-INCH CAKE

BANANA CAKE:

- 2 cups flour
- 2 teaspoons baking soda
- 1 teaspoon baking powder
- ¼ teaspoon salt
- ¼ pound unsalted butter, at room temperature
- 1⅓ cups sugar
- 4 large eggs, at room temperature
- 3 overripe medium bananas, mashed (about 1¼ cups)
- ½ cup buttermilk or plain yogurt

BANANA BUTTERCREAM FILLING:

- 2 large egg yolks
- ¾ cup confectioners' sugar
- ¼ cup milk
- ¼ cup mashed overripe banana
- ½ pound unsalted butter, at room temperature
- 1 tablespoon instant espresso powder dissolved in 2 teaspoons hot water

COFFEE FROSTING:

- 1 cup sugar
- ½ cup egg whites (from 4 to 5 large eggs)
- 10 ounces unsalted butter, cut into tablespoons
- 2 tablespoons instant espresso powder dissolved in 1 tablespoon hot water
- 1 teaspoon vanilla extract

Chocolate-covered espresso beans, for decorating

1. Heat the oven to 350°. For the cake, cover the bottom of a 9-by-3-inch round cake pan or springform pan with waxed paper and butter the paper. (If using a springform pan that doesn't seal tightly, wrap the bottom in foil to prevent leakage.)

2. Sift together the flour, baking soda, baking powder, and salt. Using an electric mixer, cream the butter with the sugar until fluffy. Add the eggs one at a time, beating for 1 minute after each addition. In a bowl, mash the bananas with the buttermilk. Beat the dry ingredients into the butter in two additions, alternating with the bananas. (The batter may appear slightly curdled.)

3. Scrape the batter into the prepared pan and smooth the top. Bake in the bottom third of the oven until a toothpick stuck in the center comes out clean, about 1 hour.

4. For the filling, in a large bowl, using an electric mixer, beat the egg yolks and confectioners' sugar at high speed until pale and thick. Meanwhile, in a medium saucepan, bring the milk and banana to a boil over moderate heat, whisking occasionally. Slowly whisk the hot milk into the egg yolks. Pour the mixture into the saucepan and cook over moderately low heat, stirring, until thick, about 5 minutes; do not boil. Pour the custard into a medium bowl and let cool briefly, whisking occasionally. Press a piece of waxed paper directly on the surface of the custard and refrigerate until chilled, at least 3 hours or overnight.

5. In a bowl, using an electric mixer, beat the butter until fluffy. Gradually beat in the cold banana custard and beat until fluffy. Then beat in the espresso.

6. Split the cake into three layers. Place one layer on a cake platter and cover with half of the buttercream filling. Top with a second layer and the remaining filling. Place the third layer on top, cover with plastic wrap, and refrigerate while you make the frosting.

7. For the frosting, in a large heatproof bowl, using an electric mixer, beat the sugar with the egg whites. Set the bowl over a large saucepan filled with about an inch of simmering water. Heat the mixture, whisking occasionally, until the sugar is dissolved, about 5 minutes. Remove the bowl from the heat and beat until fluffy, about 3 minutes. Continue beating until cool to the touch, about 5 minutes. Beat in the butter, several pieces at a time, waiting until the butter is incorporated before adding more. Whip the frosting until fluffy. If the frosting looks curdled at any time, increase the speed to high and beat until completely smooth, then reduce the speed to medium and beat in the remaining butter. If the mixture looks soft and runny, refrigerate for 5 minutes, then beat again. Beat in the espresso and vanilla until blended.

8. Set aside ½ cup of the frosting for decorating. Spread the remaining frosting on the sides and top of the cake. With the reserved frosting, using a pastry bag fitted with a star tip, pipe eight rosettes on the top edge of the cake. Place a chocolate-covered espresso bean in the center of each rosette. To serve, slice gently with a serrated cake knife.

—TRACEY SEAMAN

KEY LIME MERINGUE TORTE

This delicate cake combines sweet and tart, tender and crisp. The meringue bakes right on top of the cake batter for an effect as impressive as it is easy.

MAKES ONE 8-INCH TORTE

MERINGUE CAKE:

   1   cup cake flour

   1   teaspoon baking powder

  ⅛   teaspoon salt

  ¼   pound unsalted butter, at room temperature

1¼   cups plus 2 teaspoons sugar

   4   large eggs, separated, at room temperature

   3   tablespoons milk

   1   teaspoon vanilla extract

  ⅓   cup sliced almonds

KEY LIME CURD:

   2   large eggs

   1   large egg yolk

  ⅓   cup Key lime juice or lime or lemon juice

  ¾   cup sugar

   1   teaspoon cornstarch

      Pinch salt

   4   tablespoons unsalted butter, cut into tablespoons

1. Heat the oven to 350°. For the cake, cover the bottoms of two 8-by-2-inch round cake pans with waxed paper and butter the waxed paper.

2. Sift together the flour, baking powder, and salt. In a large bowl, using an electric mixer, cream the butter with ½ cup of the sugar until fluffy. Add the egg yolks and beat for 2 minutes. In a measuring cup, stir together the milk and vanilla and beat into the butter mixture in two batches, alternating with the dry ingredients, until just incorporated. Scrape into the prepared pans (the batter will barely reach up the sides of the pan).

3. In another large bowl, using clean beaters, beat the egg whites until they hold soft peaks. Continue beating the egg whites, adding ¾ cup of the sugar gradually, until they hold firm peaks when the beaters are lifted. Gently spread the meringue over the cake batter in the pans. Do not smooth the tops. Sprinkle the almonds, then the remaining 2 teaspoons sugar, on the meringue.

4. Bake the cakes in the bottom third of the oven until the meringue is puffed and lightly browned, about 25 minutes. Let the cakes cool completely in the pans; the tops will sink considerably.

5. For the lime curd, place the whole eggs and the egg yolk in a heatproof bowl and whisk. In a medium nonreactive

saucepan, bring the lime juice, sugar, corn-starch, and salt to a boil over moderate heat, whisking. Gradually whisk the mixture into the eggs. Scrape the lime curd into the saucepan and cook over moderate heat, stirring with a wooden spoon, until thick enough to coat the spoon, about 5 minutes. Do not boil, or it will curdle. Remove from the heat and stir in the butter.

6. Strain the curd into a clean bowl. Let cool at room temperature briefly, whisking occasionally, then press a piece of waxed paper directly on the surface and refrigerate until chilled, at least 2 hours or overnight.

7. Run a knife around the sides of the cake layers to loosen them from the pans. Carefully invert the layers onto baking sheets and remove the waxed paper. Invert one layer onto a cake platter. Spread all the lime curd on top. Cover with the other cake layer, meringue side up. To serve, slice gently with a serrated cake knife.

—Tracey Seaman

MAKE IT AHEAD

The cake can be refrigerated, loosely wrapped in plastic, for one day.

FRESH FRUIT CAKE

The inspiration for this cake comes from my mother-in-law's German apple kuchen and a fruit cake I once tasted made by the wonderful baker Jim Dodge.

MAKES ONE 9-INCH CAKE

- 1 large firm ripe pear, preferably Bosc, peeled and cut into ¾-inch dice
- 1 large tart green apple, peeled and cut into ¾-inch dice
- 6 ounces fresh or thawed frozen cranberries (about 1½ cups)
- 1 cup plus 2 tablespoons sugar
- 2 teaspoons cinnamon
- 5 tablespoons unsalted butter, at room temperature
- ⅓ cup low-fat (1.5%) buttermilk
- 2 large eggs
- 2 large egg whites
- 2 cups cake flour
- 2 teaspoons baking powder

1. Heat the oven to 350°. Lightly spray a 9-by-2-inch round cake pan with vegetable-oil cooking spray. Cover the bottom of the cake pan with parchment or waxed paper and spray the paper. Sprinkle the sides of the cake pan with sugar.

2. In a medium bowl, combine the diced pear and apple with the cranberries. Add 1 tablespoon of the sugar and the cinnamon and toss to coat.

3. In a large bowl, beat the butter until fluffy. Gradually beat in the 1 cup sugar and the buttermilk. Beat in the eggs and the egg whites until combined, then beat in the flour and the baking powder. Stir in the fruit. Spoon the batter into the prepared cake pan and sprinkle the top with the remaining 1 tablespoon sugar.

4. Bake the fruit cake until a toothpick stuck in the center comes out clean, about 1 hour. Set the cake pan on a rack and let the cake cool for 20 minutes. Invert the cake onto a plate and peel off the paper. Invert the cake again onto a large plate or platter and allow it to cool completely.

—DIANA STURGIS

MAKE IT AHEAD

You can make the cake a day in advance, then cover and store at room temperature.

UPSIDE-DOWN MANGO CORN CAKE

This quick cake is a delicious and somewhat more exotic cousin of Pineapple Upside-Down Cake.

MAKES 6 TO 8 SERVINGS

8 tablespoons unsalted butter, at room temperature

⅓ cup plus 3 tablespoons light-brown sugar

2 large mangoes, peeled and sliced ½-inch thick

½ cup coarse yellow cornmeal, preferably stone-ground

½ cup flour

1 teaspoon baking powder

¼ teaspoon cinnamon

Pinch salt

2 large eggs

2 large egg yolks

¼ teaspoon vanilla extract

1. Heat the oven to 350°. In a 9-inch cast-iron frying pan, melt 2 tablespoons of the butter over moderate heat. Stir in the 3 tablespoons brown sugar until it is melted. Arrange the mango slices in the frying pan in a tight pinwheel, filling in with scraps. Continue cooking until the mangoes are tender and lightly caramelized, about 10 minutes.

2. Meanwhile, sift the cornmeal, flour, baking powder, cinnamon, and salt into a small bowl. If any large pieces of cornmeal remain in the sifter, dump them into the bowl.

3. In a medium bowl, using an electric mixer, beat the remaining 6 tablespoons butter until light and fluffy. Beat in the remaining ⅓ cup brown sugar until fluffy. Beat in the whole eggs and the eggs yolks one at a time, blending well after each addition. Beat in the vanilla. Using a rubber spatula, fold in the dry ingredients a handful at a time, mixing lightly but thoroughly. Drop dollops of the cake batter evenly over the pinwheel of mango slices and gently spread the batter to within 1 inch of the edge of the frying pan.

4. Bake the cake in the middle of the oven, or until the top springs back when lightly touched, about 20 minutes. Remove the cake from the oven and let settle for 1 minute. Invert a large plate over the frying pan. Hold the frying pan handle with an oven mitt and with a quick motion, flip the cake onto the plate. Let the cake cool for about 10 minutes, then cut it into wedges and serve.

—MARCIA KIESEL

Stephanie's Poppy Cake

This cake begins with two 8-inch round layers that are split in half horizontally and given a light soaking with a rum-flavored syrup; it's a nice French touch that keeps the cake moist and adds a subtle extra flavor.

MAKES ONE 8-INCH CAKE

CAKE:

6 eggs, separated, at room temperature

1 cup plus 3 tablespoons sugar

3 tablespoons poppy seeds

1 tablespoon vanilla extract

1 cup plus 2 tablespoons cake flour

6 tablespoons unsalted butter, melted and cooled

RUM SYRUP:

2 tablespoons sugar

6 tablespoons hot water

1½ tablespoons rum, or 2½ teaspoons vanilla extract

LEMON CURD:

6 tablespoons unsalted butter

1⅔ cups sugar

2 whole eggs

2 egg yolks

Grated zest of 1 lemon

¼ cup lemon juice

1 tablespoon light or dark rum (optional)

LEMON BUTTER ICING:

6 ounces unsalted butter, at room temperature

3 cups sifted confectioners' sugar

⅓ cup Lemon Curd

Poppy seeds, for sprinkling

1. Heat the oven to 350°. For the cake, butter two 8-inch round cake pans and cover the bottoms with rounds of parchment or waxed paper. Butter the paper and flour the pans, tapping out the excess.

2. In a large bowl, beat the egg yolks. Continue beating the egg yolks, adding the 1 cup sugar gradually, until the mixture is as thick as mayonnaise. Beat in the poppy seeds and vanilla.

3. In another large bowl, using clean beaters, beat the egg whites until foamy. Continue beating the egg whites, adding the remaining 3 tablespoons of sugar, until they hold firm peaks when the beaters are lifted.

4. Scoop one-quarter of the whites into the yolk mixture and fold them in. Sift one-third of the flour over the batter and fold it in along with one-third of the egg whites. Continue to fold in one-third of the flour and one-third of the egg whites until everything has been incorporated. Fold in the melted butter with the last of the egg whites.

5. Scrape the batter into the prepared pans. Bang the pans once lightly on your work surface to force any air bubbles out of the batter. Bake the cakes in the lower third of the oven until they begin to shrink from the pans, 20 to 25 minutes. Cool the cakes on a rack for 30 minutes. Invert the cakes, peel off the paper, and cool completely.

6. Cut a ¼-inch wedge out of the side of each cake; this will enable you to line up the layers when assembling the cake. Using a long, serrated knife, slice each cake in half horizontally and set on a work surface, cut-side up.

7. For the rum syrup, in a small saucepan, combine all of the ingredients and stir over low heat until the sugar is completely dissolved.

8. For the lemon curd, in a medium stainless-steel saucepan, whisk all of the ingredients over very low heat until the bubbles begin to subside and a tiny wisp of steam appears. Do not boil, or it will curdle. Stir the curd over ice until cooled and lightly thickened.

9. For the lemon butter icing, in a medium bowl, beat the butter until softened, then beat in the confectioners' sugar until light and fluffy. Beat in the ⅓ cup cooled lemon curd until smooth.

10. Brush each cake layer gently with 2 tablespoons of the rum syrup. Center a bottom layer of cake on a platter and spread one-third of the remaining lemon curd over it. Cover with the top layer, cut-sides together, taking care to line up the wedges. Spread the top with lemon curd. Repeat with the remaining cake and curd, ending with a cake layer.

11. Spread a very thin layer of the icing over the top and sides of the cake to secure down the crumbs. Then spread a ¼-inch layer of icing over the top and sides. Decorate as you wish, but I suggest using a pastry bag fitted with a star tip. In any case, sprinkling the cake with poppy seeds can disguise certain ineptitudes.

—Julia Child

Make It Ahead

The cake can be made in advance. Refrigerate it first, uncovered, to firm up the icing. Then wrap in plastic and refrigerate for up to three days, or freeze for up to one month. Either way, allow the cake to come to room temperature before serving.

COCONUT LEMON ROULADE

Toasted coconut chips—fantasy birch bark—cover this classic sponge roll. You can roll and ice the cake up to four hours before serving. Let it stand at room temperature until you're ready to eat.

MAKES ONE 15-INCH ROULADE

LEMON CURD:

- 3 large egg yolks
- ¼ cup sugar
- ¼ cup lemon juice

SUGAR-TOASTED COCONUT:

- 2⅓ cups unsweetened coconut chips* (about 3½ ounces)
- 2 tablespoons sugar
- 1 tablespoon boiling water

SPONGE CAKE:

- ⅔ cup flour
- ½ teaspoon baking powder
- 4 large eggs
- 1 large egg yolk
- ¾ cup sugar
- 2 tablespoons unsalted butter, cut into small pieces
- ¼ cup milk

MARSHMALLOW FROSTING:

- 4 large egg whites
- 1 cup sugar
- ⅛ teaspoon cream of tartar
- 1 teaspoon vanilla extract
- ⅓ cup water

*Available at health-food stores and specialty-food stores.

1. For the lemon curd, in a small nonreactive saucepan, whisk the egg yolks with the sugar and lemon juice. Cook over low heat, stirring constantly, until the mixture just begins to thicken. Do not boil, or it will curdle. Immediately strain the curd into a bowl. Place plastic wrap directly on the surface of the curd and refrigerate until cold.

2. Heat the oven to 350°. For the toasted coconut, line a baking sheet with parchment or waxed paper. Put the coconut chips in a medium bowl. In a cup, combine the sugar and boiling water and stir to dissolve the sugar. Add the sugared water to the coconut and toss until thoroughly coated. Spread the coconut evenly on the baking sheet and toast it in the oven, stirring occasionally, until golden, 6 to 10 minutes. Watch the coconut carefully so that it does not burn. Remove from the baking sheet.

3. Heat the oven to 400°. For the cake, butter a 15-by-10-inch jelly-roll pan and cover it with waxed paper. Sift the flour and baking powder onto a sheet of waxed paper. In a large bowl, beat the eggs, egg yolk, and sugar. Set the bowl over a large saucepan filled with about an inch of simmering water. Using a hand-held mixer or a

whisk, beat the egg mixture until warm to the touch. Remove the bowl from the heat and beat the mixture until it is pale in color and as thick as whipped cream.

4. Meanwhile, in a small saucepan, melt the butter in the milk over low heat. Turn off the heat but leave the pan on the stove.

5. Sift one-third of the sifted flour over the egg mixture and gently fold it in with a large spatula. Repeat in two more additions. Stir the milk mixture and pour half of it in a circle on the batter, then fold it in. Repeat with the remaining milk and fold gently until incorporated. Pour the batter into the prepared jelly-roll pan and smooth the surface. Bake until the cake springs back when pressed gently, about 10 minutes. Let the cake cool completely.

6. For the frosting, put the egg whites in the bowl of a standing mixer. In a small heavy saucepan, combine the sugar and water. Bring to a boil over moderately high heat and boil, brushing the inside of the saucepan occasionally with a pastry brush dipped in water, to dissolve any sugar crystals.

7. When the sugar syrup comes to a boil, begin beating the whites at medium speed until foamy. Add the cream of tartar and continue beating the egg whites until they hold firm peaks when the beaters are lifted.

8. When the sugar syrup reaches 236° on a candy thermometer, pour it onto the whites in a slow stream and continue to beat the frosting until it is thick and fluffy, about 3 minutes, scraping down the sides of the bowl once with a rubber spatula. Add the vanilla and beat for 1 more minute. The frosting will still be a little warm.

9. Turn the cooled cake out onto a piece of foil and peel off the waxed paper. Place a piece of plastic wrap over the cake and flip it so that it is right-side up again. Remove the foil.

10 Spread the lemon curd evenly over the cake. Then spread about 2¼ cups of the frosting over the curd. Starting at a long edge, roll the cake as tightly as possible and wrap it in plastic. Let the log stand at room temperature for about 5 minutes, seam-side down.

11. Place the log on a platter and unwrap it. Spread the remaining frosting in a thick layer over the entire log. Scatter the toasted coconut over the log. Press with your hands to help the coconut adhere to the frosting. With a hot knife, slice about ½ inch off each end before serving.

—PEGGY CULLEN

PUMPKIN CARAMEL PUDDING CAKES

If you like, serve these cakes with candied ginger ice cream. To make your own easily, fold finely chopped candied ginger into slightly softened top-quality vanilla ice cream, or accompany with whipped cream and garnish with candied ginger.

MAKES 20 CAKES

1⅔ cups plus 6 tablespoons sugar

¾ cup light corn syrup

2 tablespoons water

1 cup heavy cream

¼ pound unsalted butter, cut into pieces, plus 6 tablespoons unsalted butter, melted

3 15-ounce cans unsweetened pumpkin puree

6 large eggs, separated

2 teaspoons finely grated orange zest

1½ cups cake flour

2 tablespoons baking powder

¾ teaspoon cinnamon

¾ teaspoon freshly grated nutmeg

¾ teaspoon salt

1. In a small saucepan, combine the 1⅔ cup sugar, corn syrup, and water. Simmer over moderate heat, stirring once or twice, until a deep amber caramel forms, about 15 minutes. Add the cream and the ¼ pound butter and stir over moderate heat until the caramel is smooth, about 3 minutes. Pour the caramel into a heatproof bowl and set aside to cool.

2. Heat the oven to 375°. Arrange two racks in the center part of the oven. Butter and sugar twenty ½-cup ramekins and place on two large baking sheets.

3. In a food processor, combine the caramel with the pumpkin puree, egg yolks, 6 tablespoons melted butter, and orange zest. Process until smooth and scrape it into a large bowl.

4. In another large bowl, sift the cake flour with the baking powder, cinnamon, nutmeg, and salt. Whisk to combine. Fold the flour into the pumpkin-caramel mixture until blended.

5. In a large bowl, beat the egg whites until soft peaks form. Add the remaining 6 tablespoons of sugar and continue beating until they hold firm peaks when the beaters are lifted. Fold the egg whites gently into the pumpkin batter until only a few streaks of white remain. Spoon a rounded ½ cup of the batter into each prepared ramekin. Bake until the cakes are risen and set, about 30 minutes. Carefully unmold the hot cakes onto dessert plates and serve at once.

—LYDIA SHIRE

CHOCOLATE SOUFFLÉ YULE LOG

This light, flourless roll filled with vanilla cream melts in your mouth. You'll need to start this recipe the day before you plan to serve it because the vanilla needs to stand overnight in the cream to flavor it.

MAKES ONE 17-INCH LOG

1¾ cups heavy cream

1 vanilla bean, split lengthwise

2 teaspoons vanilla extract

4 ounces best-quality semisweet chocolate, chopped

8 large eggs, at room temperature

1⅓ cups superfine sugar

⅛ teaspoon cream of tartar

3 tablespoons confectioners' sugar, more for dusting

1. In a small saucepan, scald the heavy cream and remove it from the heat just before it boils. Pour the cream into a bowl and add the vanilla bean and extract. Let cool completely, then cover and refrigerate overnight.

2. Heat the oven to 325°. Butter a 17-by-11-inch jelly-roll pan and cover the bottom with waxed paper.

3. Melt the chocolate in a double boiler, stirring occasionally, until smooth. (Or melt the chocolate in a microwave oven.) Set aside to cool slightly.

4. Meanwhile, separate the eggs into two large bowls. Beat the yolks and gradu-ally add ⅔ cup of the superfine sugar. Continue beating until the yolks are thick, stiff, and pale in color, about 5 minutes. Stir in the melted chocolate with a large rubber spatula.

5. Wash and dry the beaters. Beat the whites at medium speed until foamy. Add the cream of tartar and beat until the mixture whitens. Increase the speed to high and continue beating the egg whites, gradually beat in the remaining ⅔ cup superfine sugar until they hold soft peaks when the beaters are lifted.

6. Using a large rubber spatula, fold one-fourth of the beaten whites into the yolk mixture. Fold in the remaining egg whites in two additions. Pour the batter into the prepared pan. Use the spatula to level the batter and nudge it into the cor-ners. Bake in the middle of the oven until the cake springs back when pressed gently, about 30 minutes. Let the cake cool com-pletely in the pan.

7. Meanwhile, remove the vanilla bean from the chilled cream. Scrape the seeds from the pod into the cream and discard the pod. Add the confectioners' sugar and beat the cream until it holds firm peaks when the beaters are lifted.

8. Spread a dishcloth on a work surface and sift confectioners' sugar over it. Invert the sheet pan onto the cloth. Remove the pan and peel the waxed paper off the cake. Spread the whipped cream evenly over the cake. Starting at a long edge, and using the cloth to help, roll the cake as tightly as possible. Roll the log onto a serving dish, seam-side down. Refrigerate the cake for at least 1 hour.

9. Lightly sift confectioners' sugar over the yule log in a few spots so that it resembles a dusting of snow. Before serving, slice off the uneven ends of the log with a sharp, serrated knife.

—Peggy Cullen

Make It Ahead

You can fill and roll the cake up to six hours ahead and keep it in the refrigerator until ready to serve.

Decorating Yule Logs

To give yule logs a festive touch, try these trimmings:

• For sugared cranberries: Roll fresh cranberries in lightly beaten egg white and then in granulated sugar.

• For marzipan holly leaves: Tint marzipan using food coloring in liquid, powder, or paste form. Roll the marzipan into a rope. Cut it into 1-inch pieces. Form ovals, flatten and roll out between plastic wrap. Make the leaf points by cutting out semicircles with the back of a small piping tip. Score the leaves with a knife. Drape over egg cartons and let dry for six hours.

• For marzipan berries: Tint marzipan red and roll into small balls. Moisten and roll in sugar.

ROULÉ CONFITURE WITH RASPBERRY COULIS AND SUMMER BERRIES

When berries are out of season, try winter fruit, such as pears. This is based on a recipe that appears in *Jacques Pépin's The Art of Cooking*.

MAKES ONE 15-INCH ROULÉ

1   teaspoon unsalted butter

6   large eggs, separated

½   cup sugar

1   teaspoon vanilla extract

½   cup flour

1½ tablespoons kirschwasser

½   cup seedless raspberry preserves
    Raspberry Coulis, opposite page

12 large, fresh strawberries, sliced

2½ cups mixed fresh berries, such as blackberries, raspberries, and red currants

⅓   cup small fresh mint leaves

1   cup sour cream

1. Heat the oven to 350°. Butter a 15½-by-10½-inch jelly-roll pan. Spread the butter on a 14-by-18-inch sheet of parchment and cut a 2-inch-long diagonal slit in each corner. Press the paper into the pan buttered-side up, overlapping the cut corners.

2. In a large bowl, using an electric mixer, beat the egg yolks, sugar, and vanilla on medium speed for 2 minutes. Whisk in the flour until incorporated.

3. In another large bowl, using clean beaters, beat the egg whites at high speed until stiff peaks form. Whisk one-quarter of the beaten whites into the egg yolk mixture, then gently fold in the remaining whites with a large rubber spatula. Scrape the batter into the prepared pan and spread it evenly into the corners. Bake in the middle of the oven until golden, about 10 minutes. Let the cake cool for 30 minutes.

4. Hold the parchment at each end and lift the cake out onto a work surface. Sprinkle the cake evenly with the kirschwasser and spread the preserves in a thin layer over the entire surface. Beginning at one of the short ends, grasp the parchment with both hands and push and roll the cake into a neat, tight scroll, peeling off the paper as you go. When the cake is rolled compactly, rewrap it in the parchment and refrigerate for at least 1 hour to firm it up.

5. To assemble, spoon a few tablespoons of coulis onto dinner plates and tilt to coat evenly. Using a sharp knife, cut the roulé in ¾- to 1-inch-thick slices and place one in the center of each plate. Scatter the fresh berries around the roulé. Arrange a few mint leaves between the berries and dot

each plate with a few teaspoon-size dollops of sour cream. Serve immediately.

—JACQUES PÉPIN

MAKE IT AHEAD

The filled, rolled cake and the coulis can be made up to three days ahead. Cover and refrigerate the coulis.

RASPBERRY COULIS

When the season for fresh berries is past, I use unsweetened I.Q.F. (Individually Quick Frozen) raspberries in my coulis; since they are picked and frozen at the peak of ripeness, they're just as good as fresh berries when pureed. I do not, however, recommend serving thawed frozen berries because they tend to become mushy and bleed.

1 pound fresh raspberries
1 cup seedless raspberry preserves

In a food processor, puree the raspberries with the preserves. Press the puree through a fine sieve to remove the seeds.

DIPLOMATICO

This homey dessert, made with store-bought pound cake, can be assembled in less than half an hour.

1¼ cups strong espresso

5 tablespoons rum

7 teaspoons sugar

5 tablespoons water

1 16-ounce pound cake, cut into ¼-inch slices

4 large eggs, separated

6 ounces semisweet chocolate, chopped

1 cup very cold heavy cream

Fresh berries or walnut halves and candied fruit, for garnish

1. In a small bowl, stir together the espresso, rum, 5 teaspoons of the sugar, and the water.

2. Moisten a sheet of cheesecloth large enough to line a 9-by-5-by-3-inch glass loaf pan with plenty of overhang. Line the loaf pan with the cheesecloth. Dip the pound cake, slice by slice, in the rum-and-espresso mixture, then use the slices to line the bottom and sides of the loaf pan. (Dip the pound cake slices very quickly, or else they'll become too soggy to handle, and allow any excess liquid to drip from each slice before using it to line the pan.) Leave no gaps, patching where necessary with additional pieces of soaked pound cake.

3. In a large bowl, beat the egg yolks with 1 teaspoon of the sugar until the yolks turn pale yellow, about 4 minutes.

4. Melt the chocolate in a double boiler, stirring occasionally, until smooth. Gradually pour the melted chocolate over the beaten egg yolks, mixing quickly with a rubber spatula until combined smoothly.

5. In a medium bowl, beat the whites of the eggs until they form stiff peaks. Stir a rounded tablespoon of the beaten egg whites into the chocolate mixture to loosen it, then gently fold in the remaining beaten whites.

6. Spoon the chocolate filling into the cake-lined loaf pan. Cover the filling with more slices of rum-and-espresso-soaked pound cake. (You may have some slices of pound cake left over.) Fold the moistened cheesecloth over the top of the cake. Refrigerate the diplomatico for at least one day.

7. When you take the diplomatico out of the refrigerator, unfold the cheesecloth and pull it away from the top of the cake. Invert the loaf pan onto a platter and shake it firmly to free the cake. Peel off the cheesecloth.

8. In a large, chilled bowl, with chilled beaters, beat the cream with the remaining 1 teaspoon sugar until it holds firm peaks when the beaters are lifted. First frost the top and the sides of the diplomatico with the whipped cream, and garnish it with fresh berries, or with a simple arrangement of walnuts and candied fruit.

—MARCELLA HAZAN

MAKE IT AHEAD

The diplomatico will keep in the refrigerator for up to one week.

DIPLIMATICO TIPS

• Strong brewed espresso is very important for the flavor of Diplomatico, and using an extra-strong cup of regular coffee in its place just will not do. If you don't have an espresso machine, simply buy some espresso at your local coffee bar on your way home.

• Some pound cakes absorb too much liquid, become too soggy to handle, and break apart. Look for the cheapest brands, made with little or no butter; these cakes remain firmer and are easier to work with.

chapter 2
BARS AND COOKIES

Lovey's Brownies

LOVEY'S BROWNIES

Mother of five, including Tracey Seaman, who is formerly of FOOD & WINE's test kitchen, and grandmother of seven, Mary Seaman has made hundreds of fudgy-brownie lovers happy for years with this recipe.

MAKES 35 BROWNIES

½ pound unsalted butter

4 ounces unsweetened chocolate, chopped

2 cups sugar

4 large eggs

1 teaspoon vanilla extract

1 cup flour

½ teaspoon salt

1 generous cup chopped walnuts or pecans

1. Heat the oven to 350°. Butter a 13-by-9-inch metal or ceramic baking pan.

2. In a large saucepan, heat the butter over moderately low heat until half melted. Add the chocolate and stir until smooth. Remove from the heat and stir in the sugar with a wooden spoon.

3. Using the wooden spoon, beat in the eggs, one at a time, stirring after each addition until the eggs are fully incorporated and the chocolate mixture is shiny. Stir in the vanilla. Add the flour and salt all at once and mix until blended. Stir in the chopped nuts.

4. Scrape the batter into the prepared pan. Bake until the brownies are slightly firm to the touch and a toothpick stuck in the center shows that the brownies are moist, about 30 minutes. Let cool completely in the pan and then cut into 35 bars.

—MARY SEAMAN

CHOCOLATE PUMPKIN BROWNIES

These marbled brownies combine the flavors of rich chocolate and spicy pumpkin. They have the perfect texture, falling somewhere between cakey and fudgy. Walnuts are optional; I like them, but some chocoholics say they interfere with the brownie.

MAKES 24 BROWNIES

PUMPKIN BATTER:

- 1 tablespoon unsalted butter, at room temperature
- 3 ounces cream cheese, at room temperature
- ½ cup sugar
- 1 large egg, at room temperature
- ⅓ cup canned pumpkin puree
- 1 teaspoon vanilla extract
- ½ teaspoon cinnamon
- ½ teaspoon ground ginger
- 1 tablespoon flour

CHOCOLATE BATTER:

- 5½ ounces best-quality semisweet chocolate, chopped
- 5 ounces unsalted butter, cut into 1-inch pieces
- 4 large eggs, at room temperature
- 1½ cups sugar
- 1 teaspoon vanilla extract
- ¼ teaspoon salt
- 1⅓ cups flour
- 1 heaping cup large walnut pieces (optional)

1. Heat the oven to 350°. Butter a 13-by-9-inch baking dish. For the pumpkin batter, in a small bowl, using an electric mixer, beat the butter with the cream cheese until smooth. Beat in the sugar, scraping the bowl occasionally. Beat in the egg and then the pumpkin puree, vanilla, cinnamon, and ginger. Stir in the flour.

2. For the chocolate batter, combine the chocolate and the butter in a medium bowl. Set the bowl over a large saucepan filled with about an inch of simmering water and melt, stirring occasionally, until smooth. In a large bowl, combine the eggs with the sugar, vanilla, and salt. Set the bowl over the pan of simmering water. Using a hand-held mixer, beat at low speed until blended. Increase the speed to medium and beat until the mixture is warm to the touch. Remove the bowl from the heat and beat the mixture until thick and fluffy, about 5 minutes. Using a large rubber spatula, fold in the melted chocolate mixture. Sift the flour over the warm batter and fold it in just until combined. Fold in the walnut pieces, if using.

3. Spread the chocolate batter evenly in the prepared pan. Using a tablespoon, drop dollops of the pumpkin batter all over the top. Using the back of a butter knife, swirl the pumpkin into the chocolate but don't overdo it or the swirl pattern will be lost. Bake until a toothpick stuck in the center comes out clean, about 50 minutes. Let cool completely before cutting.

—PEGGY CULLEN

BUTTER SELECTION AND STORAGE

There are times when nothing but good butter will do—like when you're baking brownies and cookies. But before you bake, be sure the butter's not bad. Butter keeps few secrets. Look at it; it should be free of moisture at room temperature. Sniff it, and you should detect a faint, clean aroma. Then taste it. The flavor must be fresh, not too greasy, perhaps slightly nutty-sweet and seductively rich. Because butter readily picks up odors, keep it in its original wrapper, which is designed to protect it. Store it in the coldest spot in your refrigerator—the temperature should be maintained at no more than 38°—for up to one month. You can freeze butter for up to six months; enclose the original package in foil or an airtight freezer bag.

—FLORENCE FABRICANT

Heath Bar Brownies

In the immortal words of Mae West, "Too much of a good thing can be wonderful." In this recipe, the chocolate-toffee candy bars called Heath bars—a lot of them—are cut up and mixed into the brownie batter. The brownies can be served at room temperature or refrigerated; I like them best cold. The photo on the facing page pictures these brownies (left) next to Walnut Passion, page 85.

MAKES 24 SMALL BROWNIES

¼ pound unsalted butter plus 1 tablespoon for the pan

¾ cup pecan halves or pieces (2½ ounces)

5 1¼-ounce Heath candy bars or 20 miniature Heath candy bars

2 ounces unsweetened chocolate

2 large eggs

¾ cup sugar

½ teaspoon vanilla extract

¼ teaspoon salt

1 cup flour

1. Heat the oven to 350°. Turn an 8-inch square baking pan upside down. Press a 12-inch square of foil, shiny side down, onto the baking pan, shaping it to the sides and corners with your hands. Remove the foil. Run tap water into the baking pan to wet it all over. Pour out all but about 1 tablespoon of the water, then place the shaped foil in the baking pan and press it gently against the bottom and sides to adhere. Put the 1 tablespoon of butter in the pan and melt in the oven. Using a piece of crumpled plastic wrap, spread the melted butter all over the foil.

2. Toast the pecans in the oven until they are very hot and fragrant, about 12 minutes.

3. Using a large sharp knife, cut the Heath bars crosswise ¼- to ⅓-inch thick. (You will have about 1½ cups.) Chop a scant ¼ cup of the Heath bars into smaller pieces and reserve.

4. In a small double boiler, melt the unsweetened chocolate and the remaining ¼ pound of butter over warm water, stirring occasionally, until smooth. Set the melted chocolate aside to cool slightly.

5. In a medium bowl, using an electric mixer, beat the eggs, sugar, vanilla, and salt at medium speed until mixed. Add the melted chocolate and beat just to mix. Then add the flour and beat at low speed just until combined. Using a wooden spoon, stir in the toasted pecans and all but the reserved ¼ cup of the Heath bars. Scrape the batter into the prepared pan and

spread it evenly. Sprinkle the remaining Heath bars on top.

6. Bake the brownies in the bottom third of the oven until a toothpick stuck in the center comes out just barely clean, about 28 minutes. Let the brownies cool completely in the pan.

7. When the brownies are cool, cover the pan with a flat board or cookie sheet and invert. Remove the pan and peel off the foil. Cover the cake with a piece of parchment or waxed paper, and then with another board or cookie sheet, and invert again so that the cake is right side up. Refrigerate for about 1 hour.

8. Using a large, heavy, serrated knife, cut the cake into quarters, then halve each of the quarters. Now you have eight strips; cut each of the strips crosswise into three brownies, each about 2- by 1⅓-inches.

—MAIDA HEATTER

BAR COOKIE TIPS

• To get bar cookies of exactly the same size, remove the baked cake from the pan in one piece, use a ruler, and insert toothpicks along the edge to mark the cake before slicing.

• For easy slicing, use a large, heavy, serrated knife. Cut with a sawing motion.

• To store bar cookies, place them in an airtight container with waxed paper between the layers. Or wrap the bars individually in clear plastic wrap, waxed paper, or aluminum foil. They will keep for up to four days in an airtight container and up to two months in the freezer.

WALNUT PASSION

These bars are divine—a shallow, dense, chocolate cookie layer on the bottom topped with caramel loaded with walnuts. You can substitute pecans for the walnuts but be sure to toast them first. You will need a candy thermometer for testing the caramel. See photo on page 82.

MAKES 32 BARS

CHOCOLATE LAYER:

6 tablespoons unsalted butter plus 1 tablespoon for the pan

½ cup light-brown sugar

1 large egg

½ teaspoon vanilla extract

⅛ teaspoon salt

¼ cup unsweetened cocoa powder, preferably Dutch process

¼ cup sifted flour

WALNUT TOPPING:

⅓ cup heavy cream

1 tablespoon dark rum or cognac

6 tablespoons unsalted butter

1½ cups light-brown sugar

¼ cup dark corn syrup

Scant ½ teaspoon salt

2 cups walnut halves or pieces

1. Heat the oven to 375°. Turn a 9-inch square baking pan upside down on a work surface. Press a 12-inch square of foil, shiny side down, onto the pan, shaping it to the sides and corners with your hands. Remove the foil. Run some tap water into the pan to wet it all over. Pour out all but about 1 tablespoon of water, then place the shaped foil in the pan and press it gently against the bottom and sides to adhere. Put the 1 tablespoon of butter in the pan and melt in the oven. Then, using a piece of crumpled plastic wrap, spread the butter all over the bottom and sides of the foil.

2. For the chocolate layer, in a small saucepan, melt the remaining 6 tablespoons butter over moderate heat. Pour the mixture into a medium bowl and add the brown sugar, egg, vanilla, and salt. Beat with an electric mixer at medium speed to mix. At low speed, beat in the cocoa powder and the flour. Scrape the batter into the prepared pan and spread it evenly with a metal spoon.

3. Bake the layer in the bottom third of the oven until it begins to come away from the sides of the pan, about 15 minutes. Remove from the oven. Leave the oven on.

4. For the walnut topping, in a cup, combine the heavy cream and rum. In a heavy medium saucepan, melt the butter over moderate heat. Using a wooden spoon, stir in the brown sugar, dark corn syrup, and salt. Continue stirring until the mixture comes to a full boil. Place a candy

thermometer into the saucepan and boil, stirring the mixture a few times, until the temperature reaches 250°, about 2 minutes. Do not overcook.

5. Remove the mixture from the heat and quickly stir in the heavy cream (be careful, the mixture will bubble up). Stir in the walnuts. Pour the hot caramel over the chocolate layer. Using a metal spoon or fork, spread the nuts evenly and into the corners.

6. Bake the cake for 25 minutes. Remove and let cool completely.

7. To slice, cover the pan with a flat board or cookie sheet and invert. Remove the pan and peel off the foil. Cover with another board or cookie sheet and invert again so that the cake is right side up. Using a large, heavy, serrated knife, cut the cake into quarters, then halve each of the quarters. Now you have eight strips. Cut each strip crosswise into four bars. Serve the bars at room temperature.

—MAIDA HEATTER

FROSTED BUTTERSCOTCH BROWNIES

These blondies are just as good without the German chocolate cake topping.

MAKES 48 BARS

BUTTERSCOTCH BROWNIES:

1½ cups flour

½ teaspoon baking powder

¼ teaspoon salt

½ pound unsalted butter, at room temperature

1¾ cups light-brown sugar

3 large eggs, at room temperature

1½ teaspoons vanilla extract

CARAMEL FROSTING:

¾ cup pecans

¾ cup heavy cream

½ cup light-brown sugar

¼ cup granulated sugar

4 large egg yolks, at room temperature

6 tablespoons unsalted butter, cut into pieces, at room temperature

  Pinch salt

1 teaspoon vanilla extract

1 cup sweetened flaked coconut

1. Heat the oven to 350°. Butter and flour a 9-by-13-inch baking pan.

2. For the brownies, whisk together the flour, baking powder, and salt in a small bowl. Using an electric mixer, cream the butter with the sugar at medium speed until fluffy, about 3 minutes. Add the eggs one at a time, beating well after each addition. Beat in the vanilla. At low speed, mix in the dry ingredients in three additions until just blended.

3. Scrape the batter into the prepared pan and spread it evenly. Bake the brownies in the center of the oven until a toothpick stuck in the center comes out clean, 35 to 40 minutes. Cool completely.

4. Heat the oven to 350°. For the frosting, spread the pecans on a baking sheet and toast in the oven until fragrant and brown, about 8 minutes. Cool and coarsely chop.

5. In a heavy medium saucepan, combine the cream, brown sugar, granulated sugar, egg yolks, butter, and salt. Cook over moderate heat, stirring constantly with a wooden spoon, until the sugar dissolves and the mixture thickens (the spoon will start to leave a track), about 12 minutes. Do not boil. Strain the mixture into a large bowl, pressing it through a sieve with a rubber spatula. Stir in the vanilla. Stir in the coconut and toasted pecans and let cool.

6. Using the rubber spatula, spread the caramel frosting evenly over the cooled blondies. Cover the baking pan and refrigerate the blondies for 30 minutes. Cut the blondies into 48 small bars and serve them cold or at room temperature.

—JUDITH SUTTON

GANACHE-FILLED BROWN SUGAR BARS

These miniature cakes, or bar cookies, are particularly easy to transport because their "topping" of chocolate ganache (a rich mixture of melted chocolate and heavy cream) is actually inside.

MAKES 32 BARS

1¾ cups flour

¼ teaspoon salt

½ pound unsalted butter, at room temperature

1⅔ cups dark-brown sugar

2 large eggs, at room temperature

1½ teaspoons vanilla extract

½ cup heavy cream

½ pound bittersweet chocolate, chopped

1. Heat the oven to 350°. Butter the bottom of a 10-by-15-inch baking pan and cover with waxed paper. Butter and flour the paper and the sides of the baking pan and tap out the excess flour.

2. In a small bowl, whisk the flour with the salt. In a large bowl, using an electric mixer, cream the butter with the sugar at medium speed until fluffy, about 3 minutes. Beat in the eggs one at a time, beating well after each addition. Beat in the vanilla. On low speed, beat in the flour in three additions. The batter will be fairly stiff.

3. Scrape the batter into the prepared pan and spread it evenly with a metal spatula. Bake in the middle of the oven until a toothpick stuck in the center comes out clean, 18 to 20 minutes. Do not overbake. Let cool completely in the pan.

4. In a small saucepan, bring the heavy cream to a boil over moderate heat. In a food processor, finely grind the chocolate. With the machine on, add the heavy cream to the chocolate and process until completely smooth. Scrape the chocolate ganache into a medium bowl and let stand to firm up for 30 minutes to 1 hour.

5. Cover the pan of the brown sugar cake with a large wire rack and invert. Remove the pan and peel off the waxed paper. Invert the cake again onto a large cutting board. Using a large, serrated knife, cut the cake in half crosswise. Using a large, metal, icing spatula, spread the chocolate ganache evenly on one half of the brown sugar cake to within ⅛ inch of the edge. Carefully set the other half of the cake on top, matching up the cut edges. Cover and refrigerate until the chocolate ganache is set, at least 2 hours.

6. To slice, using a large, heavy, serrated knife, trim the uncut edges of the cake. Cut the cake lengthwise into four strips, then cut each of these strips crosswise into eight rectangles. Serve the bar cookies chilled or at room temperature.

—JUDITH SUTTON

MAKE IT AHEAD

The bars will keep in the refrigerator for up to two days.

GANACHE

A ganache is a rich, French concoction of cream and chocolate that may be used to glaze, frost, or fill a cake. A ganache is simple to make: Combine chopped chocolate with heated heavy cream and stir until smooth. At this point, the ganache may be cooled slightly and then, while still liquid, poured over a cake to glaze it. Or the mixture may be cooled until stiffened and spread as a frosting or filling. Or, once cooled, the ganache may be whipped until lightened and fluffy, and used as a filling. Some ganaches use butter in place of, or in addition to, the cream.

Palm Springs Lemon Squares with Dates

A layer of sliced dates lies between the shortbread on the bottom and the tart lemon custardy topping. The topping has a tendency to stick, so I use cooking-oil spray, even though the pan has also been buttered and floured. The squares cut best when frozen, and they also taste great frozen (or cold). The photo on the facing page pictures these bars (left and center) next to Creole Pecan Bars, page 93.

MAKES 32 BARS

Shortbread Crust:

¼ pound unsalted butter plus 1 tablespoon for the pan

1 cup plus 3 tablespoons sifted flour

¼ cup light-brown sugar

Pinch salt

1 cup pitted dates (about ¼ pound)

Lemon Topping:

¼ cup plus 1 teaspoon sifted flour

½ teaspoon baking powder

⅛ teaspoon salt

2 large eggs

1 cup sugar

⅓ cup lemon juice

Finely grated zest of 2 cold and firm lemons

Confectioners' sugar, for dusting

1. Heat the oven to 350°. Turn a 9-inch square baking pan upside down. Press a 12-inch square of foil, shiny side down, onto the pan, shaping it to the sides and corners with your hands. Remove the foil. Run some tap water into the pan to wet it all over. Pour out all but about 1 tablespoon of the water, then place the shaped foil in the pan and press it gently against the bottom and sides to adhere. Put the 1 tablespoon butter in the pan and melt in the oven. Using a piece of crumpled plastic wrap, spread the melted butter all over the foil. Freeze until set, then dust with flour and tap out the excess. Freeze again.

2. For the crust, in a food processor, combine the flour, brown sugar, and salt. Pulse a few times to mix. Cut the remaining ¼ pound of butter into six pieces and add it to the processor. Mix for about 30 seconds until the dough holds together. Turn the dough out of the bowl.

3. Using your hands, break off teaspoon-size pieces of dough and place them all over the bottom of the prepared pan. Flour your fingertips and press the dough evenly over the bottom of the pan,

91

reflouring your fingertips as necessary. Bake in the bottom third of the oven until lightly browned, about 28 minutes.

4. Meanwhile, for the lemon topping, in a medium bowl, sift together the flour, baking powder, and salt. In another medium bowl, beat the eggs with the granulated sugar and lemon juice. Beat in the dry ingredients until well mixed. Then stir in the lemon zest.

5. When the crust is done, remove it from the oven and lower the oven temperature to 325°. Spray the sides and corners of the foil thoroughly with vegetable-oil cooking spray. Slice the dates crosswise ¼-inch thick and arrange them in a single layer over the crust. Pour the lemon topping over the dates and press the dates down to submerge them.

6. Bake the cake until lightly golden and a little crusty, about 35 minutes. Let cool completely in the pan.

7. When the cake is cool, cover the pan with a flat board or cookie sheet and invert. Remove the pan and peel off the foil (be careful around the sides). Cover the bottom of the cake with a piece of parchment or waxed paper, and then another board or cookie sheet, and invert again so that the cake is right side up. Freeze for at least one hour.

MAKE IT AHEAD

The lemon cake can be unmolded and frozen, well wrapped, for up to four days.

CREOLE PECAN BARS

This is a very old recipe from New Orleans. The thin bars have a crisp, brown-sugar shortbread base that's completely covered with a solid pecan praline topping. See photo on page 90.

MAKES 32 BARS OR 64 BITE-SIZE PIECES

SHORTBREAD LAYER:

¼ pound unsalted butter, at room temperature

1 cup light-brown sugar

¼ teaspoon salt

2 cups sifted flour

2½ cups large pecan halves

PRALINE TOPPING:

12 tablespoons unsalted butter

⅓ cup light-brown sugar

1. Heat the oven to 350°. Turn a 9-by-13-inch baking pan upside down. Press a 17-inch length of foil, shiny side down, onto the pan, shaping it to the sides and corners with your hands. Remove the foil. Run tap water into the pan to wet it all over. Pour out all but about 1 tablespoon of the water, then place the shaped foil in the pan and press it against the bottom and sides to adhere.

2. For the shortbread layer, in a medium bowl, using an electric mixer, beat the butter at medium-high speed until soft. Add the sugar and salt and beat to mix. Add the flour and beat at low speed for 1 or 2 minutes until the ingredients form tiny crumbs that hold together when pinched.

3. Turn out the dough into the prepared pan. Using your fingertips, spread the dough to form an even layer, then press down firmly with the palm of your hand. Place the pecan halves, flat sides down, in one direction—they should be touching each other—to cover the dough.

4. For the praline topping, in a small saucepan, melt the butter and brown sugar over high heat. Stir with a wooden spatula until the mixture comes to a rolling boil. Continue to stir for 30 seconds. Remove the pan from the heat and pour the caramel over the nuts, coating the entire surface as much as possible.

5. Bake on a rack in the center of the oven for 22 minutes. Let cool, then refrigerate for at least 1 hour.

6. When the cake is cool, cover the pan with a flat board or cookie sheet and invert. Remove the pan and peel off the foil. Cover with another board or cookie sheet and invert again so that the cake is right side up. ➤

7.   Using a large, heavy, serrated knife, cut the cake crosswise into quarters, then cut each strip crosswise into eight bars, each about 3¼-inches by 1-inch (or halve the bars to make pieces about 1⅔-inches by 1-inch). Serve at room temperature.

—MAIDA HEATTER

MAKE IT AHEAD

The bars can be refrigerated in the pan for up to two days before slicing.

CHOCOLATE WALNUT BROWNIE DROPS

Stir all the ingredients together, drop the dough on cookie sheets and bake. That's all there is to these brownie-like cookies. See photo on page 118.

MAKES ABOUT 2½ DOZEN COOKIES

- 4 ounces unsweetened chocolate
- 8 tablespoons unsalted butter
- 1½ cups sugar
- 2 large eggs
- 1 cup flour
- ½ cup unsweetened cocoa powder
- ½ teaspoon baking soda
- ¼ cup milk
- 1 teaspoon vanilla extract
- 1½ cups chopped walnuts

1. Heat the oven to 375°. In a large saucepan, melt the chocolate and butter over low heat, stirring occasionally, until smooth. Remove from the heat. Whisk in the sugar and then the eggs. Using a wooden spoon, stir in the flour, cocoa, and baking soda. Add the milk and vanilla and stir until smooth. Stir in the walnuts.

2. Drop rounded tablespoons of the dough about 2 inches apart on a large cookie sheet. Bake until the cookies are set, about 12 minutes. Let cool on the cookie sheet for 2 minutes, then remove to a rack to cool completely.

—TRACEY SEAMAN

MAKE IT AHEAD

The cookies will keep in an airtight container for up to one week.

BERYL'S WALNUT TRUFFLE COOKIES

My friend Beryl Radin asked me one day about the little puddles of batter on my cookie sheets. I told her they were a mistake, but I was planning to bake them anyhow. Indeed, they tasted delicious but somehow incomplete. Beryl said, "Sandwich them with something and eat them frozen." The result—frozen chocolate mousse spread between chewy, nutty rounds—is like an ice cream sandwich. These have a third less fat than chocolate macaroon sandwich cookies.

MAKES 50 TO 55 SANDWICH COOKIES

CHOCOLATE-WALNUT COOKIES:

1½ cups sugar

1 cup plus 2 tablespoons chopped walnuts

⅓ cup unsweetened Dutch-process cocoa powder plus more for dusting

1 tablespoon plus 1 teaspoon brandy

2 teaspoons instant coffee granules

3 large egg whites

BITTERSWEET CHOCOLATE TRUFFLE MOUSSE:

1½ teaspoons unflavored powdered gelatin

¼ cup plus 2 teaspoons cold water

2 large eggs, separated

½ cup unsweetened Dutch-process cocoa powder

½ cup plus ⅓ cup sugar

1¼ cups (1%) low-fat milk

4 ounces bittersweet or semisweet chocolate, chopped

1 teaspoon vanilla extract

⅛ teaspoon cream of tartar

1. Heat the oven to 300°. For the chocolate-walnut cookies, line two cookie sheets with parchment paper.

2. In a food processor, combine the sugar, walnuts, cocoa, brandy, and coffee granules and process until finely ground. With the machine on, slowly add the egg whites to form a thick, sticky batter.

3. Drop scant teaspoons of the batter about 2 inches apart on the prepared cookie sheets. Bake on the upper and lower racks of the oven, switching the pans after 8 minutes, until the cookies puff and the tops crackle, 15 to 18 minutes. Let the cookies cool on the pans. Then carefully peel the parchment paper off the cookies.

4. For the chocolate mousse, sprinkle the gelatin into the ¼ cup cold water in a small cup. Set aside to soften for at least 5 minutes.

5. Place the egg yolks in a medium bowl near the stove to have on hand; reserve the egg whites. In a heavy medium

saucepan, combine the cocoa and the ⅓ cup sugar. Whisk in enough of the milk to form a paste. Then whisk in the remaining milk. Bring to a simmer over moderate heat, stirring frequently with a wooden spoon. Simmer gently, stirring constantly, for 1½ minutes.

6. Remove from the heat and gradually whisk about one-quarter of the hot cocoa mixture into the egg yolks. Scrape the mixture back into the pan and whisk to blend. Whisk in the softened gelatin and the chocolate and vanilla. Let sit for 1 minute, then whisk until completely smooth. Scrape the mixture into a medium bowl. Set the bowl in a larger bowl of ice water and stir occasionally until the mixture cools and starts to thicken. Remove from the ice water.

7. Place an instant-read thermometer in a mug of very hot tap water near the stove. In a medium, heat-proof bowl, combine the cream of tartar with the remaining 2 teaspoons cold water. Whisk in the egg whites and the remaining ½ cup sugar. Set the bowl in a frying pan of simmering water. Using a large rubber spatula, stir briskly, scraping all over the bottom and sides of the bowl, for 45 seconds. Remove the bowl from the pan, tilt the bowl and insert the thermometer so that at least 2 inches of the stem is immersed. If the mixture is less than 160°, rinse the thermometer in the pan water and return it to the mug, then return the bowl to the pan for

10-second intervals, stirring briskly each time, until the mixture reaches 160°. Remove from the heat.

8. Using an electric mixer, beat the reserved whites at high speed until stiff and completely cool. Fold one-quarter of the chocolate mixture into the whites with a large rubber spatula. Then fold the mixture into the remaining chocolate mixture. Cover and refrigerate for at least 4 hours.

9. To assemble, arrange five of the cookies on a work surface, bottom sides up. Scoop a heaping teaspoonful of the truffle mousse onto each cookie and gently press another cookie on top. Put the filled cookies on a baking sheet, cover with plastic wrap and place in the freezer. Repeat with the remaining cookies and mousse. Freeze overnight. Just before serving, sift a light dusting of cocoa over the cookies.

—ALICE MEDRICH

MAKE IT AHEAD

All of the elements of these sandwich cookies can be made ahead. The unfilled cookies will keep in an airtight container for up to two days and the mousse can be held in the refrigerator for up to 24 hours. Once filled, the cookies will keep frozen, in an airtight container, for up to two months.

GINGERBREAD COOKIES

These cookies make a perfect canvas for the royal icing recipe on the next page. Once decorated, the cookies make great hanging Christmas tree ornaments. See Cookie Ornament Tips on the next page.

MAKES ABOUT 7 DOZEN 2½-INCH COOKIES

- 4 cups flour
- 2 tablespoons unsweetened cocoa powder
- 5 teaspoons ground ginger
- 2 teaspoons cinnamon
- 1 teaspoon ground cloves
- 1 teaspoon baking soda
- 1 teaspoon salt
- ½ pound unsalted butter, at room temperature
- 1 cup sugar
- 1 egg, at room temperature, lightly beaten
- ½ cup unsulphured molasses
   Royal Icing, next page

1. In a large bowl, sift together the flour, cocoa powder, ground ginger, cinnamon, cloves, baking soda, and salt. Whisk well to combine.

2. In a large bowl, using an electric mixer, cream the butter with the sugar until fluffy. Beat in the egg, then gradually beat in the molasses. Scrape down the bowl with a rubber spatula and mix again for a few seconds. On low speed, gradually beat in the dry ingredients until combined.

3. Turn out the cookie dough onto a lightly floured surface and knead it gently a few times. Divide the dough into four equal pieces and flatten each piece into a 6-inch disk. Cover each piece of dough with plastic wrap and refrigerate for at least 4 hours or overnight.

4. Heat the oven to 350°. Line two cookie sheets with parchment paper. On a lightly floured surface, using a floured rolling pin, roll out one piece of the dough ⅛-inch thick for cookies or ½-inch thick for ornaments. Cut with cookie cutters. Using a long, wide, metal spatula, transfer the cookies to the prepared cookie sheets. Repeat with the remaining pieces of dough. Reroll all the dough scraps and cut out more cookies.

5. Bake the cookies until the edges just begin to brown, 10 minutes for the thin cookies and 20 minutes for the thick ones. Let the cookies cool on the cookie sheets until firm, then remove to a rack to cool completely.

—PEGGY CULLEN

ROYAL ICING

MAKES 2 CUPS

2 large egg whites, at room
temperature

About 1 pound confectioners'
sugar

¼ teaspoon cream of tartar

1 tablespoon lemon juice

Liquid, paste, or powdered food
coloring

1. In a large bowl, combine all the ingredients except the food coloring. Using a hand-held electric mixer, beat at high speed until fluffy, thick, and shiny, 2 to 3 minutes.

2. Divide the icing into small batches and adjust the consistency as needed. To thin for painting, beat in water. For a stiffer icing that holds its shape, add more sugar. Tint the icing with food coloring. Cover tightly with plastic wrap to prevent the icing from drying out.

MAKE IT AHEAD

The gingerbread cookies will keep for up to one week in an airtight container and for up to one month in the freezer. You can refrigerate the icing on its own for up to one week.

COOKIE ORNAMENT TIPS

For hanging cookie ornaments: Roll and cut the cookies and then pierce each with the blunt end of a bamboo skewer. Repierce after baking while still warm. To make a ribbon border, punch holes around the edge of an unbaked cookie with a chopstick. Repunch the holes after baking, while still warm. Weave a ribbon through the holes after the cookie has cooled.

MOLASSES SPICE COOKIES

These sugar-coated, richly spiced cookies are a snap to make and make an excellent addition to any holiday cookie plate.

MAKES ABOUT 4 DOZEN COOKIES

- 12 tablespoons unsalted butter
- 1½ cups sugar
- ¼ cup dark, unsulphered molasses
- 1 large egg
- 2 cups sifted flour
- 2 teaspoons baking soda
- 1 teaspoon cinnamon
- ¼ teaspoon ground ginger
- ½ teaspoon salt
- ¼ teaspoon ground cloves

1. In a medium saucepan, melt the butter over low heat, then let cool to room temperature.

2. Stir 1 cup of the sugar, the molasses, and eggs into the butter.

3. Sift together the flour, baking soda, cinnamon, ginger, salt, and cloves. Add to the butter mixture and mix well. Cover and chill the dough until stiff, about 45 minutes.

4. Heat the oven to 375°. Shape the dough into balls 1 inch in diameter. Roll each ball in the remaining ½ cup sugar and place about 2 inches apart on buttered cookie sheets. Bake in the middle of the oven until the cookies are golden brown and the tops are cracked, 8 to 10 minutes. Using a wide spatula, remove the cookies to racks to cool.

—JOANNA PRUESS

CHRISTMAS COOKIES

These buttery, decorated cookies are particularly special because they're layered with jam.

MAKES ABOUT 4 DOZEN COOKIES

10 ounces unsalted butter, at room temperature

1 cup sugar

Pinch salt

4 large egg yolks, at room temperature

1 teaspoon finely grated lemon zest

1 teaspoon vanilla extract

3 cups flour

Small silver dragées,* for decorating

Apricot or seedless raspberry jam

*Available at pastry-supply shops

1. Using an electric mixer, beat the butter with the sugar and salt until fluffy. Beat in the egg yolks, lemon zest, and vanilla. On low speed, beat in the flour, 1 cup at a time, until just combined. Divide the dough into four equal pieces and flatten into smooth disks. Wrap separately in waxed paper and refrigerate until firm, at least 30 minutes.

2. Heat the oven to 350°. On a lightly floured surface, roll one disk of the dough ⅛-inch thick. Using cookie cutters, cut it into star and moon shapes. Use mini cutters to stamp out patterns in half of the cookies and decorate with dragées. With a metal spatula, transfer the cookies to a large cookie sheet lined with parchment paper. Bake until pale golden, 15 to 20 minutes. Let cool on the parchment, then transfer to a rack to cool completely. Repeat with the remaining disks.

3. Spread a rounded teaspoon of jam on each of the solid cookies and top with a decorated cookie.

—SUSAN LANTZIUS

MAKE IT AHEAD

The cookie dough can be refrigerated for up to two days or frozen for up to one month. Once baked and filled, the cookies can be stored for up to three days in an airtight container.

ALMOND COOKIES

This version of *ricciarelli* comes from my pastry chef, Sandy Soto Teich. It is the apotheosis of a macaroon—soft and chewy, not too sweet, with just a lingering hint of orange. Finely ground almond flour is also sold as blanched almond meal. The cookies will keep for up to three days in an airtight container.

MAKES 3½ DOZEN COOKIES

2 egg whites, at room temperature

Pinch salt

1¼ cups granulated sugar

2 teaspoons grated orange zest (from 1 orange)

1 teaspoon vanilla extract

½ teaspoon almond extract

3 scant cups almond flour *

¼ cup all-purpose flour

Confectioners' sugar, for dusting

*Available at specialty food shops

1. Heat the oven to 250°. Spray two nonstick cookie sheets with vegetable-oil cooking spray.

2. In a medium bowl, beat the egg whites with the salt until they hold soft peaks when the beaters are lifted. Gradually beat in 1 cup of the granulated sugar and continue beating until the whites hold firm peaks when the beaters are lifted. Stir in the orange zest, vanilla and almond extracts, and finally the almond flour until incorporated and the dough is thick and stiff.

3. In a small bowl, toss the remaining ¼ cup granulated sugar with the all-purpose flour. Lightly dust the prepared cookie sheets with this mixture and scatter the rest on a work surface.

4. With greased hands, divide the dough in three pieces. Roll one piece into a rope at least ¾ inch in diameter and flatten slightly. Using a wet knife, cut the strip of dough on the diagonal to form 1-inch diamonds. Arrange the diamonds on one of the prepared cookie sheets. Repeat with the remaining dough.

5. Bake the cookies until puffed and set, about 15 minutes. They should not color. Remove from the oven and immediately sift confectioners' sugar generously over the tops. Place the cookies on wire racks to cool completely.

—EVAN KLEIMAN

GINGER ALMOND COOKIES

This recipe was inspired by a mail-order catalogue from Penzey's Ltd., the peerless Milwaukee spice house. This particular catalogue introduced vibrant, lemony China #1 gingerroot, which is sold in three dried forms—whole, cracked, and ground. This recipe uses ground ginger. Be sure to allow time for the cookie dough to chill.

MAKES ABOUT 4 DOZEN

- ½ cup whole almonds, toasted
- 6 tablespoons sugar
- 1 cup flour
- 2 teaspoons ground ginger
-   Pinch Salt
- ¼ pound unsalted butter, at room temperature
- 1 teaspoon vanilla extract

1. In a food processor, combine the almonds with 3 tablespoons of the sugar and process to a coarse powder. Transfer to a bowl and stir in the flour, ginger, and salt.

2. In a large bowl, beat the butter with the remaining 3 tablespoons of sugar and the vanilla until well blended. Add the flour mixture and beat until combined.

3. Divide the dough in half and shape each half into a 6-inch-long log. Wrap each log in plastic and chill until firm, at least 3 hours or for up to three days.

4. Heat the oven to 350° and line two cookie sheets with parchment paper. Slice the dough logs ¼-inch thick and arrange the slices 1 inch apart on the prepared cookie sheets. Bake the cookies until golden on the bottoms and edges, about 18 minutes. Shift the pans halfway through baking. Slide the parchment with the cookies onto wire racks and let the cookies cool completely before serving.

—JAN NEWBERRY

MAKE IT AHEAD

The cookies will keep in an airtight container for up to three days.

BUTTER PECAN SANDIES

Pecans, brown sugar, and butter—a combination favored by Southern bakers—team up in these crisp cookies. For optimal results, be sure to use fresh, top-quality pecans.

MAKES ABOUT 3½ DOZEN COOKIES

1½ cups pecan halves

½ cup light-brown sugar

2½ cups flour

½ teaspoon baking powder

Scant ½ teaspoon salt

¼ teaspoon baking soda

10 tablespoons plus 2 teaspoons unsalted butter, at room temperature

¼ cup corn oil or other vegetable oil

1¼ cups confectioners' sugar, sifted

1 large egg

1½ teaspoons vanilla extract

1. Heat the oven to 350°. Butter several cookie sheets and set them aside. Spread the pecan halves in a roasting pan and toast, stirring frequently, until the nuts are nicely darkened and fragrant, about 8 minutes. Let cool completely.

2. Measure ¾ cup of the toasted pecans and chop them finely and evenly. Reserve.

3. Put the remaining toasted pecan halves and the brown sugar in a food processor and pulse to coarsely chop the pecans. Then process continuously until the pecans form a slightly dry paste, about 3 minutes longer. Scrape down the sides and bottom of the bowl several times during processing.

4. Sift together the flour, baking powder, salt, and baking soda. In a large bowl, using an electric mixer, beat the butter and oil at medium speed until well blended and lightened. Add the pecan paste and the confectioners' sugar and beat until fluffy and smooth. Beat in the egg and the vanilla until well blended. Beat or stir in the dry ingredients and ¼ cup of the reserved chopped pecans until thoroughly mixed. Reserve the remaining nuts for garnish.

5. Halve the cookie dough and, using your hands, flatten each piece of dough into a disk. Place each disk between long sheets of waxed paper. Roll out each piece of dough ¼-inch thick, smoothing out any wrinkles that form in the paper. Put the paper-covered cookie dough on large baking sheets and freeze until the dough is firm, at least 45 minutes.

6. Heat the oven to 350°. Peel off one sheet of waxed paper from one of the dough layers (to loosen it), then replace

the waxed paper and flip over the dough layer. Peel off the top sheet of waxed paper and discard.

7. Using a 2-inch round cookie cutter or juice glass, cut out the cookies. Using a metal spatula, place the cookies about 1½ inches apart on the prepared cookie sheets. Garnish the center of each of the cookies with a generous pinch or two of the reserved chopped pecans. Lightly press the nuts into the dough. Repeat the procedure with the second piece of dough. Reroll all the dough scraps and cut out more cookies (freeze for a few minutes if the dough is soft). Then continue cutting out cookies until all of the dough has been used. Place the cookies on the cookie sheets and garnish with the pecans, as above.

8. Bake the cookies one sheet at a time in the upper part of the oven until they are just tinged with brown and slightly darker around the edges, 9 to 12 minutes. Rotate the cookie sheet halfway through baking to ensure even browning.

9. Let the cookies firm up slightly on the cookie sheet on a rack, 2 to 3 minutes. Using a metal spatula, carefully remove the cookies to racks to cool completely.

—Nancy Baggett

MAKE IT AHEAD

The dough sheets can be frozen for up to 24 hours; allow the dough to thaw slightly at room temperature before rolling. Once baked, the cookies will keep for up to ten days in an airtight container at room temperature or for up to two months wrapped airtight and frozen.

SUGAR COOKIES

This dough is ideal for cutting into shapes and decorating with royal icing, page 100. It's also delicious simply sprinkled with cinnamon sugar, which is made with two to three teaspoons of cinnamon per ¼ cup granulated sugar.

MAKES ABOUT 6 DOZEN COOKIES

3¾ cups flour

2 teaspoons baking powder

½ teaspoon salt

½ pound unsalted butter, at room temperature

1⅔ cups sugar

2 large eggs, at room temperature, lightly beaten

2 teaspoons vanilla extract

Cinnamon sugar, for sprinkling (optional)

1. In a medium bowl, whisk together the flour, baking powder, and salt.

2. In a large bowl, using an electric mixer, cream the butter and sugar until fluffy. Add the eggs one at a time, beating well after each addition until thoroughly combined. Scrape down the bowl with a rubber spatula and beat for a few more seconds. Beat in the vanilla. On low speed, mix in half the dry ingredients. Stir in the remainder with the spatula or your hands.

3. Turn out the dough onto a lightly floured work surface and cut it in half. Pat the dough into two disks and wrap them in plastic wrap. Refrigerate the dough until it is firm, at least 4 hours or overnight.

4. Heat the oven to 350°. Line two cookie sheets with parchment paper. On a lightly floured surface, roll out the cookie dough about ³⁄₁₆-inch thick. Cut the dough with cookie cutters and sprinkle generously with cinnamon sugar, if using. Transfer the cookies to the cookie sheets.

5. Bake the cookies until the edges just begin to turn golden, about 10 minutes. Let cool on the sheet until firm, then remove to a rack to cool completely.

—PEGGY CULLEN

MAKE IT AHEAD

The cookies will keep for up to one week in an airtight container and for up to one month in the freezer.

CHOCOLATE CHIP COOKIES THREE DIFFERENT WAYS

Here are three variations on a chocolate chip cookie recipe. The first is a thin, crisp cookie. Since it contains butter, which melts quickly, it spreads easily. A little corn syrup is added for crispness and color, and all-purpose flour, which doesn't absorb much liquid, is used to encourage spreading. The second, a soft, puffy cookie, contains cake flour (instead of all-purpose flour), baking powder (instead of baking soda), shortening (instead of butter, and a little less than usual), and a slightly reduced amount of sugar to help limit spreading. It is made with an egg, which lifts and puffs the dough. The third, an in-between cookie, contains half butter for tenderness and half shortening to limit spreading. An egg and a little corn syrup add body, crispness, and color.

MAKES ABOUT 2½ DOZEN COOKIES

FOR THIN, CRISP COOKIES:

- 1 cup chopped nuts plus 2 tablespoons unsalted butter
- 1½ cups flour
- ¾ teaspoon salt
- ¾ teaspoon baking soda
- 10 tablespoons unsalted butter
- ½ cup granulated sugar plus ⅓ cup light-brown sugar plus 3 tablespoons light corn syrup
- 2 tablespoons milk
- 1 tablespoon vanilla extract
- 1 cup semisweet chocolate chips

FOR PUFFED, SOFT COOKIES:

- 1 cup chopped nuts plus 2 tablespoons unsalted butter
- 1½ cups cake flour
- ¾ teaspoon salt
- 1½ teaspoons baking powder
- 9 tablespoons shortening
- ¾ cup plus 3 tablespoons light-brown sugar
- 1 large egg
- 1 tablespoon vanilla extract
- 1 cup semisweet chocolate chips

FOR IN-BETWEEN COOKIES:

- 1 cup chopped nuts plus 2 tablespoons unsalted butter
- 1½ cups cake flour
- ¾ teaspoon salt
- 1½ teaspoons baking powder
- 5 tablespoons unsalted butter plus 5 tablespoons shortening
- ¾ cup light-brown sugar plus 2 tablespoons light corn syrup
- 1 large egg
- 1 tablespoon vanilla extract
- 1 cup semisweet chocolate chips

1. Heat the oven to 350°. On a large baking sheet, toast the nuts until golden brown, about 10 minutes. Remove from the oven and immediately stir in the 2 tablespoons butter. Increase the oven temperature to 375°.

2. In a medium bowl, sift together the flour, salt, and baking soda or baking powder.

3. In a large bowl, using a hand-held electric mixer, cream the butter or shortening and the sugar at medium-high speed until light and fluffy. Beat in the corn syrup, if using. Beat in the milk or egg thoroughly. Beat in the vanilla. On low speed, gradually beat in the dry ingredients until thoroughly combined. Scrape down the sides once with a rubber spatula. Add the toasted nuts and the chocolate chips and beat on low speed for about 5 seconds. Using the rubber spatula, thoroughly mix in the chips and the toasted nuts.

4. Spray cookie sheets lightly with vegetable-oil cooking spray. Drop slightly heaping tablespoons of the cookie dough about 2 inches apart on the prepared sheets. Bake the cookies until the edges are just beginning to brown, about 12 minutes. Let the cookies cool on the sheets on racks for 3 minutes, then transfer the cookies to the racks to cool completely.

—SHIRLEY CORRIHER

TIPS ON KEEPING COOKIES FROM SPREADING

If you like, you can also control the spreading of other of your favorite cookies. Here's how:

• Refrigerate the dough before you form or cut the cookies. A chilled dough limits spreading as the cookies bake.

• Decrease the sugar a little; sugar encourages spreading.

• Substitute shortening for some of the butter. Shortening maintains a more solid texture than butter over a wider temperature range. This suggestion best applies to cookies made with chocolate, spices, nuts, and other flavorings rather than a simple butter cookie whose pure flavor might be compromised.

Old-Fashioned Oatmeal Chocolate Chip Cookies

These plain-looking cookies are just the sort that seem made for keeping in an old-fashioned cookie jar. The rolled oats lend a pleasant nutty flavor and a slightly nubby texture. The cookies will keep for up to ten days in an airtight container at room temperature. You may also freeze them, wrapped airtight, for up to two months.

MAKES ABOUT 3 DOZEN COOKIES

1	cup flour
½	teaspoon baking soda
½	teaspoon baking powder
¼	teaspoon salt
10	tablespoons unsalted butter, at room temperature
	Scant 1 cup dark-brown sugar
1	large egg, lightly beaten
2	teaspoons vanilla extract
2⅓	cups old-fashioned rolled oats
1⅓	cups mini chocolate chips
2	to 3 tablespoons granulated sugar

1. Heat the oven to 350°. Butter several cookie sheets. In a small bowl, stir together the flour, baking soda, baking powder, and salt.

2. In a large bowl, using an electric mixer, beat the butter at medium speed until fluffy. Add the brown sugar and beat until fluffy and smooth. Beat in the egg and vanilla. Beat in the flour mixture. Using a large wooden spoon, stir in the oats and chocolate chips until combined.

3. Break off tablespoon-size portions of dough and roll between your palms into generous 1½-inch balls. Place the balls about 2½ inches apart on the prepared cookie sheets.

4. Butter the bottom of a large drinking glass. Place the granulated sugar in a shallow bowl. Dip the bottom of the glass into the sugar and use it to flatten the cookies into 2-inch rounds. Dip the glass into the sugar again between cookies.

5. Bake the cookies one sheet at a time in the upper part of the oven until the cookies are lightly colored and just slightly darker at the edges, about 13 minutes. Rotate the cookie sheet halfway through baking to ensure even browning.

6. Transfer the cookie sheet to a rack and let the cookies firm up slightly, 2 to 3 minutes. Using a metal spatula, transfer the cookies to racks to cool completely.

—Nancy Baggett

CHOCOLATE PEANUT COOKIES

Peanuts lend a salty crispness to these chocolate cookies, and peanut-butter chips add a sweet creaminess. If you like, you can use two additional cups of peanuts in place of the peanut-butter chips.

MAKES 2 DOZEN COOKIES

½ pound good-quality semisweet chocolate, chopped

1¾ cups flour

⅓ cup unsweetened cocoa powder

1 teaspoon baking soda

½ teaspoon salt

½ pound unsalted butter, at room temperature

1 cup light-brown sugar

½ cup granulated sugar

2 teaspoons vanilla extract

2 large eggs

2 large egg whites

1 cup unsalted peanuts

1 cup peanut-butter chips (about 6 ounces)

1. Heat the oven to 375°. Butter two large baking sheets. Melt the chocolate in a double boiler, stirring occasionally, until smooth. Let cool.

2. In a small bowl, combine the flour, cocoa powder, baking soda, and salt. In a large bowl, beat the butter until it is light and fluffy. Add the brown sugar, granulated sugar, and vanilla to the butter and blend until smooth. Add the melted semisweet chocolate, the whole eggs, and egg whites and mix until combined. Stir in the dry ingredients just until combined, then stir in the unsalted peanuts and the peanut-butter chips.

3. For each cookie, scoop a scant ¼ cup of the dough onto the prepared baking sheets, leaving about 2 inches between each of the cookies. Bake the cookies until they are just set in the middle, 10 to 12 minutes. Bake them for about 3 minutes longer if you want crisper cookies. Transfer the cookies to a wire rack to cool.

—PAMELA MORGAN

MAKE IT AHEAD

The cookies will keep in an airtight container for up to three days.

Brown-Sugar Icebox Cookies

Use this as a basic cookie dough and flavor it to suit your taste.

MAKES ABOUT 5 DOZEN COOKIES

- ¼ pound unsalted butter, at room temperature
- ½ cup light-brown sugar
- ¼ cup granulated sugar
- 1 large egg
- 1½ teaspoons vanilla extract
- 1⅔ cups flour
- ½ teaspoon baking soda
- ⅛ teaspoon salt

1. In a bowl, beat the butter with an electric mixer until fluffy. Add the brown sugar and granulated sugar and beat until well blended. Beat in the egg and vanilla until thickened. Beat in ⅔ cup of the flour along with the baking soda and salt. Stir in the remaining 1 cup flour. The dough will be soft.

2. Divide the dough in half. Wrap each half in waxed or parchment paper or plastic wrap and shape it into a 6-inch log. Refrigerate until firm.

3. Heat the oven to 350°. Using a thin knife, slice each log ⅛- to ¼-inch thick. Arrange the cookies 1 inch apart on buttered cookie sheets and bake until lightly golden, 10 to 15 minutes.

—Jim Fobel

Variations

- Add ½ cup finely chopped crystallized ginger to the dough with the final portion of flour. Roll each log in ⅓ cup finely chopped blanched almonds before chilling.

- Add 3 tablespoons poppyseeds and 1 tablespoon grated lemon zest to the dough with the final portion of flour. Roll each log in 1 tablespoon poppyseeds before chilling.

- Add 1 teaspoon freshly ground nutmeg, 1 teaspoon cinnamon, and ¼ teaspoon ground cloves to the dough with the final portion of flour. Roll each log in ⅓ cup finely chopped walnuts before chilling.

- Roll each log in 1½ cup very finely ground French-roast coffee to coat before chilling.

- Add 1 cup finely chopped toasted pecans to the dough with the final portion of flour. Roll each log in ⅓ cup finely chopped toasted pecans before chilling.

BUTTER COOKIES

To my mind, there is no first bite as luxurious as that of a butter cookie. When baked just right, the cookie melts in your mouth. A dusting of confectioners' sugar just before serving adds a touch of elegance.

MAKES ABOUT 2 DOZEN COOKIES

½ pound unsalted butter, at room temperature

⅔ cup superfine sugar, more for sprinkling

1 teaspoon vanilla extract

¼ teaspoon salt

2 cups flour

¼ cup confectioners' sugar

1. In a medium bowl, using an electric mixer, cream the butter with the superfine sugar, vanilla, and salt. Do not overmix. (The butter should not be fluffy.) Using a wooden spoon or a rubber spatula, stir in the flour in two batches. Mix just until the flour is incorporated.

2. Shape the cookie dough into a log. Cover well with plastic wrap and refrigerate until firm, at least 2 hours or overnight.

3. Heat the oven to 350°. Line two baking sheets with parchment or waxed paper. Remove the dough from the refrigerator and let it soften slightly before rolling.

4. Cut the cookie dough into four pieces. On a well-floured work surface, roll out one piece of dough ¼-inch thick. Run a long metal spatula under the dough to loosen it from the work surface. Using a 3-inch cookie cutter, cut out shapes as close together as possible. Transfer the shapes to one of the prepared baking sheets with a spatula, leaving about 1 inch between them. Repeat with the remaining pieces of dough. Reroll all the dough scraps and cut more cookies.

5. Sprinkle the shapes with superfine sugar and bake until the edges are just barely golden brown, 15 to 20 minutes. Remove from the oven and let the cookies cool on the baking sheets for 10 minutes. Transfer to a wire rack with a metal spatula and let them cool completely. Sift confectioners' sugar over the cookies just before serving.

—SHEILA LUKINS

MAKE IT AHEAD

The cookies can be stored in an airtight container for up to two days.

Mexican Wedding Cookies

These buttery cake mounds are so-called because they are served at weddings in Mexico. They're traditionally made with pecans but you can substitute walnuts or even pine nuts, if you like.

MAKES 16 COOKIES

4 tablespoons unsalted butter, at room temperature

2 tablespoons chopped pecans

¼ teaspoon vanilla extract

¾ cup confectioners' sugar

½ cup flour

Pinch salt

1. In a medium bowl, beat the butter, pecans, and vanilla until creamy, about 1 minute. Beat in ⅓ cup of the confectioners' sugar. Sift in the flour and salt and mix well. Shape the dough into an 8-inch log, wrap in plastic and refrigerate until chilled, at least 1 hour or overnight.

2. Heat the oven to 350° and line a large cookie sheet with parchment paper. Using a sharp knife, quarter the dough lengthwise, then cut the quarters crosswise into four equal slices. Roll each piece of dough into a ¾-inch ball and arrange about 1 inch apart on the cookie sheet. Bake until lightly golden, about 15 minutes. Let cool slightly.

3. In a large bowl, gently toss the cookies in the remaining confectioners' sugar. Let cool completely.

—Jonathan Eismann

SIMPLE SHORTBREAD

Ground cloves and mace give this familiar, melt-in-your-mouth cookie a new twist. A light coating of egg white makes a pretty, translucent glaze. Cut them into rectangles as suggested below, or, for fun, mix shapes with squares and diamonds.

MAKES 27 COOKIES

12 tablespoons unsalted butter, at room temperature

½ cup sugar

1 large egg, separated

1¾ cups flour

½ teaspoon ground cloves

⅛ teaspoon ground mace

1. Heat the oven to 325°. In a medium bowl, cream the softened butter. Add the sugar and stir to blend. Beat in the egg yolk and then the flour, cloves, and mace. Press the dough into a 9-inch-square baking pan.

2. Beat the white of the egg and brush it over the shortbread dough. Bake until the shortbread is golden, about 45 minutes. Cut the warm shortbread into 3-by-1-inch pieces. Allow it to cool in the baking pan before serving.

—SARAH FRITSCHNER

CANE SUGAR VS. BEET SUGAR

Because the chemical composition of sugar from a sugar beet and from sugar cane is identical, it makes no difference if you use cane or beet sugar. They taste, smell, and behave exactly the same. Beet sugar is more abundant. Unless a package is marked "pure cane" sugar, it's a good bet that it's beet sugar.

—CAROLE BLOOM

FIG MOONS

These are like the fig cookies of your childhood—only better. If you don't have dried fruit for the filling, substitute any fruit preserves that you have on hand in the refrigerator. The photo on the facing page pictures these cookies (right) next to Chocolate Walnut Brownie Drops, page 95.

MAKES 2 DOZEN COOKIES

1½ cups flour

½ teaspoon baking powder

½ teaspoon baking soda

¼ teaspoon cinnamon

¼ teaspoon salt

4 tablespoons unsalted butter, at room temperature

¼ cup vegetable shortening

⅓ cup light-brown sugar

1 large egg

½ teaspoon finely grated lemon zest

8 medium dried figs (about 6 ounces), stemmed and quartered

½ cup pitted dates (about 3 ounces)

⅓ cup water

2 teaspoons cognac or water

1. In a medium bowl, stir the flour with the baking powder, baking soda, cinnamon, and salt.

2. In a large bowl, using an electric mixer, cream the butter and shortening with the brown sugar until fluffy. Beat in the egg and zest. Using a wooden spoon, stir in the dry ingredients. Shape into a disk, wrap in waxed paper and refrigerate until firm, at least 3 hours or overnight.

3. In a small nonreactive saucepan, combine the figs, dates, and water. Bring to a simmer over moderate heat and cook until the figs are tender, about 12 minutes. Transfer the fruit and its cooking liquid to a food processor, add the cognac and puree until smooth. Let cool completely.

4. Heat the oven to 375°. Cut the chilled dough into quarters. On a lightly floured work surface, roll out one piece of the dough ⅛-inch-thick. Cut with a 3-inch fluted round cookie cutter. Arrange the rounds about 1 inch apart on a large cookie sheet. Continue rolling and cutting the dough until the cookie sheet is full. Knead the scraps together and refrigerate until chilled.

5. Spoon 1 teaspoon of the fig filling into the center of each round. Fold the dough over the filling to form a half-moon and press the edges with the tines of a fork to seal. Using a small sharp knife, cut two vents in the top of each cookie. Bake until golden and set, about 12 minutes. Cool completely. Continue making cookies with the remaining dough, scraps, and filling.

—TRACEY SEAMAN

CHOCOLATE SHORTBREAD HEARTS

These shortbread cookies are laden with chocolate and are sinfully rich. Heart shapes are perfect for Valentine's Day, but you can, of course, cut these cookies into any other shapes as well.

MAKES ABOUT 10 COOKIES

4 tablespoons unsalted butter, at room temperature

2½ tablespoons sugar

½ teaspoon vanilla extract

½ cup flour

2½ tablespoons unsweetened cocoa powder

⅛ teaspoon salt

1. Heat the oven to 275°. In a small bowl, cream the butter until fluffy. Add the sugar and vanilla and beat until well blended.

2. On a piece of waxed paper, sift together the flour, cocoa, and salt. Stir the dry ingredients into the butter mixture until smooth. Wrap the dough in plastic and refrigerate for at least 15 minutes.

3. On a lightly sugared surface, roll out the dough to form a ⅜-inch-thick circle. Stamp out the cookies with a 2½-inch heart-shaped cookie cutter. Transfer the hearts to a lightly buttered cookie sheet and prick all over with the tines of a fork.

4. Bake the cookies in the middle of the oven until firm to the touch, 40 to 45 minutes. Let rest for 5 minutes on the sheet, then remove from the sheet and let cool completely.

—BOB CHAMBERS

MAKE IT AHEAD

You can make the cookies ahead and store them for up to one week in an airtight container.

BITTERSWEET CHOCOLATE WAFERS

You will need a pastry bag to pipe out this dough, which you can make into cookies of any size, from little chocolate dots to rounds big enough to make sandwiches with ice cream, ganache, or buttercream filling. You can also layer the wafers with whipped cream and refrigerate for a soft, cakey dessert. Here, each of the wafers is topped with a nut for a simple, elegant look.

MAKES ABOUT 4 DOZEN COOKIES

- ¾ cup flour
- ½ teaspoon baking soda
- ¼ pound unsalted butter, at room temperature
- ⅔ cup dark-brown sugar
- ½ teaspoon salt
- ¼ cup plus 2 tablespoons unsweetened cocoa powder, sifted
- 1 teaspoon vanilla extract
- 2 large egg whites, at room temperature
  About 2 ounces assorted nuts, such as walnut and pecan halves, pine nuts, and whole almonds

1. Heat the oven to 325°. In a small bowl, sift the flour and baking soda and whisk to combine. In a medium bowl, using an electric mixer, cream the butter, brown sugar, and salt until fluffy. Beat in the unsweetened cocoa powder and vanilla. Scrape down the bowl with a rubber spatula. Add the egg whites one at a time, beating well after each addition. Stir in the sifted dry ingredients.

2. Line two cookie sheets with parchment paper. Fit a pastry bag with a round tip approximately ⅜ inch in diameter. Pipe thick 1¼-inch mounds about 2 inches apart on the prepared cookie sheets. Place one large nut or four to five pine nuts in the center of each of the mounds.

3. Bake the cookies until the centers spring back somewhat when they are gently pressed, 15 to 20 minutes. Let the cookies cool for about 10 minutes on the cookie sheets, then transfer the cookies to racks to cool completely.

—PEGGY CULLEN

LEMON PAPER THINS

Spreading the dough for these delicate wafers is a little tricky, but definitely worth the effort. You'll need a metal icing spatula, preferably offset, which is available at kitchenware stores. You can cut the cookies into any shape, but I prefer the look of diamonds. If you like, flavor the sugar with a seasoning other than lemon, such as orange zest or ground cinnamon. Make the flavored sugar a day ahead.

MAKES ABOUT 5 DOZEN COOKIES

- ½ cup granulated sugar
- 2 tablespoons finely grated lemon zest
- ¼ pound plus 2 tablespoons unsalted butter, at room temperature
- ¾ cup plus 2 tablespoons confectioners' sugar, sifted
- 1 teaspoon vanilla extract
- 1½ cups flour, sifted
- ½ cup milk

1. In a small bowl, stir together the granulated sugar and lemon zest. Leave uncovered overnight to dry out, stirring once or twice. The next day, sift the lemon sugar with your fingers to break up any remaining lumps.

2. Heat the oven to 325°. Using a pastry brush, spread 2 tablespoons of the butter on two 16-by-14-inch unrimmed cookie sheets. Refrigerate the cookie sheets while you make the dough.

3. In a medium bowl, using an electric mixer, cream the remaining ¼ pound butter with the confectioners' sugar. Beat in the vanilla. Stir in the flour alternately with the milk, beginning and ending with the flour. Beat for a few seconds until the dough is completely smooth and has the consistency of soft mashed potatoes.

4. Divide the dough in half. Using a metal icing spatula, preferably offset, spread half the dough on one of the chilled cookie sheets in a thin, even layer, covering the sheet completely. Take care that the edges are as thick as the center. Sprinkle the dough with half of the lemon-sugar. Repeat with the remaining dough and lemon-sugar.

5. Using a blunt table knife, score parallel vertical lines 2 inches apart from one edge of the dough to the other, wiping the knife clean between each cut. Then cut another set of parallel lines, also 2 inches apart, at a 45° angle to the first set of lines, to form diamonds.

6. Bake the cookies, turning the cookie sheets once (and switching them if the cookies are coloring unevenly), until the cookies are golden, 18 to 20 minutes. Do not let them get too dark. Remove the

cookie sheets from the oven and, working quickly, use a large sharp knife to recut the diamonds. (If you wait too long, the cookies will harden and break.) Using a metal spatula, transfer the cookie diamonds to a rack to cool.

—PEGGY CULLEN

MAKE IT AHEAD

The cookies will keep for up to a week in an airtight container. Or you can freeze them for up to one month.

HOW SUGAR IS PROCESSED

• First, sugarcane stems or sugar-beet roots are cut, crushed, and washed with hot water. Their juice is extracted and clarified or filtered.

• The resulting liquid is put in a centrifuge, which separates molasses from concentrated crystals. (The molasses you find in the market is from sugarcane; molasses from sugar beets is unpalatable.) The crystals formed at this stage are sometimes partially refined and sold as raw sugar.

• The sugar then goes through a process of liquefaction and crystallization until equal-size crystals of pure white sugar (99.8 percent sucrose) are produced and mechanically sorted into various sizes.

• Light- or dark-brown sugar is made by adding varying amounts of molasses back into the white sugar crystals (from sugarcane, not sugar beets); the molasses contributes the characteristic flavor and color.

—CAROLE BLOOM

LEMON POPPY STARS

This rich, delicate cream-cheese dough softens quickly; so roll out small amounts at a time, leaving the remainder refrigerated while you work. The photo on the facing page pictures these cookies next to PB and Js, page 126.

MAKES ABOUT 4½ DOZEN COOKIES

2 cups flour

¼ teaspoon baking soda

¼ teaspoon salt

2 tablespoons poppy seeds, more for sprinkling

12 tablespoons unsalted butter, at room temperature

4 ounces cream cheese, at room temperature

¾ cup sugar, more for sprinkling

1 large egg, at room temperature

1 tablespoon finely grated lemon zest

1 teaspoon vanilla extract

1 large egg white, lightly beaten

1. In a medium bowl, sift the flour with the baking soda and salt. Stir in the 2 tablespoons poppy seeds.

2. In a large bowl, using an electric mixer, cream the butter and the cream cheese with ¾ cup of sugar until fluffy. Beat in the egg, lemon zest, and vanilla. Using a wooden spoon, stir in the dry ingredients.

3. Divide the dough in half. Pat each half into a disk and wrap in waxed paper. Refrigerate until firm, at least 2 hours or overnight.

4. Heat the oven to 350°. Cut each disk of dough into quarters. Set one quarter on a well-floured work surface. Cover and refrigerate the remaining dough. Roll out the dough to about ⅛-inch thick. Cut with a 3-inch, star-shaped cookie cutter. Transfer the poppy stars to a large cookie sheet, spacing them about ½ inch apart. Repeat with another piece of dough until the cookie sheet is filled. Knead any scraps together and refrigerate until chilled.

5. Brush each cookie with the beaten egg white and sprinkle lightly with poppy seeds and sugar. Bake the cookies until golden, about 12 minutes. Transfer the cookies to a rack to cool completely. Continue making cookies with the remaining dough and scraps.

—TRACEY SEAMAN

MAKE IT AHEAD

You can make the cookies up to a week ahead and store them in an airtight container.

PB AND JS

Peanut butter and jelly sandwiches inspired these large thumbprint cookies. Kids love them for an after school treat and adult "kids" hardly ever turn them down either. Chop the peanuts in a food processor or by hand. See photo on page 124.

MAKES 2½ DOZEN COOKIES

½ pound unsalted butter, at room temperature

½ cup sugar

¼ cup creamy peanut butter

1 large egg yolk

1 teaspoon vanilla extract

1½ cups flour

¼ teaspoon salt

Scant ½ cup unsalted roasted peanuts, very finely chopped

About ⅔ cup good-quality strawberry or apricot jam

1. Heat the oven to 375°. In a medium bowl, using an electric mixer, cream the butter and sugar until fluffy. Beat in the peanut butter, egg yolk, and vanilla. Using a wooden spoon, stir in the flour and salt.

2. Form the dough into 1-inch balls. Roll the balls in the chopped peanuts and place them about 2 inches apart on a large cookie sheet. Bake the cookies for 5 minutes. Using your thumb or a small melon baller, make a deep indentation in the center of each cookie so that it will flatten slightly. Spoon about 1 teaspoon of jam into each cookie. Do not overfill. Bake until the cookies are golden and cracked, about 15 minutes longer. Let cool completely.

—TRACEY SEAMAN

MAKE IT AHEAD

The cookies can be stored for up to three days in an airtight container.

Chocolate Walnut Biscotti

These biscotti—studded with chocolate and walnuts—are Italy's answer to chocolate chip cookies. For a slightly different cookie, replace the chocolate chunks with raisins.

MAKES ABOUT 4 DOZEN BISCOTTI

1	cup walnut halves
4½	cups flour
1	tablespoon baking powder
½	teaspoon salt
½	pound unsalted butter, at room temperature
1½	cups sugar
4	large eggs
1	tablespoon vanilla extract
5½	ounces bittersweet chocolate, cut into ½-inch chunks (about 1 cup)

1. Heat the oven to 400°. Spread the walnuts on a baking sheet and toast until golden brown, about 8 minutes. Let the nuts cool, then coarsely chop. Lower the oven temperature to 325°.

2. In a large bowl, sift together the flour, baking powder, and salt. In a large bowl, cream the butter with the sugar. Beat in the eggs, one at a time, blending thoroughly after each addition. Add the vanilla. Gradually stir in the flour mixture, then fold in the nuts and the chocolate until just blended. Divide the dough into four pieces and shape each piece into a 12-inch log. Set the logs on two lightly buttered baking sheets and refrigerate until chilled, at least 30 minutes.

3. Bake the dough logs for about 20 minutes, or until they are firm and starting to brown. Transfer to a rack and let cool slightly. Lower the oven temperature to 250°. Using a serrated knife, cut the logs crosswise diagonally, ½-inch thick. Set the cookies on their side on the baking sheets and bake until golden brown, about 15 minutes. Let cool before serving.

—Anne Quatrano and Clifford Harrison

Make It Ahead

The biscotti can be stored in an airtight container for up to three days.

PISTACHIO ORANGE BISCOTTI

Serve these "twice-baked" cookies after dinner with a sweet dessert wine or coffee.

MAKES ABOUT 120 BISCOTTI

1½ cups shelled unsalted pistachios

4½ cups flour

1 tablespoon baking powder

½ teaspoon salt

½ pound unsalted butter, at room temperature

1¾ cups granulated sugar

4 large eggs, lightly beaten

1 tablespoon plus 1 teaspoon finely grated orange zest

2 teaspoons vanilla extract

3 tablespoons confectioners' sugar, for dusting

1. Heat the oven to 325°. Line two baking sheets with parchment paper.

2. In a food processor, finely chop ¼ cup of the pistachios. Add the remaining pistachios and pulse four times, leaving some of the nuts coarsely chopped.

3. In a medium bowl, whisk together the flour, baking powder, and salt. In a standing electric mixer fitted with the paddle, beat the butter with the granulated sugar until blended. Add the eggs, orange zest, and vanilla, and beat until blended. Beat in the dry ingredients on low speed. Fold in the pistachios.

4. Divide the dough into six equal pieces. On a work surface dusted with the confectioners' sugar, shape each piece of dough into a 12-inch log about 1½-inches wide. Transfer to the prepared baking sheets, arranging the logs about 3 inches apart. Bake in the upper and lower thirds of the oven, switching the pans halfway through baking, until golden and the tops spring back when lightly touched, about 30 minutes. Let cool on the baking sheets for 10 minutes. Lower the oven temperature to 300°.

5. Carefully remove one of the logs to a cutting board. Using a serrated knife, cut the log diagonally into ½-inch slices. Arrange the slices on the baking sheet, cut sides down, and repeat with the remaining logs. Bake the biscotti, switching the pans halfway through baking, until golden and dry, about 20 minutes. (The slices don't need to be turned.) Let cool completely on the baking sheets.

—GRACE PARISI

PINE-NUT ALMOND MACAROONS

These are classic southern Italian cookies—chewy almond macaroons covered with pine nuts. In this case, they are not cloyingly sweet. They evoke a Mediterranean Easter and, being flourless, are an ideal Passover cookie. If you can, buy Mediterranean or Italian pine nuts. They have a more delicate flavor than the Chinese pine nuts.

MAKES ABOUT 3 DOZEN MACAROONS

7 ounces almond paste

½ cup superfine sugar

3 tablespoons egg whites (from 2 lightly beaten whites), at room temperature

⅔ cup pine nuts

1. Heat the oven to 350°. Line two cookie sheets with parchment paper.

2. In a standing electric mixer, beat the almond paste and the superfine sugar for 1 minute. Scrape down the bowl and beat for 30 seconds longer. Beat in the egg whites, 1 tablespoon at a time, until blended. Scrape down the bowl and beat for a few seconds; the batter will be soft but not runny.

3. Scrape the batter into a pastry bag fitted with a #5 plain tip (about ½ inch). Pipe 1¼-inch rounds about 1½ inches apart on the prepared cookie sheets and sprinkle the pine nuts all over the tops and sides of the mounds. Bake the macaroons, turning the cookie sheets once, until the cookies are golden brown, about 20 minutes. Slide the parchment paper onto a rack and allow the macaroons to cool completely. Remove the macaroons from the parchment paper and serve.

—PEGGY CULLEN

MAKE IT AHEAD

The macaroons will keep in an airtight container for one week. Or you may freeze them for up to one month.

chapter 3
TARTS AND PIES

Hazelnut Tart

HAZELNUT TART

The tart shell recipe on the next page makes enough dough for two 11-inch tarts. Wrap and chill half of the dough for another use.

MAKES ONE 11-INCH TART

1⅔ cups shelled hazelnuts

1½ tablespoons unsalted butter

4 large eggs

1 large egg yolk

¾ cup sugar

½ cup dark corn syrup

2 tablespoons cider vinegar

1 teaspoon vanilla extract

⅛ teaspoon salt

Sweet Tart Shell, next page

Lightly sweetened whipping cream, for serving

1. Heat the oven to 350°. Spread the hazelnuts on a baking sheet and toast until the skins are blistered, about 15 minutes. Rub the nuts together in a towel to remove as much of the skin as possible. Let the nuts cool, then coarsely chop. Leave the oven on.

2. In a small saucepan, cook the butter over moderate heat until browned, about 1 minute. In a medium bowl, whisk together the eggs, egg yolk, and sugar until light and fluffy. Whisk in the corn syrup, vinegar, browned butter, vanilla, and salt, and stir in the hazelnuts. Pour the filling into the tart shell, spreading it evenly. Bake on the bottom rack of the oven until the filling is set, about 30 minutes. Let cool for at least 1 hour or up to 8 hours. Serve warm or at room temperature with whipped cream.

—SANFORD D'AMATO

STORING SUGAR

All forms of white sugar will last indefinitely if stored in airtight containers in a cool, dry place. A tightly sealed glass jar in the pantry works well. When brown sugar is exposed to air, it becomes hard because its moisture evaporates. Store it in a thick plastic bag or an airtight container. If it dries out, try one of these remedies.

• Add a slice of fresh apple to the sugar and set the sugar aside for about three days.
• Heat the sugar in a microwave oven at high power for about thirty seconds, or up to a minute.
• Warm the sugar in a shallow baking pan in a conventional oven at 250° for about five minutes.

—CAROLE BLOOM

Sweet Tart Shell

**MAKES ENOUGH DOUGH FOR TWO
11-INCH TART SHELLS**

½ pound unsalted butter, at room
   temperature

½ cup sugar

1 large egg, at room temperature

½ teaspoon vanilla extract

2¾ cups flour

1. In a medium bowl, cream the butter with the sugar. Beat in the egg and vanilla. Stir in the flour just until combined. Shape the dough into a ball and cut it in half. Flatten each piece into a 6-inch disk and wrap separately in plastic wrap. Refrigerate one half until chilled, for at least 1 hour or overnight. Freeze the other half for up to a month for another use.

2. On a lightly floured sheet of parchment paper, roll the dough out to a 13-inch round. (If the pastry becomes too soft, slide the paper onto a cookie sheet and refrigerate for 10 minutes.) Invert the dough onto an 11-inch tart pan with a removable bottom and peel off the paper. Press the pastry into the pan and against the sides. Trim the pastry even with the rim of the pan. Refrigerate for 30 minutes.

3. Heat the oven to 350°. Line the shell with a large piece of foil and fill it with pie weights, dried beans, or rice. Bake on the bottom rack of the oven for 15 minutes. Remove the foil and weights. Bake until the pastry is pale golden, about 15 minutes longer. Let cool before filling.

Make It Ahead

You can bake the tart shell and toast the nuts a day ahead. Keep them both at room temperature.

PEAR AND HAZELNUT TART

To toast the hazelnuts, spread them in a pie plate and put them in a 400° oven for about eight minutes, or until fragrant and browned. Let cool. Rub the nuts together in a kitchen towel to remove the skins.

MAKES ONE 11½-INCH TART

¾ cup granulated sugar

½ cup hazelnuts, toasted (see above) and chopped

2 tablespoons finely grated fresh ginger

5 Bosc pears, peeled, cored, and cut into 1-inch dice

3 tablespoons flour

Hazelnut Spice Tart Shell, next page

1 cup heavy cream

½ cup confectioners' sugar

1½ teaspoons chopped fresh thyme

1. In a food processor, combine ¼ cup of the granulated sugar with the hazelnuts and ginger and process to a coarse powder. In a large bowl, toss the pears with the remaining ½ cup of granulated sugar and the flour. Remove the tart shell from the refrigerator. Spread the hazelnut-and-ginger mixture over the bottom of the shell and top with the pears. Arrange the frozen dough strips over the filling and pears in a lattice pattern.

2. Heat the oven to 350°. Bake the tart in the center of the oven until the pastry is brown and the filling is bubbling, about 1½ hours. Let cool for at least 10 minutes.

3. Meanwhile, in a large bowl, whip the cream until it holds soft peaks when the beaters are lifted. Add the confectioners' sugar and thyme. Beat until firm. Don't overbeat. Serve the tart warm, with the whipped cream.

—GORDON HAMERSLEY

Hazelnut-Spice Tart Shell

MAKES ONE 11½-INCH TART SHELL

- 2 cups flour
- ½ cup hazelnuts, toasted (see page 135) and chopped
- 1 tablespoon cinnamon
- ½ teaspoon ground cloves
- ½ teaspoon ground allspice
- ½ pound cold unsalted butter, diced
- 2 hard-cooked egg yolks, pressed through a strainer
- 1½ tablespoons finely grated lemon zest
- ¼ cup ice water

1. In a food processor, combine the flour, hazelnuts, cinnamon, cloves, and allspice and process until the nuts are finely ground. Add the butter, egg yolks, and lemon zest and pulse until the mixture resembles coarse meal. Add the ice water and pulse just until the dough comes together. Scrape the dough onto a lightly floured work surface and knead briefly. Pat the dough into a disk, wrap in plastic and refrigerate until firm, about 1 hour.

2. Heat the oven to 350°. Cut off a third of the dough and keep it refrigerated. On a lightly floured surface, roll out the remaining dough to a 13-inch round. Fold the dough in half and transfer it to an 11½-inch tart pan with a removable bottom. Unfold the dough and press it into the pan and against the sides. Trim the pastry even with the rim of the pan. Refrigerate 30 minutes before filling.

3. On a lightly floured surface, roll out the remaining piece of dough to a 13-by-8-inch rectangle. Place the rectangle on a baking sheet and freeze until very firm. Using a pizza cutter or a sharp knife, cut the rectangle lengthwise into ten strips, cutting the pastry directly on the pan. Refreeze the strips until needed.

Make It Ahead

The unfilled tart shell and the lattice top can be made ahead and frozen for up to a week.

ITALIAN ALMOND TART

Regional variations of this tart are found all over Italy, but the addition of bits of chocolate makes this one unusual. The silken mascarpone and the bittersweet chocolate sauce perfectly complement the tart's not-too-sweet, macaroon-like filling.

MAKES ONE 9-INCH TART

- 2 cups flour
- 1¼ cups granulated sugar
- ¼ teaspoon salt
- ¼ pound plus 2 tablespoons cold unsalted butter, cut into small pieces
- 4 to 5 tablespoons ice water
- 4 large egg whites
- 2 cups blanched whole almonds, ground
- 3 ounces semisweet chocolate, finely chopped (generous ½ cup)
- 1 large egg yolk beaten with 2 tablespoons water, for glazing
- 8 ounces mascarpone cheese
- 2 tablespoons confectioners' sugar
  Bittersweet Chocolate Sauce, next page

1. In a medium bowl, stir together the flour, ½ cup of the granulated sugar, and the salt. Using your fingertips, a pastry blender, or two knives, cut the butter into the flour until it resembles coarse meal. Drizzle 4 tablespoons of the ice water all over the top and, using a fork, stir until the dough just holds together when pinched, adding up to 1 tablespoon more ice water, if necessary. Divide the dough in half. Shape each half into a disk, wrap well, and refrigerate for 30 minutes.

2. On a lightly floured surface, roll out one disk of dough into a 12-inch round. Fold the dough in quarters and place in a 9-inch fluted tart pan with a removable bottom. Unfold the dough and press it gently into the pan and against the sides without stretching. Trim the overhang to ½ inch and fold it in, pressing it against the sides to form a lip ¼ inch above the pan rim. Using a fork, prick the bottom of the tart shell at 1-inch intervals. Refrigerate the tart shell for 30 minutes to firm up.

3. On a lightly floured surface, roll out the remaining disk of dough to an 11-inch round. Transfer the round to a baking sheet and refrigerate until ready to use.

4. Heat the oven to 375°. Line the tart shell with a large piece of foil and fill it with pie weights, dried beans, or rice. Bake the shell for 15 minutes. Remove the foil and weights and bake just until the dough has lost its raw look, about 5 minutes longer. Let the tart shell cool slightly. Leave the oven on.

5. In a large bowl, using an electric mixer, beat the egg whites at medium speed until they hold soft peaks when the beaters are lifted. Gradually beat in the remaining ¾ cup granulated sugar. Increase the speed to high and beat until the whites are stiff and glossy. Using a large rubber spatula, fold in the ground almonds and then the chopped chocolate. Scrape the filling evenly into the partially baked tart shell and smooth the surface.

6. Remove the rolled-out dough from the refrigerator and, with a sharp knife, cut it into ten ¾-inch-wide strips. Evenly lay five parallel strips across the tart. Lay the remaining strips diagonally across them to form a diamond lattice. Trim the ends of the strips flush with the tart shell and press them into the filling. Brush the pastry with the egg glaze.

7. Bake the tart until the filling is puffed and golden and the pastry is light golden brown, about 30 minutes. Let cool to room temperature.

8. Place the mascarpone cheese in a medium bowl. Using a wooden spoon, beat in the confectioners' sugar. Refrigerate until serving time.

9. To serve, using a fork, spoon, or plastic squeeze bottle, decoratively drizzle 1 tablespoon of the bittersweet chocolate sauce over eight large dessert plates. Set a slice of the tart on each of the plates and place a dollop of the sweetened mascarpone cheese next to it.

—JUDITH SUTTON

BITTERSWEET CHOCOLATE SAUCE

MAKES ABOUT ½ CUP

1½ ounces bittersweet chocolate, chopped (generous ¼ cup)

⅓ cup heavy cream

2 tablespoons sugar

⅛ teaspoon vanilla extract

In a small heavy saucepan, combine the chocolate, cream, and sugar. Cook over low heat, stirring with a wooden spoon, until the chocolate is completely melted and the sugar is dissolved, 2 to 3 minutes. Transfer to a small bowl and stir in the vanilla. Let the sauce cool to room temperature.

MAKE IT AHEAD

The tart dough can be made a day ahead and refrigerated. You may also fill and bake the tart a day ahead; just set it aside at room temperature. The sauce can be covered and refrigerated for up to four days; reheat it in a double boiler before serving.

TYPES OF SUGARS

WHITE SUGAR

• Granulated sugar is the most common form of sugar and the type most frequently used in recipes. Its distinguishing characteristics are a paper-white color and fine crystals.

• Sugar cubes, made from moist granulated sugar that is pressed into molds and dried, can be crushed and used like granulated.

• Superfine sugar is similar to granulated except that it has very tiny crystals. Since it dissolves quickly and completely, leaving no grainy texture, it's perfect for caramel, meringues, drinks, cold desserts, and fine-textured cakes. If you can't find it, you can approximate it by grinding granulated sugar for one minute in a food processor.

• Confectioners' sugar is the granulated variety ground to a powder and sifted. Because powdered sugar tends to hold moisture and is prone to clumping, it is blended with about three percent corn-starch during processing. Always sift it before using. Confectioners' sugar is ideal for uncooked icings and frostings because it leaves no graininess. It also looks pretty dusted over the top of a dessert.

• Coarse sugar is shaped into small pearl-like balls that are several times as big as granulated sugar crystals. It is used to decorate and garnish confections and baked goods. Because its large crystals do not dissolve easily, it is not used as a sweetener.

• Crystal sugar is similar to coarse except that it is cylindrical, not round. It, too, is used for decorating and garnishing, and is often tinted with food coloring and sold as "rainbow sugar."

BROWN SUGAR

• Dark- and light-brown sugar are made up of sugar crystals coated with molasses, which lends a slightly grainy, moist texture. This moisture creates small pockets of air, so the sugar must be tightly packed when measuring. Dark-brown sugar (about 6.5 percent molasses) has a stronger, more full-bodied flavor than light-brown sugar (about 3.5 percent), though they're often interchangeable. Use them instead of white sugar when you want a distinct, rich flavor.

• Muscovado sugar is a dark and sticky variety noted for its deep molasses flavor. Its crystals tend to be a little larger than those of the regular brown sugars.

• Demerara sugar has crystals that are slightly larger than muscovado's. It has less molasses, and thus a lighter taste and color.

RAW SUGAR

• Raw sugar is essentially the product at the point before the molasses is removed. True raw sugar is unrefined and contains various molds and bacteria considered unsafe for human consumption. What we buy as raw sugar is partially refined: It is washed with steam to purify it. With crystals about the size of coarse sugar, it can be used in place of brown sugar.

• Turbinado is a form of raw sugar with light amber cylindrical crystals and a mild brown sugar flavor.

—CAROLE BLOOME

ALMOND AND STRAWBERRY TART

Juicy ripe strawberries make a refreshing topping for a rich, buttery tart. If you hate to roll pastry, try this technique: Chill the dough and coarsely grate it into the tart pan, then pat it into the base and sides.

The nonvintage Le Filigare Vin Santo is a perfect accompaniment to this tart; it has all the perfume and aroma of a classic vin santo without being too intense. Or, you might try other drier vin santos, such as the 1990 Selvapiana and the 1991 Isole e Olena.

MAKES ONE 9½-INCH TART

½ pound whole blanched almonds

¾ cup superfine sugar

6 ounces unsalted butter, at room temperature

2 large eggs, at room temperature

Sweet Tart Shell, next page

2 pints fresh strawberries, bottoms trimmed flat and berries quartered lengthwise

1½ tablespoons confectioners' sugar

Crème fraîche, for serving

1. In a food processor, pulse the almonds and ¼ cup of the superfine sugar until the nuts are finely ground. In a medium bowl, beat the butter with the remaining ½ cup of superfine sugar until the mixture is fluffy. Add the butter mixture to the almonds and process until combined. Add the eggs to the almond mixture one at a time, processing until the mixture is smooth after each addition.

2. Spread the almond mixture in the tart shell. Bake the tart in the lower third of the oven until the top is golden, about 45 minutes. Let cool completely.

3. Remove the cooled tart from the pan. Transfer the tart to a large platter. Arrange the quartered strawberries upright on the tart and then sift the confectioners' sugar over the strawberries. Serve the strawberry tart with crème fraîche.

—RUTH ROGERS AND ROSE GRAY

Sweet Tart Shell

MAKES ONE 9½-INCH TART SHELL

1⅔ cups flour

5 ounces cold unsalted butter, cut into ½-inch pieces

Pinch salt

⅔ cup confectioners' sugar

2 large egg yolks

1. Heat the oven to 350°. In a food processor, combine the flour, butter, and salt and pulse until the mixture resembles coarse bread crumbs. Pulse in the confectioners' sugar and then the egg yolks until combined and the pastry pulls away from the side of the bowl. Pat the pastry into a smooth round disk.

2. On a lightly floured surface, roll the pastry out to a 12-inch round. Drape it over a 9½-inch fluted tart pan with a removable bottom. Press the dough into the pan and against the sides. Trim the pastry even with the rim of the pan. Line the shell with a large piece of foil and fill it with pie weights, dried beans, or rice. Bake the tart shell until the edges are lightly colored, about 20 minutes. Remove the foil and weights. Bake until the pastry is dry and firm to the touch, about 10 minutes longer. Let cool before filling.

Make It Ahead

You can make the tart without the strawberries up to six hours ahead. Just set it aside at room temperature and add the strawberries when you're ready to serve.

Brown-Butter Pecan Tart with Bourbon Vanilla Ice Cream

Rich pecan pie is better than ever with toasted pecans, brown butter, and a touch of bourbon. We love it with bourbon-vanilla ice cream, but plain old vanilla ice cream or softly whipped cream will do fine.

8 TO 10 SERVINGS

2½   cups chopped pecans

4   tablespoons unsalted butter

½   cup light-brown sugar

¼   cup granulated sugar

1¼   cups light corn syrup

¼   cup bourbon

1   teaspoon vanilla extract

2   large whole eggs

3   large egg yolks

    Tart Shell, next page

¾   cup pecan halves

    Bourbon Vanilla Ice Cream, page 145

1. Heat the oven to 350°. Spread the chopped pecans on a baking sheet and toast until fragrant, about 7 minutes. Leave the oven on.

2. In a small frying pan, cook the butter over moderate heat until lightly browned, about 3 minutes. Transfer to a medium bowl. Whisk in the brown and granulated sugars, corn syrup, bourbon, and vanilla. Finally, whisk in the whole eggs and egg yolks.

3. Spread the toasted pecan pieces in the tart shell. Arrange the pecan halves in a neat ring around the outer edge. Gently pour the filling over the nuts so that they are evenly covered.

4. Bake the tart until the filling is set, about 45 minutes. Let cool completely. Remove the sides of the pan, put the tart on a large plate, and serve it with a scoop of bourbon vanilla ice cream.

—Karen Barker

Tart Shell

MAKES ONE 11-INCH TART SHELL

1¼ cups plus 2 tablespoons flour

1 tablespoon plus 1 teaspoon sugar

Pinch salt

¼ pound cold unsalted butter, cut into ½-inch pieces

1 large egg, separated, white lightly beaten

1 tablespoon milk

1. In a food processor, combine the flour, sugar, and salt and pulse to blend. Add the butter and pulse until the mixture resembles coarse meal. In a small bowl, combine the egg yolk and milk. Add to the processor and pulse just until the dough comes together. Pat the dough into a disk, wrap in plastic, and refrigerate until firm, at least 1 hour or overnight. Let the dough soften slightly before rolling out.

2. Heat the oven to 350°. On a lightly floured surface, roll the dough out to a 13-inch round. Drape the dough over an 11-inch tart pan with a removable bottom and press the dough into the pan and against the sides. Trim the pastry even with the rim of the pan. With a fork, prick the bottom of the tart shell every inch or so with a fork and freeze until firm, about 5 minutes.

3. Line the pastry with a large piece of foil and fill with pie weights, rice, or dried beans. Bake until set, about 20 minutes. Remove the foil and weights and bake until golden, about 15 minutes. Immediately brush the pastry with the beaten egg white. Put the pan on a baking sheet and fill the tart shell.

BOURBON VANILLA ICE CREAM

MAKES 1 QUART

1¾ cups half-and-half

1½ cups heavy cream

1 large vanilla bean, split lengthwise

7 large egg yolks

¾ cups sugar

Pinch salt

¼ cup bourbon

1. In a large nonreactive saucepan, combine the half-and-half and heavy cream. Scrape all the seeds from the vanilla bean into the cream and add the pods of the beans. Cook over moderate heat just until the cream comes to a boil.

2. Meanwhile, in a large bowl, whisk the egg yolks with the sugar and salt. Gradually whisk in the hot cream, then return the mixture to the saucepan. Cook over moderate heat, stirring constantly, until the custard is just thick enough to coat the back of a spoon, about 3 to 5 minutes. Strain the custard into a large bowl and refrigerate until cold, about 2 hours.

3. Stir the bourbon into the cold custard. Pour the custard into an ice cream maker and freeze the custard according to the manufacturer's instructions. Transfer the ice cream to a chilled container and freeze until hard enough to scoop, for at least 3 hours or up to three days.

CHOCOLATE PECAN TART

Unlike most pies, this tart is just as good when baked a day ahead as long as it is not refrigerated. This is a light, elegant version of the American classic.

MAKES ONE 11-INCH TART

    French Pastry Shell, opposite page

4   ounces unsalted butter

¼   cup honey

¾   cup dark-brown sugar

3   tablespoons granulated sugar

⅓   cup plus ¼ cup heavy cream

2   cups pecans, chopped

1½ ounces imported bittersweet chocolate, cut into small pieces

    Cocoa powder and confectioners' sugar, for dusting

    Fresh mint sprigs, for garnish

1. Heat the oven to 400°. Line the pastry shell with a large piece of foil and fill it with pie weights, dried beans, or rice. Bake for 15 minutes. Remove the foil and weights. Bake until the bottom dries out, about 3 minutes longer. Let cool. Reduce the oven temperature to 350°.

2. In a small saucepan, melt the butter and honey together over high heat. Add the brown and granulated sugars and stir until dissolved, then boil for 1 minute without stirring. Add the ⅓ cup heavy cream and stir constantly until smooth. Remove from the heat and stir in the chopped pecans.

3. Pour the mixture into the baked pastry shell. If necessary, spread the pecans to evenly distribute them over the bottom of the tart. Bake until bubbles appear around the edges and the center is slightly firm, about 20 minutes. Cool.

4. In a small saucepan, bring the remaining ¼ cup heavy cream to a boil over high heat. Remove from the heat, add the chocolate and stir until melted. Spread the chocolate evenly over the cooled tart.

5. Cut out an 11-inch circle from a piece of parchment or waxed paper. Fold it in eighths, then open it and cut out every other wedge, leaving four wedges held together at the center. Place it on top of the tart. Using a fine sieve, dust the cocoa over the exposed tart. Carefully lift the paper and shake off excess cocoa. Set the paper over the cocoa-dusted sections and sift confectioners' sugar over the tart. Carefully remove the paper. Remove the rim of the pan and transfer the tart to a serving platter. Place a cluster of mint sprigs in the center of the tart.

—LYDIE MARSHALL

FRENCH PASTRY SHELL

MAKES ONE 11-INCH TART SHELL

1   cup flour
¼   pound unsalted butter, cut into small pieces
1   tablespoon sugar
    Pinch salt
2   to 3 tablespoons cold water

1.   In a food processor, combine the flour, butter, sugar, and salt and process for 10 seconds. Add 2 tablespoons of the water and pulse just until the mixture resembles coarse cornmeal. Pinch the dough; it should hold together. If not, add up to 1 more tablespoon of water.

2.   Turn the dough out on a work surface and, using the heel of your hand and working a little of the dough at a time, knead lightly and quickly to blend the butter and flour. Gather the dough into a ball and flatten slightly. Wrap in waxed paper and refrigerate just long enough to firm up the butter, about 15 minutes.

3.   Roll the dough out to a 13-inch circle. Drape over a fluted 11-inch tart pan with a removable bottom. Press into the pan and against the sides. Trim the pastry even with the rim of the pan. With a fork, prick the bottom of the tart shell every inch or so. Wrap well with plastic wrap and freeze at least 5 minutes or until ready to bake.

MAKE IT AHEAD

The tart can be made up to a day ahead but without the dusting of confectioners' sugar and cocoa powder. Leave it uncovered at room temperature and just before serving, decorate with the sugar and cocoa.

CHOCOLATE CARAMEL TART

Caramel is used both as a flavoring and a garnish for this tart that layers rich chocolate ganache with an airy caramel cream.

MAKES ONE 10-INCH TART

- 2 cups heavy cream
- 4½ ounces bittersweet chocolate, chopped
  Sweet Tart Shell, opposite page
- ½ cup granulated sugar
- 3 tablespoons water
- 3 tablespoons unsalted butter, cut into 6 pieces, at room temperature
- 2 large egg whites, at room temperature
  Pinch salt
- 2 tablespoons superfine sugar

1. In a small saucepan, bring ¾ cup of the heavy cream to a boil over moderate heat. Meanwhile, in a food processor, finely grind the chocolate. With the machine on, add the hot cream to the chocolate and process until completely smooth. Scrape the ganache into a medium bowl. Refrigerate, stirring occasionally with a rubber spatula, until the ganache is cold to the touch but not set, 1 to 1½ hours.

2. Using an electric mixer, beat the ganache on low speed just until it lightens in color and holds soft peaks, about 1 minute. Do not overbeat. Scrape the ganache into the cooled tart shell, spreading it evenly. Cover and refrigerate the tart while you prepare the caramel cream.

3. In a small, deep heavy saucepan, combine the granulated sugar with the water. Bring the mixture to a boil over moderately high heat and boil (brushing the inside of the saucepan occasionally with a pastry brush dipped in water to dissolve any sugar crystals) until the caramel turns a rich, tea-like brown, 5 to 8 minutes. Remove from the heat and immediately add ½ cup of the cream. Stand back to avoid spatters. Cook over low heat, stirring, until completely smooth, about 1 minute. Remove from the heat, add the butter, and stir until melted. Transfer the caramel to a large bowl and let cool to room temperature.

4. Transfer 3 tablespoons of the cooled caramel to a small saucepan and reserve. In a medium bowl, beat the remaining ¾ cup heavy cream until it holds soft peaks when the beaters are lifted. Do not overbeat. In a large bowl, using an electric mixer, beat the egg whites and salt at medium speed until soft peaks form. Gradually beat in the superfine sugar. Increase the speed to high and beat until the whites are stiff and glossy. Stir 3 tablespoons of the whites into the caramel in the bowl. Fold in the remaining whites, then fold in the whipped cream. Spread the cream over the chilled ganache and refrigerate.

5. Rewarm the reserved caramel over low heat, stirring, until it begins to liquefy and is barely warm, not hot, about 30 seconds. Using a fork, drizzle the caramel over the top of the tart. Refrigerate the tart for at least 2 and up to 6 hours. Cut into wedges and serve.

—JUDITH SUTTON

MAKE IT AHEAD

The tart shell may be filled with ganache and refrigerated for up to one day. The caramel may also be made up to a day ahead. Cover and refrigerate it, and then bring to room temperature before using.

SWEET TART SHELL

MAKES ONE 10-INCH TART SHELL

1⅓ cups flour

3 tablespoons light-brown sugar

2 tablespoons granulated sugar

⅛ teaspoon salt

4 ounces cold unsalted butter, cut into ½-inch pieces

1 large egg yolk

2 to 2½ tablespoons ice water

1. In the bowl of a food processor, combine the flour, brown sugar, granulated sugar, and salt, and pulse to blend. Scatter the butter on top and pulse 10 to 15 times, until the mixture resembles coarse meal. Add the egg yolk and pulse just to blend. Drizzle 2 tablespoons of the ice water on top and pulse until the dough just comes together, adding up to ½ tablespoon more ice water if necessary. Using your hands, shape and pat the dough into a disk, wrap well, and refrigerate for at least 1 hour and up to two days.

2. Roll the dough out between two sheets of waxed paper to a 13-inch round. Peel off the top sheet of waxed paper and invert the dough into a 10-inch fluted tart pan with a removable bottom. Peel off the remaining paper and fit the dough into the pan and against the sides. Trim the pastry even with the rim of the pan. Refrigerate for 30 minutes.

3. Heat the oven to 375°. Line the shell with a large piece of foil and fill it with pie weights, dried beans, or rice. Bake for 18 minutes. Remove the foil and weights. Bake until the pastry is pale golden, about 15 minutes longer. Let cool before filling.

Pumpkin and Apple Tart with Ginger

This luscious dessert pairs two Thanksgiving favorites—pumpkin and apple—in a sophisticated tart spiked with fresh and ground ginger, allspice, and black pepper. Serve it with whipped cream or vanilla ice cream.

MAKES ONE 11-INCH TART

- 3 large eggs
- 1 cup dark-brown sugar
- 2 cups unsweetened pumpkin puree
- 1 cup heavy cream
- 2 tablespoons finely grated fresh ginger
- 2 tablespoons lemon juice
- 2 teaspoons cinnamon
- 1 teaspoon salt
- 1 teaspoon vanilla extract
- ½ teaspoon ground ginger
- ½ teaspoon freshly ground pepper
- ¼ teaspoon ground allspice
- 2 Granny Smith apples, peeled, halved, cored, and sliced ⅛-inch-thick
- ¼ cup granulated sugar
- 2 tablespoons unsalted butter, melted
- Tart Shell, opposite page
- 4 amaretti cookies, coarsely crumbled (about ⅓ cup)

1. Heat the oven to 400°. In a large bowl, using an electric mixer, beat the eggs with the brown sugar until light, about 2 minutes. Add the pumpkin puree, cream, fresh ginger, 1½ tablespoons of the lemon juice, 1½ teaspoons of the cinnamon, the salt, vanilla, ground ginger, pepper, and allspice. Beat until thoroughly blended.

2. In a bowl, toss the apples with the granulated sugar, the butter, and the remaining ½ tablespoon lemon juice, and ½ teaspoon cinnamon.

3 Pour the filling into the cooled tart shell. Starting at the outside, overlap the apple slices in concentric circles over the filling. Bake until the apples are tender and golden and the custard is set in the center, about 1 hour. Let cool completely, then sprinkle with the amaretti crumbs.

—Jody Adams

TART SHELL

MAKES ONE 11-INCH TART SHELL

1½ cups flour

 2 tablespoons sugar

 1 teaspoon salt

½ teaspoon finely grated lemon zest

¼ pound plus 1 tablespoon cold
     unsalted butter, diced

 4 to 5 tablespoons ice water

1. In a food processor, combine the flour, sugar, salt, and lemon zest and pulse to blend. Scatter the butter on top and pulse until it is in pea-size pieces. Transfer the dough to a lightly floured surface and drizzle on 4 tablespoons of the ice water, adding more ice water if the dough seems dry. Knead briefly to blend. Pat the dough into a disk, wrap in plastic, and refrigerate for at least 1 hour.

2. Heat the oven to 425°. On a lightly floured surface, roll the dough out to a 15-inch round. Drape the dough over an 11-inch tart pan with a removable bottom. Firmly press the dough into the pan and against the sides. Trim the overhang to ½ inch and fold it in to reinforce the sides.

3. Line the shell with a large piece of foil and fill it with pie weights, dried beans, or rice. Set the pan on a baking sheet and bake until the sides of the pastry shell are lightly colored, about 25 minutes. Remove the foil and weights. Bake until the base of the shell is golden, about 5 minutes longer. Let cool before filling.

MEME'S APPLE TART

I remember well the apple tart my mother made every day as a dessert offering in her small Lyons restaurant. Unlike any other dough, hers achieved its tender, crumbly, airy texture from the combination of vegetable shortening, baking powder, and warm milk mixed with the flour. This recipe also appears in *Jacques Pépin's Kitchen: Cooking with Claudine* (Bay Books, 1996).

MAKES ONE 9-INCH TART

- 2 pounds sweet apples (about 4), such as Golden Delicious

  Tart Shell, see box at right

- 3 tablespoons sugar

- 2 tablespoons unsalted butter, cut into small pieces

1. Heat the oven to 400°. Peel, quarter, core, and cut the apples into 1-inch-thick wedges. Arrange the wedges in a concentric circle in the tart shell. Sprinkle evenly with the sugar and the butter.

2. Set the tart on a baking sheet. Bake until the fruit is tender and the pastry golden, about 1 hour. Cover the tart loosely with foil after 45 minutes to prevent over-browning. Cut into wedges and serve warm.

—JACQUES PÉPIN

MAKE IT AHEAD

The pastry dough can be made ahead and refrigerated for up to a day.

TART SHELL

MAKES ONE 9-INCH TART SHELL

- ¼ cup milk
- 1¼ cups flour
- 1 teaspoon sugar
- ½ teaspoon baking powder
- ⅛ teaspoon salt
- 6 tablespoons vegetable shortening

1. In a small pan, heat the milk to lukewarm. In a bowl, mix the flour, sugar, baking powder, and salt. Add the shortening and mix with a spoon or your hands until the dough feels and looks sandy. Add the milk and mix rapidly until the dough forms a ball.

2. Roll the dough out between two sheets of plastic wrap to an 11- to 12-inch round. Remove the top piece of plastic. Using the bottom piece, invert the dough into a 9-inch tart pan with removable bottom. Peel off the remaining plastic. Press the dough into the pan and against the sides. Trim the pastry even with the rim of the pan.

Apple Tartlets with Browned Butter Filling

These delicate, individual tarts are as delicious as they are beautiful. The secret is a filling made with beurre noisette, browned butter, which is cooked until it acquires a nutty flavor.

MAKES 8 INDIVIDUAL TARTLETS

- 1 large egg
- ⅓ cup plus 4 teaspoons sugar
- 3½ tablespoons flour
- 4 tablespoons unsalted butter
- ½ vanilla bean, split lengthwise
- ½ pound frozen puff pastry, thawed but cold
- 6 small Granny Smith or Golden Delicious apples
- 1 lemon, halved
- ¼ cup apricot preserves
- 2 tablespoons water

  Chopped toasted pecans or walnuts, for garnish

  Crème fraîche or vanilla ice cream, for serving

1. In a small bowl, whisk the egg with the ⅓ cup of sugar until well blended. Whisk in the flour until combined.

2. In a small heavy saucepan, combine the butter and vanilla bean. Cook over high heat until the butter is golden brown and smells nutty, about 10 minutes. Remove the vanilla bean, rinse, and save for another use. Gradually whisk the browned butter into the egg-flour mixture. Let cool to room temperature, then cover and refrigerate for at least 1 hour, until the mixture is chilled.

3. Halve the puff pastry. On a lightly floured surface, roll one half of the pastry out to a 12-inch square. Using a sharp knife and a pot lid or a small plate as a guide, cut out four 5½-inch rounds of dough. Arrange the dough rounds about 1 inch apart on a large, ungreased baking sheet. Cover with plastic wrap and refrigerate. Repeat with the remaining pastry on another baking sheet, for a total of eight rounds. Refrigerate the pastry for at least 30 minutes or overnight.

4. Heat the oven to 400°. Using a small, sharp knife, slice about ½ inch off the top and bottom of each of the apples. Peel, halve, and core the apples. Rub the apple halves with the lemon halves to prevent discoloring. Place one apple half, cut side down, on a work surface and carefully slice the apple crosswise about 1/16-inch thick. Do not separate the apple slices. Repeat with the remaining apple halves. Squeeze lemon juice over them to prevent discoloration.

5. Place 1 tablespoon of the browned butter filling in the center of each puff pastry round. Cut across the tips of the apple slices to even the ends. Set aside eight apple slices. Using about three quarters of a whole apple for one pastry round, arrange the apple slices in a tight overlapping circle, placing their trimmed ends flush with the edge of the dough. Repeat with the remaining pastry rounds and apples. Then cut the eight reserved apple slices into short wedges and arrange in the center of each tartlet to form rosettes. Sprinkle ½ teaspoon sugar evenly over each tartlet. Bake until the apples are tender and lightly browned on the edges, 18 to 20 minutes. Let cool on the baking sheets.

6. In a small nonreactive saucepan, combine the apricot preserves and the water. Melt over low heat, stirring, until smooth, 1 to 2 minutes. Brush the warm apricot glaze evenly over the apples.

7. Place the apple tartlets on individual dessert plates. Sprinkle chopped toasted nuts over them and place a dollop of crème fraîche or a small scoop of ice cream next to each serving.

—JUDITH SUTTON

MAKE IT AHEAD

The browned butter filling can be prepared up to three days ahead. Or, if you like, you can make the tartlets in advance and keep them in the kitchen, uncovered, for up to six hours. Just reheat the tartlets in a 375° oven for about 5 minutes before serving.

PUFF PASTRY

If possible use all-butter puff pastry, such as the Saucier or Dufour brand, which is available in the frozen-food section of gourmet markets and some supermarkets. Pepperidge Farm brand puff pastry, available at most supermarkets, is a good variety that is made with shortening.

PEAR AND GINGER CUSTARD TART

A tender cookie-like crust, soft pears, and bits of chewy crystallized ginger give a wealth of textures and flavors to this tart. The recipe for the pastry on the opposite page makes enough dough for two 9-inch tart shells. You can either double the filling below and bake two tarts—if you are cooking for a crowd— or fill and bake one shell and save the second for another use; it will keep, well wrapped in the freezer, for up to a week.

MAKES ONE 9-INCH TART

Sweet Tart Shell, opposite page

2 pears, preferably Bartlett or Comice

½ cup heavy cream

2 large eggs

¼ cup granulated sugar

1 ½ tablespoons blanched almonds, finely ground

2 tablespoons chopped crystallized ginger, (about 1 ounce)

1. Heat the oven to 375°. Bake the tart shells for 10 minutes, then set aside to cool. Leave the oven on.

2. Using a small, sharp knife, peel, quarter, and core the pears. Slice them lengthwise ¼-inch thick. In a medium bowl, whisk the cream with the eggs, granulated sugar, and ground almonds. Arrange the pear slices in concentric circles in the cooled tart shell, sprinkle the ginger over the pears, and carefully pour the egg mixture over the fruit.

3. Bake the tart until the custard is firm and the crust is browned, 25 to 35 minutes. Transfer the tart to a rack and let cool to room temperature before serving.

—FRAN GAGE

SWEET TART SHELLS

MAKES TWO 9-INCH TART SHELLS

¼ pound plus 2 tablespoons unsalted butter, at room temperature

1¼ cups plus ⅓ cup pastry flour

¾ cup confectioners' sugar

¼ cup blanched almonds (about 1¼ ounces), finely ground

1 large egg

¾ teaspoon vanilla extract

¼ teaspoon salt

1. In an electric mixer, beat the butter at moderate speed until softened. Add the ⅓ cup flour, the confectioners' sugar, ground almonds, egg, vanilla, and salt. Beat until well blended, scraping down the sides of the bowl once or twice. Add the remaining 1¼ cups flour and beat on low speed just until combined. Do not overmix.

2. Halve the dough and flatten into two disks. Wrap in waxed paper and refrigerate for at least 1 hour or overnight.

3. Line two baking sheets without sides with parchment paper and dust very lightly with flour. Place one pastry disk on a prepared baking sheet. The dough will be sticky. Working quickly and using as little extra flour as possible, roll it out to an 11-inch round about ⅛-inch thick. Repeat with the other pastry disk. Refrigerate the pastry rounds on the baking sheets until firm, about 1 hour.

4. Flip one round of dough into a 9-inch fluted tart pan with a removable bottom. Peel off the parchment paper. Press the dough into the pan and against the sides. Prick the tart shell all over with a fork. Repeat with the other round of dough. Freeze the unbaked tart shells for at least 30 minutes or up to one week.

INDIVIDUAL QUINCE TARTES TATIN WITH SHEEP'S MILK ICE CREAM

Poached quinces have a delicate sweetness and rosy color, making them a fine alternative to apples in this version of the classic French dessert developed by Melissa Kelly, chef at the Old Chatham Sheepherding Company Inn. To remove the quinces' tough centers, cut the peeled fruit into wedges and then remove the cores with an apple corer or small biscuit cutter.

8 SERVINGS

1½ cups plus 1⅓ cups sugar

6 cups water

1 vanilla bean, split lengthwise

6 large quinces, peeled, cut into 12 wedges each, and cored

4 tablespoons unsalted butter

½ cup golden raisins (optional)

2 pounds all-butter puff pastry, chilled

Sheep's Milk Ice Cream, next page, or vanilla ice cream, for serving

1. In a large saucepan, combine the 1½ cups sugar with the water. Scrape the seeds from the vanilla bean into the pan and add the pod of the bean. Cook over high heat, stirring, until the sugar dissolves, about 8 minutes. Add the quince wedges and bring just to a boil. Reduce the heat to low, cover, and simmer until tender, about 2 hours. Occasionally submerge the quinces in the poaching liquid. Let the quinces cool in the liquid.

2. Heat the oven to 375°. Melt the butter in a medium frying pan. Sprinkle the remaining 1⅓ cups of sugar over the butter and cook over moderate heat, without stirring, until the sugar just begins to brown around the edges, about 2 minutes. Cook, stirring gently, until the caramel turns dark golden, 6 to 8 minutes. Immediately pour the caramel into eight 4-inch-wide ramekins (1⅓-cup capacity). Swirl the caramel in the ramekins to coat the bottoms.

3. Drain the quinces and arrange the wedges in the ramekins in overlapping circles. Scatter the raisins on top, if using.

4. On a lightly floured surface, roll out the puff pastry ⅛-inch thick. Using a large biscuit cutter or small bowl, cut eight 4-inch rounds from the pastry and make two 1-inch slits in the center of each. Top the quinces with the dough rounds and bake until the crust is golden and the juices are bubbling, about 45 minutes. Let cool slightly, then invert onto plates. Serve with sheep's milk ice cream.

—MELISSA KELLY

SHEEP'S MILK ICE CREAM

MAKES ABOUT 1½ QUARTS

1½   cups sheep's milk or whole milk
 ½   cup light-brown sugar
     Pinch salt
 1   vanilla bean, split lengthwise
 7   large egg yolks
 ¼   cup granulated sugar
2¼   cups heavy cream

1. In a medium saucepan, combine the milk, brown sugar, and salt. Carefully scrape the seeds from the vanilla bean into the pan and add the bean. Cook over moderately low heat, stirring occasionally, until the milk is steaming, about 8 minutes. Do not boil. Remove from the heat and keep warm. Discard the vanilla bean.

2. Meanwhile, in a bowl, whisk the egg yolks with the granulated sugar until thick and pale. Whisk in half of the warm milk, then whisk in the remaining milk. Pour all of the mixture back into the saucepan and cook, stirring frequently, until the custard thickens slightly and coats the back of a spoon, 8 to 10 minutes. Stir in the cream. Strain the custard into a bowl and chill thoroughly. Transfer to an ice cream maker and freeze according to the manufacturer's instructions.

MAKE IT AHEAD

The quinces can be refrigerated in their liquid for up to three days; drain just before using. The tarts can also be made ahead. Set them aside at room temperature for up to eight hours and then reheat them in a 325° oven for 10 minutes before unmolding.

CRANBERRY, CARAMEL, AND ALMOND TARTLETS

The pastry dough for these tartlets, from The City Bakery in New York City, was designed to be flaky and tender even after being kneaded well. The sweet and creamy caramel filling balances the tartness of the cranberries.

MAKES EIGHT INDIVIDUAL TARTLETS

¾ cup plus 2 tablespoons heavy cream

¾ cup granulated sugar

4 cups fresh cranberries, picked over

1 cup sliced almonds

   Sweet Tart Shells, next page

1. Heat the oven to 375°. In a small saucepan, bring the cream to a simmer over low heat. In a heavy medium saucepan, cook the sugar over moderately high heat, stirring constantly with a wooden spoon, until melted, about 5 minutes. Swirling the pan occasionally, cook until the sugar is a rich, tea-like brown, about 2 minutes. Immediately whisk the hot cream into the caramel, taking care to avoid splatters. Do not let the mixture boil over. Cook, whisking constantly, until smooth. Strain the caramel into a medium bowl. Add the fresh cranberries and the sliced almonds and stir to coat completely.

2. Place the baking sheets with the tartlet shells on top of another baking sheet (to prevent the bottoms of the tartlets from burning). Mound the filling into the tartlet shells and bake them until the cranberries have burst and the edges of the pastry are nicely browned, 25 to 35 minutes.

3. Remove the flan rings from the tartlets with tongs. If they stick, run a small, sharp knife around the tartlet rims and then lift off the rings. Using a metal spatula, carefully transfer the tartlets to a rack to cool slightly. Serve warm or at room temperature.

—MAURY RUBIN

SWEET TART SHELLS

MAKES EIGHT 4-INCH TART SHELLS

¼ pound plus 5 tablespoons cold unsalted butter, cut into ½-inch slices, at room temperature

⅓ cup confectioners' sugar

1 large egg yolk

¾ cup unbleached all-purpose flour, sifted

¾ cup bread flour, sifted

1. In a medium bowl, using an electric mixer, beat the butter with the confectioners' sugar on medium speed for 2 minutes. Beat in the egg yolk, scraping the bowl with a rubber spatula. Using a wooden spoon, stir in half of the all-purpose flour and the bread flour until combined. Mix in the remaining all-purpose flour and bread flour to form a soft, sticky dough. Scrape the dough onto a piece of waxed paper and form it into a flat disk. Wrap and refrigerate the dough until firm, at least 2 hours or overnight.

2. On a lightly floured surface, cut the dough into 1-inch pieces. Using the heel of your hand, knead the pieces together until the dough is smooth but still cool, using a pastry scraper or metal spatula to free the dough from the work surface. Roll the dough into a 12-inch-long log and cut into eight equal pieces. Transfer to a plate, cover with plastic wrap and refrigerate until the dough is cold, about 20 minutes.

3. Line a large baking sheet with parchment paper. Place eight 4-inch flan rings or 4½-inch fluted tartlet pans with removable bottoms on the baking sheet. Remove one piece of dough from the refrigerator and, on a lightly floured surface, roll it out to a 5½-inch round. Drape the dough over one of the flan rings. Using your thumbs, gently but firmly press the dough into the ring, taking care to form a close fit around the base. Trim the dough even with the rim of the ring. Prick the dough all over with a fork. Repeat with the remaining pastry dough. Freeze the rings on the baking sheet until the pastry is chilled and firm, about 15 minutes.

4. Meanwhile, heat the oven to 375°. Bake the tartlet shells on the baking sheet until golden, about 12 minutes. (If the dough puffs up, tap it with a spoon. Do not prick it.) Remove the tartlet shells and let cool on the baking sheet before filling.

MIDSUMMER FRUIT TART

The tart base here consists of a cleverly constructed free-form crust that is baked with a thin layer of cheesecake filling. If you happen to have a quiche ring, you could certainly use it here: Butter the ring, set it on a buttered baking sheet, and line it with the dough. If not, try my associate Stephanie's free-form solution. It seems a little fussy, I know, but it works admirably.

MAKES ONE 9-INCH TART

¼ pound whipped cream cheese, at room temperature

2 tablespoons unsalted butter, at room temperature

1 teaspoon cornstarch, sifted

5 tablespoons sugar

¼ cup sour cream, at room temperature

1 large egg

1½ teaspoons vanilla extract

Free-Form Tart Shell, next page

1 cup apricot jam

3 tablespoons white rum, cognac, or orange liqueur (optional)

1 pint strawberries, hulled and thickly sliced lengthwise

3 kiwis, peeled and sliced

½ cup raspberries

½ cup blackberries

1. Heat the oven to 350°. Using a hand-held mixer, beat the cream cheese until smooth and fluffy, then cream in the butter. Slowly beat in the cornstarch, then 2 tablespoons of the sugar, the sour cream, egg, and vanilla.

2. Prepare a folded strip of aluminum foil 1-inch wide and long enough to surround the tart shell with an inch extra. Butter the foil and pin the buttered side closely around the tart shell. Pour in the filling. Bake on the lower shelf of the oven until the shell is lightly browned and crisp, about 20 minutes. The filling will puff up to the top of the tart shell. Remove the tart to a rack; the filling will sink down. Let cool completely to set the crust.

3. Slide the tart onto a serving platter and remove the foil. Push the jam through a sieve into a 6-cup saucepan, stir in the remaining 3 tablespoons sugar and the rum, if using, and simmer over moderate heat for 2 minutes. Brush a thin layer of the glaze inside the tart. Arrange the strawberries in a circle around the inside edge. Overlap the kiwis inside and mound the berries in the center. Brush the warm glaze over the fruit and serve.

—JULIA CHILD

Free-Form Tart Shell

MAKES ONE 9-INCH TART SHELL

½ cup unbleached all-purpose flour plus more for dusting

½ cup cake flour, sifted

¼ pound cold unsalted butter, quartered lengthwise and crosswise

¼ teaspoon salt

1 tablespoon sugar

5 tablespoons cold vegetable shortening

1 large egg

1½ teaspoons vanilla extract

1. In a food processor, combine the flours, butter, and salt and process for about 30 seconds to blend. Add the sugar, shortening, egg, and vanilla and process until the dough just comes together. On a lightly floured work surface, shape and pat the dough into a disk 1-inch thick, sprinkling on a little flour if the dough is sticky. Wrap in plastic and refrigerate for at least 1 hour, or until firm.

2. Set the dough on a lightly floured work surface and start beating it with your rolling pin, frequently rotating the dough as you gradually form a circular shape. When soft enough to roll, transfer the dough to a lightly floured 18-inch square of heavy-duty aluminum foil. Working rapidly so the dough remains cold, roll it out to a 12-inch round, ³⁄₁₆-inch thick. You'll have a handful of leftover scraps to freeze for your next tart. Slide the dough on its foil onto a cookie sheet and freeze for 5 minutes.

3. Roll the edge of the dough up over itself to make a ¾-inch border. Then roll the border over onto itself, making an upstanding edge. With lightly floured fingers, pinch the thick, raised edge of the dough to form a rim ¾-inch tall and ³⁄₁₆-inch thick. Make the height even all around, since the filling will leak out at any low spots. Decorate the outside of the tart shell's rim by supporting the inside with your fingers as you press the outside with the tines of a table fork held vertically. Trim off any extra foil, cover the tart shell and freeze for at least 30 minutes before filling.

LEMON LOVER'S TART

Lemon is one of my preferred winter flavors, and this rich, creamy tart is the perfect ending to a festive family dinner. The lemon-curd filling thickens slowly; you may find the hand-beating a bit tedious, but the results are well worth it. The tart can be prepared several hours in advance and requires no last-minute fussing, making it ideal for entertaining.

MAKES ONE 9-INCH TART

2 large eggs, at room temperature

3 large egg yolks, at room temperature

1 cup sugar

¼ pound unsalted butter, at room temperature, cut into 8 tablespoons

Finely grated zest of 2 lemons, blanched and refreshed

½ cup lemon juice, strained

Lemon Pastry Shell, next page

Fine strips of lemon zest, blanched and refreshed, for garnish (optional)

1. In the top of a nonreactive double boiler set over, but not touching, simmering water, combine the eggs, egg yolks, and sugar. Cook, whisking frequently, until the mixture is thick and pale yellow, about 10 minutes.

2. Whisk in the butter, piece by piece, allowing each piece to melt before adding the next. Add the grated zest and the lemon juice and whisk frequently until the mixture is thick and the first bubbles appear, about 10 minutes longer. Do not let the mixture boil, or it will curdle.

3. Pour the filling into the pastry shell. Smooth the top with a spatula and set the tart aside at room temperature until the filling firms up, about 30 minutes, before unmolding and serving. Garnish with the strips of lemon zest, if using.

—PATRICIA WELLS

LEMON PASTRY SHELL

MAKES ONE 9-INCH TART SHELL

¼ pound unsalted butter, melted and cooled

¼ teaspoon vanilla extract

¼ teaspoon almond extract

Grated zest of 1 lemon, blanched and refreshed

¼ cup confectioners' sugar

Pinch fine sea salt

1¼ cups plus 1 tablespoon flour

1. Heat the oven to 350°. Butter a 9-inch fluted tart pan with a removable bottom.

2. In a medium bowl, using a wooden spoon, combine the melted butter, vanilla and almond extracts, lemon zest, confectioners' sugar, and salt, and stir to blend. Gradually stir in the flour to form a smooth, soft dough. Place the dough in the center of the prepared pan. Using the tips of your fingers, evenly press the dough along the bottom and up the sides of the pan. The dough will be quite thin.

3. Bake the pastry shell in the center of the oven just until the dough is firm and lightly browned, 12 to 15 minutes. Let the shell cool completely before filling. Do not remove from the pan before the tart is filled and set.

BLANCHING LEMON ZEST

To blanch lemon zest, boil it in water for three minutes; drain, rinse in cold water to refresh it and drain again.

CITRUS CUSTARD TARTS WITH CARAMELIZED FIGS

Buttery citrus custard, made with lemon, grapefruit, and orange juices and zests, fills these elegant individual tart shells. The tarts should be refrigerated overnight before serving to firm up the custard.

Serve these tarts with a luscious dessert wine with a ripe but tart flavor of its own, such as the 1994 Far Niente Dolce from California or the 1990 Château Guiraud Sauternes from France.

MAKES EIGHT INDIVIDUAL TARTLETS

½ cup lemon juice

¼ cup grapefruit juice

¼ cup orange juice

3 large eggs

1 cup sugar

4 tablespoons unsalted butter, cut into pieces

½ tablespoon finely grated lemon zest

½ tablespoon finely grated grapefruit zest

½ tablespoon finely grated orange zest

Tart Shells, page 169

12 ripe fresh figs, preferably green and purple, cut into thin wedges

½ cup water

1. In a double boiler or heatproof bowl set over a saucepan filled with about an inch of simmering water, whisk the citrus juices together with the eggs and ½ cup of the sugar until blended. Cook, stirring constantly with a wooden spoon, until the custard is smooth and thick, 10 to 12 minutes. Do not boil, or it will curdle. Remove from the heat. Stir in the butter.

2. Strain the custard into a bowl and stir in the citrus zests. Divide the custard among the tart shells and let cool completely. Cover with a sheet of waxed paper and refrigerate overnight.

3. Remove the tarts from the pans and arrange the figs on top. In a small saucepan, cook the remaining ½ cup of sugar with the water over moderate heat, stirring occasionally, until the sugar is dissolved and the syrup slightly thickened, about 5 minutes. Let the syrup cool and then brush over the figs to glaze.

—RORI SPINELLI

TART SHELLS

MAKES EIGHT 4½-INCH TART SHELLS

2½ cups flour

2 teaspoons sugar

¾ teaspoon salt

½ pound cold unsalted butter, cut into ½-inch pieces

1 teaspoon finely grated lemon zest

¼ cup plus 3 tablespoons cold skim milk

1. In a food processor, combine the flour, sugar, and salt and pulse to blend. Add the butter and lemon zest and pulse until the mixture resembles coarse meal. Add the milk and pulse just until combined. Transfer the dough to a lightly floured work surface and gently knead until smooth. Divide the dough in half and pat each half into a smooth disk. Wrap in plastic and refrigerate until the dough is chilled, about 1 hour.

2. Arrange eight 4½-inch fluted tart pans with removable bottoms on a baking sheet. Divide one disk of dough into four equal pieces and roll each piece out to a 6½-inch round. Press each round into a tart pan and against the sides. Trim the the pastry even with the rims of the pan. Refrigerate the tart shells for 30 minutes.

3. Heat the oven to 375°. Line each shell with a piece of foil and fill with pie weights, dried beans, or rice. Bake until the edges are lightly golden, about 25 minutes. Remove the foil and weights. Bake until the pastry bottoms are golden, about 7 minutes longer. Let cool before filling.

PLUM GALETTE

The thin-crusted, open-faced fruit tart known as a galette is a quintessential French bistro dessert. This version is made with fresh plums, but the same tart can be made throughout the year with a variety of other seasonal fruits—peaches, cherries, and apricots in summer; apples, pears, or grapes in fall and winter, and rhubarb stalks in spring. This recipe is based on a recipe that appears in *Jacques Pépin's The Art of Cooking*.

8 SERVINGS

¼ cup plus ⅓ cup sugar

3 tablespoons ground almonds

3 tablespoons flour

Food Processor Pâte Brisée, next page, rolled to an oval

2½ pounds large plums, halved, pitted, and cut into ½-inch wedges

3 tablespoons unsalted butter, cut into small pieces

½ cup good-quality plum, apricot, or raspberry preserves, strained if necessary

1. Heat the oven to 400°. In a small bowl, combine the ¼ cup sugar with the ground almonds and flour. Spread this mixture evenly over the chilled pastry to within 2 inches of the edge. Arrange the plum wedges on top and dot all over with the pieces of butter. Sprinkle all but 1 teaspoon of the remaining ⅓ cup sugar over the fruit. Fold the edges of the dough up over the plums to create a 2-inch border. (If the dough feels cold and firm, wait for a few minutes until it softens to prevent it from cracking.) Sprinkle the border with the reserved 1 teaspoon sugar.

2. Bake the galette in the middle of the oven until the fruit is very soft and the crust is richly browned, about 1 hour. If any juices have leaked onto the baking sheet, slide a knife under the galette to release it from the sheet. Spoon the preserves over the hot fruit and spread evenly with a pastry brush. Brush some up onto the crust, if desired. Let the galette cool to room temperature before serving.

—JACQUES PÉPIN

Food Processor Pâte Brisée

MAKES ENOUGH FOR ONE GALETTE

1½ cups flour

12 tablespoons unsalted cold butter, cut into ½-inch pieces

¼ teaspoon salt

⅓ cup ice water

1. In a food processor, combine the flour, butter, and salt and process for about 5 seconds. The butter should still be in pieces. Add the ice water and process just until the dough comes together, about 5 seconds longer. Do not overprocess; the butter should still be visible in the dough.

2. Remove the dough from the processor and gather it into a ball. On a lightly floured surface, roll the dough out to a 16- by 18-inch oval ¹⁄₁₆- to ¹⁄₁₈-inch thick. Drape the dough over the rolling pin and transfer it to a large heavy baking sheet. Chill the dough until firm, about 20 minutes before filling.

STARS AND STRIPES BERRY PIE

This berry pie is decorated in the spirit of our flag, with star cutouts and striped fork marks for the Fourth of July. If blackberries are unavailable, increase the other berries to equal 5¾ cups, keeping the proportion of blueberries low since they can easily overwhelm other berries.

MAKES ONE 9-INCH PIE

2 cups strawberries, hulled and halved, or quartered if large

1¼ cups raspberries

1¼ cups blackberries

1¼ cups blueberries

Juice of ½ lemon

⅔ cup plus 1 tablespoon sugar

1½ tablespoons cornstarch

1½ tablespoons instant tapioca

Flaky Double-Crust Pie Shell, page 191

1. Using your hands, gently toss all the berries with the lemon juice. In a small bowl, whisk the ⅔ cup sugar with the cornstarch and tapioca. Sprinkle over the berries and toss gently to combine. Let sit for 15 minutes.

2. Heat the oven to 450°. Place a piece of foil on the bottom of the oven to catch any drips. Using a pastry brush, moisten the rim of the chilled pie shell bottom with cold water. Pour the fruit into the pie shell and distribute it evenly. Scrape in all the liquid and any undissolved sugar clinging to the bowl.

3. To make decorative vents, using a 1-inch star cookie cutter, cut the chilled pie shell top in five spots placed evenly apart. Save the cutouts. Peel the dough off the parchment paper, then center the dough over the pie. Press all around the edge of the pie to seal. Cut any overhanging dough flush with the edge of the pan. Press around the rim with a fork, angling it for decorative effect, to seal the dough. Lightly brush the top of the pie with cold water and decorate with the cutout stars. Stamp extra cutouts out of any dough scraps if desired. Lightly brush the cutouts with cold water. Sprinkle the remaining 1 tablespoon sugar over the top of the pie.

4. Bake the pie on the bottom rack of the oven until the crust begins to brown, about 20 minutes. Then lower the oven temperature to 375° and bake until the juices are bubbling out through the vents, about 35 minutes longer. Cool for at least 2 hours. Serve cold.

—PEGGY CULLEN

173

BLEEDING HEART PLUM PIE

Here, a crunchy top crust is created by overlapping heart-shaped cutouts of dough and sprinkling the whole surface with sugar. You can use any cookie cutter to vary the top of the pie (leaf shapes, for example, are pretty). Because this pie has no bottom crust, use a glass or ceramic pie plate, which won't react with the acidic fruit.

To begin this recipe, make the dough for the Flaky Double-Crust Pie Shell, page 191, but don't roll it out.

MAKES ONE 9-INCH PIE

- ¾ cup plus 1 tablespoon sugar
- 2 tablespoons instant tapioca
- 1 tablespoon cornstarch
- ¼ teaspoon cinnamon
- ¼ teaspoon ground ginger
- 3 pounds red or black plums, or a mixture, sliced ⅜-inch thick (about 6 cups)
  Dough for Flaky Double-Crust Pie Shell, page 191
- 1 tablespoon unsalted butter, cut into small pieces

1. In a large bowl, whisk the ¾ cup sugar with the tapioca, cornstarch, cinnamon, and ginger. Add the sliced plums and toss to mix.

2. Heat the oven to 450°. Keep one disk of the chilled dough refrigerated while you work with the other. Roll the dough out to a 12-inch round. Using a 9-inch glass or ceramic pie plate as a template, place it rim down on the dough and cut around it with a small, sharp knife. Remove the pie plate and cut a second circle ½ inch outside the perimeter of the first circle. Using a pastry brush, lightly moisten the ½-inch-wide ring of dough with cold water and invert it onto the rim of the plate; press gently to adhere. Don't worry if it breaks. Simply pinch the dough back together where it is torn.

3. Using heart-shaped cookie cutters (the same size or different sizes), cut hearts as close together as possible out of the remaining dough. Slide a long metal spatula underneath the hearts to loosen them from the work surface. Roll the second disk of dough out into a 12-inch round and cut out more hearts as close together as possible.

4. Toss the plums to redistribute the liquid and then pour them into the pie plate. Scrape in all the liquid and any undissolved sugar clinging to the bowl. Dot the filling with the butter.

5. Using a pastry brush, lightly moisten the dough ring on the pie plate with cold water. Affix the heart cutouts, tips toward

the pie's center, to the ring, overlapping them slightly to form a ring of hearts (see photo on page 174). Affix another ring of hearts to the first ring, moistening the dough on the underside where they overlap (if you used different-size cutters, use the larger cutouts near the edge of the pie and the smaller ones in the center). Continue to cover the pie in this fashion, leaving a few open spaces here and there to act as vents.

6. Using a pastry brush, moisten the surface of the dough with cold water. Sprinkle the remaining 1 tablespoon sugar on top. Bake in the middle of the oven until the crust begins to brown, about 20 minutes. Place a piece of foil underneath it to catch drips, lower the temperature to 375° and bake until the top is nicely browned, about 20 minutes longer. Let cool for at least 2 hours.

—Peggy Cullen

BLUEBERRY CROSTATA WITH A CORNMEAL CRUST

The fruit filling for this Italian tart is like a blueberry jam. When blueberries are in season, make extra filling to spread on toast and other breakfast breads.

MAKES ONE 9-INCH CROSTATA

- 3 cups blueberries
- 1 cup granulated sugar
- ⅛ teaspoon cinnamon
- 2 cups flour
- ⅓ cup yellow cornmeal
- 1 teaspoon baking powder
- ½ teaspoon salt
- 6 ounces cold unsalted butter, cut into pieces
- 2 teaspoons finely grated lemon zest
- 1 egg plus 1 egg yolk, lightly beaten
  Confectioners' sugar, for dusting

1. In a medium nonreative saucepan, combine the blueberries, ½ cup of the granulated sugar, and the cinnamon. Cover and bring to a simmer over moderate heat. Uncover and cook, stirring occasionally, until the mixture has thickened slightly, about 20 minutes. Transfer to a small container and let cool, then cover tightly and refrigerate while you proceed. The mixture will thicken further as it cools.

2. In a large bowl, toss the flour with the cornmeal, baking powder, salt, and the remaining ½ cup granulated sugar. Using a pastry blender or two knives, cut in the cold butter until the mixture resembles coarse crumbs. Stir in the lemon zest. Using a fork, stir the beaten eggs into the flour mixture until the dough is moist and crumbly.

3. Scatter about two-thirds of the crumb mixture in a 9-inch round tart pan with a removable bottom. Pat the crumbs evenly over the bottom and up the sides of the pan to form a shell. Spoon the chilled blueberry mixture into the shell and smooth the surface.

4. Heat the oven to 350°. On a very lightly floured work surface, pat the remaining crumb mixture into a square and cut the square into nine even strips. Roll each strip into a ½-inch-thick rope. Crisscross the ropes 1 inch apart over the surface of the tart to form a lattice. Press the rope ends against the inside rim of the shell.

5. Bake the blueberry crostata until golden brown, 45 to 50 minutes. Let cool in the pan for 10 minutes then remove it from the pan and let cool completely. Just before serving, sift confectioners' sugar over the top.

—MICHELLE SCICOLONE

INDIAN APPLE PIE

This homespun pie, with its spiced apple filling and buttery cornmeal-brown sugar topping, is a cross between Indian pudding and apple pie. Serve it with vanilla or caramel ice cream.

MAKES ONE 9-INCH PIE

TOPPING:

- ¾ cup light-brown sugar
- ½ cup flour
- ¼ cup coarse cornmeal or polenta
- 1 teaspoon cinnamon
- 4 tablespoons unsalted butter, cut into ½-inch pieces
- 1½ tablespoons heavy cream

FILLING:

- 2 pounds Granny Smith apples (about 4), peeled, halved, cored, and cut into 12 wedges each
- 1 teaspoon flour
- 4 tablespoons unsalted butter, at room temperature
- 2 tablespoons granulated sugar
- ⅓ cup mild unsulphured molasses
- 1½ teaspoons cinnamon
- ¼ teaspoon ground ginger

Maury's Pie Shell, opposite page

1. For the topping, in a large bowl, rub together the brown sugar, flour, cornmeal, and cinnamon between your fingertips. Add the butter and rub into the mixture to form pea-size lumps. Using a blunt knife, stir in the cream.

2. Heat the oven to 375°. For the filling, in a large bowl, toss the apples with the flour. In another large bowl, combine the butter, sugar, molasses, cinnamon, and ginger and whisk until smooth. Add the apples and stir well. Pour the filling into the pie shell, mounding it in the center. Scrape the sticky topping over the apples. It will melt and cover most of them as it cooks.

3. Bake the pie on the middle shelf of the oven for 30 minutes, then cover loosely with foil and place a baking sheet on the lower shelf to catch any drips. Bake until the apples are tender when pierced, 30 to 40 minutes longer. Let the pie cool for 30 minutes and serve it while it is still warm.

—MAURY RUBIN

MAURY'S PIE SHELL

MAKES ONE 9-INCH PIE SHELL

1¼ cups flour

1 tablespoon sugar

⅛ teaspoon salt

6 tablespoons cold unsalted butter, cut into pieces

2 tablespoons cold vegetable shortening

2½ to 3 tablespoons ice water

1. In a food processor, combine the flour, sugar, and salt and pulse to combine. Add the butter and shortening and pulse until the pieces are the size of small peas. Drizzle in 2½ tablespoons of the ice water and pulse a few times, adding a little more water if necessary until the dough can be gathered into a ball. Pat the dough into a 6-inch disk. Wrap it in plastic wrap or waxed paper and refrigerate for at least 1 hour or overnight. Let the dough soften at room temperature for 5 minutes before rolling it out.

2. On a lightly floured work surface, roll the dough out to a 12-inch round. Fit the dough into a 9-inch pie plate. Tuck in the overhang to reinforce a generous rim and crimp the rim decoratively. Refrigerate the pie shell until firm, at least 1 hour or overnight, before filling.

CHEF'S TIP

Granny Smith apples are the best choice for Indian Apple Pie. They hold their shape during cooking—essential for baking apples—and offer a pleasantly tart contrast to the sweet blend of molasses and granulated sugar in the filling and the brown sugar in the topping. Other baking apples to look for, especially at local farmers' markets, include Mutsu, Golden Delicious, Greening, and Idared.

Deep-Dish Apple Pie with a Cheddar Crust

Nothing evokes memories of the old-time diners like a classic apple pie. You can assemble this pie and wrap and freeze it, unbaked, for up to two weeks.

MAKES ONE 9-INCH PIE

2½ pounds Golden Delicious apples (about 6), peeled, cored, and sliced ¼-inch thick

Juice of ½ large lemon

¾ cups light-brown sugar

2 tablespoons flour

½ teaspoon coarse salt

Cheddar Double-Crust Pie Shell

1. Heat the oven to 375°. In a large bowl, toss the apples with the lemon juice. Sprinkle on the brown sugar, flour, and salt and toss well. Mound the apples in the lined pie pan. Moisten the pie-shell rim with water and cover with the dough round. Trim any overhang and crimp the edge to seal. Cut four steam vents in the top of the pie.

2. Bake the pie on the bottom shelf of the oven until golden and bubbly and the apples are tender when pierced, about 1 hour. Cover the pie with foil halfway through if browning too fast. Let cool for about 1 hour before serving.

—Waldy Malouf

Cheddar Double-Crust Pie Shell

MAKES ONE 9-INCH DOUBLE-CRUST PIE SHELL

1½ cups flour

¼ pound sharp cheddar cheese, grated

¼ teaspoon coarse salt

¼ pound cold unsalted butter, cut into tablespoons

1 egg, lightly beaten

1. In a food processor, combine the flour, cheese, and salt and pulse to mix. Add the butter and pulse until the mixture resembles coarse meal. Transfer the mixture to a large bowl and make a well in the center. Stir in the egg and work the dough into a ball.

2. Flatten the dough into two disks. Roll one of the disks out between two sheets of waxed paper to an 11-inch round. Remove the waxed paper and line a 9-inch pie plate with a dough round. Repeat to roll the second disk out to an 11-inch round. Refrigerate both until chilled.

JESSIE'S SOUR-CHERRY PIE

The complex taste of sour cherries is the perfect foil for this sweet, simple crust. Frozen sour cherries are available all year by mail—order from Orchard Harvest, 1-800-286-7209.

MAKES ONE 8-INCH PIE

1¼ cups sugar

¼ cup cornstarch, sifted

1¼ pounds fresh or frozen pitted sour cherries

3 tablespoons unsalted butter

1 teaspoon almond extract

2 cups flour

½ teaspoon salt

¾ cup vegetable shortening or lard

4 to 5 tablespoons ice water

1. In a nonreactive saucepan, combine the sugar and cornstarch. Stir in the cherries and let stand until soupy, about 15 minutes. Cook over moderate heat, stirring, until thickened, 8 to 10 minutes. Stir in the butter and almond extract. Let cool.

2. Heat the oven to 450°. In a bowl, mix the flour and salt. Cut in the shortening until the mixture resembles small peas. Stir in the ice water until the dough forms a ball. Divide the dough in half and pat each half out to a 6-inch disk.

3. Lightly flour the disks and place each between two sheets of waxed paper. Roll one disk out to a 10-inch round. Peel off the top sheet of paper and invert the dough into an 8-inch pie plate. Peel off the paper and fit the dough into the plate. Roll out the remaining disk, remove the paper and cut a few slits in the center of the round to vent steam.

4. Pour the filling in the pie dish. Wet the rim of the bottom crust and top with the vented crust. Trim and crimp the edge. Bake for 15 minutes. Lower the temperature to 400°. Bake until the crust is golden, about 40 minutes. Let cool.

—JESSIE CROMWELL

PEACH POUCH PIE WITH BERRIES

In this peasant-style pie, the edges of the dough are folded over the fruit to form a rustic pouch. Allow time to make the dough and let it chill for four hours before using.

MAKES ONE 9-INCH PIE

- ⅔ cup plus 1 teaspoon sugar
- 3 tablespoons cornstarch
- 3 pounds ripe but firm peaches, peeled and sliced ½-inch-thick (about 6 cups)
  Pie Shell, next page
- ½ cup blueberries
- ½ cup raspberries

1. Heat the oven to 450°. Place a piece of foil on the bottom of the oven to catch any drips.

2. In a large bowl, whisk the ⅔ cup of sugar with the cornstarch. Gently toss in the peaches. Let sit for 10 minutes.

3. Meanwhile, remove the pie shell from the refrigerator. Gently toss the peaches. Let sit for 5 minutes longer. Combine the blueberries and raspberries and gently stir them into the peaches. Pour the fruit into the pie shell and distribute it evenly. Scrape in all the liquid and any undissolved sugar clinging to the bowl. When the dough is pliable, fold the overhanging edge to cover the outer portion of the filling, leaving a 5-inch opening of exposed fruit in the center of the pie.

4. Using a pastry brush, moisten the surface of the dough with cold water. Sprinkle the remaining 1 teaspoon sugar over the dough. Bake the pie on the lower rack of the oven until the crust begins to brown, about 20 minutes. Then lower the temperature to 375° and bake until the fruit is bubbling and the crust is nicely colored, 35 to 45 minutes longer. Cool for at least 2 hours.

—PEGGY CULLEN

Pie Shell

MAKES ONE 9-INCH PIE SHELL

1⅓ cups flour

1 teaspoon salt

1 teaspoon sugar

4 tablespoons cold unsalted butter, cut into ½-inch pieces

4 tablespoons cold vegetable shortening, cut into small pieces

¼ cup ice water

1. In a food processor, combine the flour, salt, and sugar and pulse to mix. Add the butter and shortening and pulse until the mixture resembles coarse meal.

2. Drizzle the ice water evenly over the mixture and pulse eight to twelve times, until the dough forms small clumps. Turn out the dough onto a work surface, scraping the bowl well. Using the heel of your hand, gently press the dough into the table with a few quick strokes. Gather the dough together and flatten it into a disk about 4 inches in diameter. Wrap the dough in plastic wrap and refrigerate for at least 4 hours or overnight.

3. On a lightly floured surface, roll the chilled dough out to a 14-inch round. Using a 9-inch pie plate as a template, place it rim down on the dough and cut out a circle about 2 inches larger than the rim with a pastry wheel. Slide a long metal spatula underneath the dough to loosen it. Fold the dough round in half, center it over the pie plate and open it. Gently press the dough against the bottom and sides of the pie plate. The dough should drag on the table. Set the pie plate on a bowl to allow the edge to hang down and refrigerate for 30 minutes before filling.

BLUEBERRY LEMON SOUFFLÉ PIE

Sweetened, lightly cooked blueberries are covered with melt-in-your-mouth lemon soufflé in this fruit pie and soufflé in one.

MAKES ONE 9-INCH PIE

- 3 cups blueberries
- 6 tablespoons granulated sugar
- 3 large eggs, separated
- 7 tablespoons superfine sugar
- ¼ cup plus 3 tablespoons fresh lemon juice
  Grated zest of 2 lemons
- ⅛ teaspoon salt
  Flaky Pie Shell, page 187

1. Heat the oven to 400°. In a nonreactive saucepan, toss the blueberries and granulated sugar. Cook over moderately high heat, stirring occasionally, until the juices begin to bubble, 3 to 5 minutes. Do not overcook or the berries will burst. Pour into a stainless steel strainer set over a bowl. Reserve the drained juices.

2. Using an electric mixer, beat the egg yolks with 4 tablespoons of the superfine sugar until pale and thick, about 2 minutes. Gradually beat in the lemon juice and then the zest.

3. Transfer the mixture to a nonreactive saucepan and cook over low heat, stirring, until it thickens, about 8 minutes. Do not boil, or it will curdle. Scrape into a bowl and set aside on a rack to cool.

4. Using clean beaters, beat the egg whites until foamy. Add the salt and beat until the whites hold soft peaks when the beaters are lifted. Add the remaining 3 tablespoons superfine sugar, ½ tablespoon at a time, beating well after each addition. Beat at high speed until the whites are glossy but not dry, about 20 seconds longer.

5. Using a rubber spatula, stir one-fourth of the beaten whites into the yolk mixture. Gently fold into the remaining whites in three additions.

6 Spoon the blueberries into the baked pie shell and drizzle 2½ tablespoons of the drained juices over them. Mound all the soufflé mixture over the berries. Spread the mixture gently to cover the berries, touching the pie crust all around. Bake in the middle of the oven until the top is nicely browned, about 15 minutes. Cool slightly and serve warm or at room temperature.

—PEGGY CULLEN

Flaky Pie Shell

This pie dough may be made ahead, wrapped, and refrigerated for up to two days. Once rolled and wrapped, the pie shell can be frozen for up to two months. Just defrost the shell overnight in the refrigerator before baking.

MAKES ONE 9-INCH PIE SHELL

- 1 cup plus 2 tablespoons flour
- ¾ teaspoon salt
- ¾ teaspoon sugar
- 3 tablespoons cold unsalted butter, cut into ½-inch pieces
- 3½ tablespoons cold vegetable shortening, cut into small pieces
- 3 tablespoons ice water

1. In a food processor, combine the flour, salt, and sugar and pulse to mix. Add the butter and shortening and pulse until the mixture resembles coarse meal with particles the size of peas.

2. Drizzle the ice water evenly over the mixture and pulse eight to twelve times, until the dough forms small clumps. Turn out the dough onto a work surface, scraping the bowl well. Using the heel of your hand, gently press the dough into the table with a few quick strokes. Gather the dough together and flatten it into a disk about 4 inches in diameter. Wrap the dough in plastic wrap and refrigerate for at least 4 hours or overnight.

3. Place the disk of chilled dough on a lightly floured surface and flour the top of the dough. Roll the dough out lightly with a floured rolling pin to a 9-inch round, rotating and flipping the dough over every few strokes to ensure even thickness. Now roll out the round of dough from the center until it reaches a diameter of about 12 inches.

4. Fold the dough round in half. Center it over the pie plate and unfold it. Gently press the dough against the bottom and sides of the pie plate. Trim the dough so that it overhangs the rim of the pie plate by 1 inch. The dough should touch but not drag on the table. Fold the overhanging dough under and crimp decoratively. Prick a few holes in the bottom of the shell with a fork. Refrigerate the pie shell for at least 30 minutes.

5. Heat the oven to 450°. Line the chilled pie shell with foil, making sure the foil completely covers the crimped edge (this may take an extra piece of foil) and fill with pie weights, dried beans, or rice. Bake the shell in the center of the oven until the edges are lightly golden, about 20 minutes. Remove the foil and weights. Bake until the center has lost its raw look and the shell is golden brown all over, 12 to 15 minutes longer.

DOUBLE-DECKER PUMPKIN CHIFFON PIE

This delectable two-tone dessert features the standard pumpkin-pie filling topped with a layer of fluffy pumpkin-flavored chiffon. Sweetened whipped cream completes the holiday picture.

The dough can be refrigerated overnight, or fitted into a pie plate and frozen for up to one month. You can hold the pumpkin pie (without the chiffon layer) overnight in the refrigerator, and add the chiffon the day you plan to serve it.

MAKES ONE 9-INCH PIE

PUMPKIN PIE:

1   cup canned pumpkin puree

¼   cup granulated sugar

¼   cup light-brown sugar

½   teaspoon cinnamon

½   teaspoon ground ginger

¼   teaspoon freshly grated nutmeg

¼   teaspoon ground allspice

¼   teaspoon unsweetened cocoa powder

¼   teaspoon salt

2   large eggs, lightly beaten

⅔   cup heavy cream

1   tablespoon molasses

1   teaspoon vanilla extract
    Pie Shell, opposite page

PUMPKIN CHIFFON:

1½   teaspoons unflavored powdered gelatin

2   tablespoons cold water

1   cup canned pumpkin puree

¼   cup light-brown sugar

¼   teaspoon cinnamon

¼   teaspoon ground ginger

¼   teaspoon freshly grated nutmeg

⅛   teaspoon salt

2   large eggs, separated

2   teaspoons vanilla extract

½   cup heavy cream

⅓   cup plus 1½ tablespoons granulated sugar

1. Heat the oven to 350°. For the pumpkin pie, in a medium bowl, whisk the pumpkin puree with the granulated sugar, brown sugar, cinnamon, ginger, nutmeg, allspice, cocoa powder, and salt. Whisk in the eggs, cream, molasses, and vanilla. Pour the custard into the prebaked pie shell, spreading it evenly. Bake until the surface is puffed, the edges are firm and the center is slightly shaky, 35 to 40 minutes. Transfer to a rack and let cool completely.

2. For the pumpkin chiffon, in a small cup, sprinkle the gelatin over the cold water. In a medium saucepan, combine the pumpkin puree, brown sugar, cinnamon, ginger, nutmeg, and salt. Put the egg whites in a clean medium bowl and cover with

plastic wrap. Stir the egg yolks into the pumpkin mixture and bring just to a boil over moderately high heat, stirring gently. Whisk in the dissolved gelatin and the vanilla. Transfer to a bowl and let cool to room temperature.

3. In a medium bowl, beat the cream with the 1½ tablespoons granulated sugar until soft peaks form when the beaters are lifted.

4. Using a hand-held mixer, beat the remaining ⅓ cup of granulated sugar into the egg whites. Set the bowl over a large saucepan that contains about an inch of simmering water. Beat the egg whites at low speed until warm to the touch. Remove from the heat and continue beating at high speed until the whites are glossy and hold semi-firm peaks when the beaters are lifted.

5. Fold the meringue into the pumpkin mixture just until combined. Fold in the whipped cream. Spoon the chiffon over the pumpkin pie and refrigerate until set, at least 1 hour and up to 6 hours.

—PEGGY CULLEN

PIE SHELL

MAKES ONE 9-INCH PIE SHELL

- 1 cup plus 2 tablespoons flour
- ¾ teaspoon sugar
- ¾ teaspoon salt
- 3½ tablespoons cold vegetable shortening, cut into small pieces
- 3 tablespoons cold unsalted butter, cut into ½-inch pieces
- 3 tablespoons ice water

1. In a food processor, combine the flour with the sugar and salt and pulse to blend. Add the shortening and butter and pulse until the mixture resembles coarse meal. Drizzle in the ice water and pulse until the dough forms small clumps. Turn the dough onto a lightly floured work surface and press it out with the heel of your hand. Gather the dough together and flatten it into a 4-inch disk. Wrap in plastic wrap and refrigerate for at least 1 hour.

2. On a lightly floured surface, roll the dough out to a 12-inch round. Drape the dough over a 9-inch glass pie plate. Press the dough against the bottom and sides of the pie plate. Trim any overhanging dough and flute the edges. Prick the bottom all over with a fork and freeze until firm, about 20 minutes.

3. Heat the oven to 450°. Line the shell with a large piece of foil and fill with pie weights, dry beans, or rice. Bake until the edges are slightly golden, 20 to 25 minutes. Remove the foil and weights. Bake until the center loses its raw look, 5 to 8 more minutes. The shell should be a little light; it will be baked again. Cool before adding the filling.

CHERRY APRICOT LATTICE PIE

The bottom of this lattice-top pie is lined with a layer of crushed amaretti cookies that absorb the cherry and apricot juice. If you don't care for almond flavor, just eliminate the cookies.

If you use sour cherries instead of sweet ones, increase the sugar to three-quarters of a cup.

MAKES ONE 9-INCH PIE

1 pound sweet cherries, pitted and halved (about 2½ cups)

6 apricots, halved, pitted, and cut into sixths or eighths (about 2 cups)

⅔ cups plus 2 teaspoons sugar

1½ tablespoons cornstarch

1½ tablespoons instant tapioca

⅓ cup coarsely crushed amaretti cookies

Flaky Double-Crust Pie Shell, opposite page

1. Toss the cherries and apricots together in a medium bowl. In a small bowl, whisk the ⅔ cup sugar with the cornstarch and tapioca. Sprinkle this mixture over the fruit and toss gently. Let sit for 15 minutes, tossing the mixture once after about 10 minutes.

2. Heat the oven to 450°. Sprinkle the amaretti cookies over the chilled pie shell bottom. Using a pastry brush, lightly moisten the rim with cold water. Pour the fruit into the pie shell and distribute it evenly. Scrape in all the liquid and any undissolved sugar clinging to the bowl.

3. Using a long metal spatula, loosen the chilled lattice pastry strips from the paper-lined baking sheet. Place the longest strip across the center of the pie. Place a strip on either side, each about 1 inch apart. Weave in the remaining strips at an opposing angle. Press gently to seal the lattice to the rim. Using scissors, trim the ends of the lattice even with the overhanging bottom crust, then fold this dough under and crimp decoratively. Lightly brush the lattice with cold water and sprinkle the remaining 2 teaspoons sugar on top.

4. Bake the pie on the bottom rack of the oven until the lattice begins to brown, about 20 minutes. Then lower the temperature to 375° and bake until the lattice is nicely colored and the filling bubbles up through the lattice, about 35 minutes longer. Cool at least 2 hours. Serve the pie warm or cool.

—PEGGY CULLEN

FLAKY DOUBLE-CRUST PIE SHELL

MAKES ONE 9-INCH DOUBLE-CRUST OR LATTICE-TOP PIE SHELL

2　cups flour

1　teaspoon salt

1　teaspoon sugar

6　tablespoons cold unsalted butter, cut into ½-inch pieces

6　tablespoons vegetable shortening, cut into small pieces

⅓　cup ice water

1. In a food processor, combine the flour, salt, and sugar and pulse to mix. Add the butter and shortening and pulse until the mixture resembles coarse meal.

2. Drizzle the ice water evenly over the mixture and pulse eight to twelve times, until the dough forms small clumps. Turn out the dough onto a work surface, scraping the bowl well. Using the heel of your hand, gently press the dough into the table with a few quick strokes. Gather the dough together and flatten it into two 4-inch disks. Wrap the dough in plastic wrap and refrigerate for at least 4 hours or overnight.

3. Keep one disk refrigerated while you work with the other. On a floured work surface, heavily dust both sides of the dough with flour. Press the dough into a 6-inch round. Roll the dough out with a floured rolling pin to a 9-inch round, rotating and flipping the dough over every few strokes to ensure even thickness. Now roll out the round of dough from the center until it reaches a diameter of about 12 inches.

4. Fold the dough round in half. Center it over the pie plate and unfold it. Gently press the dough against the bottom and sides of the pie plate. Then trim the overhanging dough edge to ½ inch for a double-crust pie, 1 inch for a lattice-top pie. Do not crimp the edge. Refrigerate the pie shell for at least 30 minutes or up to two days before filling.

5. Roll out the remaining disk of dough to a 12-inch round, as above. Fold the round in half and unfold onto a baking sheet lined with parchment or waxed paper. At this point, if you are making a lattice top, use a pastry wheel (fluted or not) to cut the round of dough into parallel strips about 1½-inches wide (the wider the strips, the easier they are to handle). Cover the solid round or the lattice strips with plastic wrap and refrigerate for 30 minutes before using.

MANGO PIE

While you're waiting for peaches to come into season, treat yourself to a slice of this exotic peach-like pie. You can tell a ripe mango by its perfume (spicy and peach-like) and its color: An unripe mango is green and develops splashes of yellow, orange, and red as it ripens.

MAKES ONE 9-INCH PIE

Pie Dough, opposite page

3   large ripe mangoes, peeled and cut into ¼-inch slices

⅓   cup sugar, more for sprinkling

2   tablespoons instant tapioca

1½   tablespoons lemon juice

Large pinch cinnamon

Milk or heavy cream, for brushing

1. Divide the pie dough in half. On a lightly floured surface, roll one piece of the pie dough out to a 12-inch round about ¼-inch thick. Fold the round of dough in half and transfer it to a 9-inch glass pie plate. Unfold the pie dough and gently press it against the bottom and sides of the pie plate. Trim the overhanging dough to ¼ inch. Freeze the pie shell for about 20 minutes to firm it up.

2. Heat the oven to 375°. Bake the pie shell on the bottom shelf of the oven for 10 minutes. Transfer to a rack to cool. Leave the oven on.

3 Meanwhile, in a large bowl, toss the mango slices with the sugar, instant tapioca, lemon juice, and cinnamon. Let the mixture stand for about 5 minutes to soften the tapioca.

4. On a lightly floured surface, roll out the second piece of pie dough as you did the first. With a slotted spoon, transfer the mango slices to the baked bottom pie crust. Spoon just enough of the juices over the fruit to moisten.

5. Dampen the rim of the bottom pie crust with water. Drape the rolled-out dough over the mango filling and press all around the rim to seal. Trim off any excess pie dough. Make a decorative border with a fork by pressing the tines all around the rim of the pie. Cut three long narrow crescents in the top crust, brush the crust with milk or cream, and then sprinkle the crust generously with sugar.

6. Bake the pie on the bottom shelf of the oven until the crust is golden brown and juices are bubbling through the steam vents, about 45 minutes. Transfer the pie to a rack and let cool for a few hours before serving. Serve the pie warm or at room temperature.

—MARCIA KIESEL

PIE DOUGH

MAKES ENOUGH FOR ONE 9-INCH DOUBLE-CRUST PIE SHELL

2 cups flour, sifted

½ teaspoon salt

¼ pound cold unsalted butter, cut into small pieces

½ cup cold vegetable shortening

About 5 tablespoons ice water

In a medium bowl, combine the flour and salt. Using a pastry blender or two knives, cut in the butter until the mixture resembles coarse meal. Cut in the vegetable shortening until blended. Dribble in 4 tablespoons of the ice water, mixing lightly with a fork until the pie dough begins to come together. Gather the pie dough into a ball. If the dough seems dry, add the remaining 1 tablespoon ice water. Pat the pie dough into a disk, wrap the disk in waxed paper, and refrigerate for at least 30 minutes or overnight before rolling.

BANANA, CHOCOLATE, AND COCONUT-CREAM PIE

The sweet, crunchy brittle that tops this pie makes a fun snack on its own or a decoration for sundaes, cakes, and pies.

MAKES ONE 9-INCH PIE

1 cup heavy cream

6 ounces semisweet chocolate, chopped

Pinch salt

3 large ripe bananas, sliced crosswise 1½-inches thick

Pie Shell, opposite page

1¼ cups milk

¼ cup sugar

2 tablespoons plus 2 teaspoons cornstarch

2 large egg yolks

½ cup shredded sweetened coconut

¼ teaspoon vanilla extract

2 cups Banana Brittle, opposite page (optional)

1. In a small saucepan, heat the cream just until boiling. Remove from the heat and stir in the chocolate until melted. Transfer to a bowl and add the salt. Refrigerate, stirring often, until the mixture is cooled and thickened, about 45 minutes. Arrange the banana pieces vertically in the pie shell in concentric circles. Pour the chocolate mixture over them and refrigerate until firm, about 2 hours.

2. Meanwhile, heat the milk in a heavy saucepan. In a bowl, mix the sugar and cornstarch. Stir in the egg yolks, then whisk the mixture into the milk. Whisk over low heat until the custard thickens and almost boils, about 4 minutes. Transfer to a bowl, add the coconut and vanilla and let stand until cooled, stirring. Refrigerate until chilled, about 20 minutes.

3. Spread the coconut custard over the chilled pie and refrigerate until firm, about 2 hours. Just before serving, arrange the banana brittle, if using, over the top of the pie.

—MARCIA KIESEL

PIE SHELL

MAKES ONE 9-INCH SHELL

1¼ cups flour

½ teaspoon sugar

Pinch salt

¼ cup plus 1 tablespoon chilled vegetable shortening

About ¼ cup ice water

1. In a bowl, combine the flour, sugar, and salt. Cut in the shortening until the mixture resembles coarse meal. Add the water and stir just until the dough comes together. Shape into a disk, cover with plastic wrap, and refrigerate until chilled, at least 30 minutes or overnight.

2. Heat the oven to 375°. On a floured surface, roll the dough out to an 11-inch round. Drape the dough over a 9-inch pie plate. Gently press the dough against the bottom and sides of the pie plate. Trim the overhang to ½ inch, fold it under itself and crimp decoratively. Freeze the pie shell until firm, about 10 minutes. Bake the pie shell until golden, about 25 minutes. Let cool on a rack before filling.

BANANA BRITTLE

MAKES ABOUT 4 CUPS

2 tablespoons unsalted butter

1 tablespoon vegetable oil

5 tablespoons sugar

3 semi-ripe medium bananas, very thinly sliced crosswise

¾ teaspoon cinnamon

¼ cup minced unsalted peanuts

Heat the oven to 350°. On a large baking sheet, melt the butter in the oil. Spread to coat the pan evenly and sprinkle with 3 tablespoons of the sugar. Cover with the banana slices in a slightly overlapping layer and sprinkle with the remaining 2 tablespoons sugar, the cinnamon, and the peanuts. Bake until the slices around the edge are crisp and golden, about 20 minutes. Let cool slightly so they firm up. Transfer the browned slices to a plate and bake the rest until browned, about 3 minutes.

MAKE IT AHEAD

The banana brittle can be wrapped in waxed paper and stored in an airtight container for up to five days.

CHOCOLATE SILK PIE

Use a standing electric mixer and beat well. This will give the filling its rich, silky-smooth texture. A hand-held electric mixer will also do the job.

MAKES ONE 9-INCH PIE

- 2 ounces bittersweet chocolate, chopped
- 2 ounces unsweetened chocolate, chopped
- 6 ounces unsalted butter, at room temperature
- 1 cup plus 1 tablespoon superfine sugar
- 2 teaspoons bourbon
- 2 teaspoons vanilla extract
- 3 large eggs, at room temperature
  Pie Shell, opposite page
- 1 cup heavy cream

1. In a small heatproof bowl set over a saucepan of barely simmering water, melt the chocolates, stirring occasionally, until smooth. Let cool slightly.

2. In a large bowl, using an electric mixer, cream the butter and the 1 cup superfine sugar until fluffy, about 3 minutes. Beat in the bourbon and 1½ teaspoons of the vanilla, then beat in the melted chocolate. Beat in the eggs one at a time, beating for 5 minutes after each addition and scraping down the bowl several times.

3. Scrape the filling into the pie shell and smooth the top with a rubber spatula. Refrigerate until set, at least 4 hours or overnight.

4. Shortly before serving, in a medium bowl, beat the cream with the remaining 1 tablespoon superfine sugar and the remaining ½ teaspoon vanilla, until the cream holds firm peaks when the beaters are lifted. Using a long metal spatula, spread the whipped cream over the top of the pie. (Alternatively, spoon the topping into a pastry bag fitted with a large star tip. Pipe a border of rosettes around the edge of the pie.) Cut into wedges and serve.

—JUDITH SUTTON

PIE SHELL

MAKES ONE 9-INCH PIE SHELL

1⅓ cups flour

3 tablespoons sugar

⅛ teaspoon salt

¼ pound cold unsalted butter, cut into ½-inch pieces

3 to 3½ tablespoons ice water

1. In a food processor, combine the flour, sugar, and salt and pulse to blend. Scatter the butter pieces over the flour mixture and pulse 10 to 15 times, until the mixture resembles coarse meal. Drizzle 3 tablespoons of the ice water on top and pulse until the dough just comes together, adding up to ½ tablespoon more ice water, if necessary.

Using your hands, shape the dough into a disk, wrap well, and refrigerate for at least 1 hour or overnight.

2. On a lightly floured surface, roll the dough out to a 13-inch round. Drape the dough over a 9-inch pie plate. Gently press the dough against the bottom and sides of the pie plate. Trim the overhang to ½ inch. Fold under the overhanging dough and crimp the edge decoratively. Refrigerate the pie shell for 30 minutes.

3. Heat the oven to 375°. Line the shell with a large piece of foil and fill it with pie weights, dried beans, or rice. Bake for 15 minutes. Remove the foil and weights. Bake until the pastry is pale golden, about 10 to 12 minutes longer. Let cool before filling.

chapter 4

FRUIT DESSERTS

Peaches in Muscat with Honey

GINGER STAR SHORTCAKES WITH SUMMER BERRIES

For a show-stopping dessert, fill gingerbread shortcakes with rich mascarpone cream and sweet ripe berries.

16 SERVINGS

BERRIES:

1½ pints strawberries, sliced

1½ pints blueberries

1½ pints blackberries

1½ pints raspberries

1 cup sugar

MASCARPONE CREAM:

¾ pound mascarpone cheese (1½ cups) or cream cheese, at room temperature

¼ cup plus 2 tablespoons chopped candied ginger (about 1½ ounces)

3 tablespoons sugar

1½ teaspoons vanilla extract

3 cups heavy cream

SHORTCAKES:

4½ cups flour

1 cup plus 1½ tablespoons sugar

1 tablespoon plus 1 teaspoon ground ginger

1 tablespoon baking powder

2 teaspoons ground cinnamon

1½ teaspoons baking soda

1 teaspoon ground allspice

½ teaspoon salt

½ teaspoon freshly ground white pepper

¾ cup cold Molasses Butter, next page, cut into 1-inch pieces

1⅓ cups buttermilk

2 large egg yolks

About ¾ cup Molasses Butter, next page, at room temperature

1. For the berries, in a large bowl, toss the berries with the sugar and let macerate at room temperature for at least 1 or up to 4 hours, stirring gently from time to time.

2. For the mascarpone cream, in a medium bowl, beat the mascarpone with the ginger, sugar, and vanilla until well blended. Slowly beat in the heavy cream just until the mixture holds soft peaks when the beaters are lifted. Refrigerate for up to 3 hours.

3. Heat the oven to 425°. For the shortcakes, butter two baking sheets. In a large bowl, sift the flour with the 1 cup sugar, the ginger, baking powder, cinnamon, baking soda, allspice, salt, and pepper and whisk to combine. Using a pastry cutter or two knives, cut in the cold molasses butter until the mixture resembles small peas. ➤

4. In a large measuring cup, whisk the buttermilk and egg yolks. Stir one cup into the dry ingredients. Using your hands, squeeze the dough until smooth. If necessary, stir in a little more liquid, but don't let the dough become sticky. Reserve the remaining liquid for glazing.

5. Turn the dough onto a lightly floured surface and roll out to a ½-inch thickness. Using a lightly floured 3-inch, star-shaped or round biscuit cutter, cut out as many shortcakes as you can. Pat the scraps together and continue cutting to make a total of sixteen shortcakes. Arrange the shortcakes on the prepared baking sheets so they don't touch, then brush the tops lightly with the remaining buttermilk mixture and sprinkle with the remaining 1½ tablespoons of sugar.

6. Bake the shortcakes, a tray at a time, until the bottoms are lightly browned, about 15 minutes. Cool 5 minutes. Split with a serrated knife and then set each base on a plate and spread with a thin layer of the room temperature molasses butter. Mound berries on each. Whip the mascarpone cream briefly and add a dollop to the berries. Cover each shortcake with a top.

—Joe Abuso

Molasses Butter

MAKES ABOUT 1½ CUPS

½ pound unsalted butter, at room temperature
¼ cup dark-brown sugar
⅓ cup unsulphured molasses

In a medium bowl, beat the butter with the brown sugar until light and creamy. Beat in the molasses.

Make It Ahead

The molasses butter can be made ahead and refrigerated overnight.

CINNAMON CRUNCH SHORTCAKES WITH MIXED BERRIES

These individual shortcake biscuits are dipped in butter and then coated with cinnamon sugar to create a crunchy topping. Don't use a knife to split biscuits; it will crush their flaky layers. Use your fingers to open them.

8 SERVINGS

Biscuit Dough, next page, patted into a rectangle

2 cups raspberries

1½ cups blackberries

2 cups blueberries

⅔ cup plus ½ cup sugar

2 teaspoons water, more if needed

¼ pound unsalted butter

2 teaspoons cinnamon

Ginger Whipped Cream, page 220

1. Heat the oven to 450°. On a lightly floured surface, roll the biscuit dough out ½- to ¾-inch thick. Using a heart-shaped or any other biscuit cutter that measures 3 inches at its widest point, cut out five shortcakes as close together as possible. Press the cutter straight down; don't twist it. If the cutter sticks to the dough, dip it in flour between cuts. Gather the scraps together and press or roll out as before. Cut out two more shortcakes. Press the remaining scraps into a ball, flatten, and cut out the last shortcake. (Alternatively, on a lightly floured surface, pat the dough into an 8-inch round. Halve the round, then cut each half into three wedges for a total of six triangular shortcakes.) Place the shortcakes on an ungreased baking sheet, cover with the plastic wrap, and refrigerate.

2. In a medium bowl, gently toss the raspberries and blackberries to combine. In a medium nonreactive saucepan, gently toss the blueberries with the ⅔ cup sugar and the water. Cover and cook over moderate heat, stirring once or twice and brushing down the sides of the pan, just until the blueberries start to pop and release their juices, about 5 minutes. If the sugar hasn't dissolved, stir in a few more drops of water. Remove the pan from the heat and add the raspberries and blackberries. Do not stir. Put the berries into the bowl.

3. Bake the shortcakes on a rack in the middle of the oven until golden brown, about 15 minutes.

4. Meanwhile, melt the butter in a small saucepan over low heat. In a small bowl, combine the remaining ½ cup sugar and the cinnamon.

5. Immediately after removing the shortcakes from the oven, dip them in the butter and cinnamon sugar as follows.

Holding a shortcake right side up, dip the bottom in the melted butter. Place the shortcake, buttered side down, in the cinnamon sugar and shake the bowl so that the sugar adheres to and completely covers the bottom. Then turn the shortcake over and dip the top in the butter and cinnamon sugar in the same manner. Place the shortcake right side up on a plate. Continue with the remaining shortcakes. (If the level of the butter is too low for dipping the last shortcake, use a pastry brush to generously brush the butter on the top and bottom of the biscuit.)

6. Using your fingers, gently split open the shortcakes. Spoon about ½ cup of the mixed berries over the bottom of each shortcake. Cover the berries with the shortcake tops and spoon a dollop of the ginger whipped cream alongside. Serve the mixed berry shortcakes at once.

—PEGGY CULLEN

BISCUIT DOUGH

MAKES 8 SHORTCAKE BISCUITS

2 cups flour

1 tablespoon baking powder

½ teaspoon salt

¼ pound cold unsalted butter, cut into ½-inch dice

¾ cup cold milk

1. In a food processor, pulse the flour, baking powder, and salt until mixed. Add the butter and pulse until the mixture resembles coarse meal with particles the size of peas and lentils, about forty times.

2. Drizzle the milk evenly over the dry ingredients and pulse a few times, just until incorporated and the dough forms small clumps.

3. Turn out the dough onto a work surface and knead once or twice to gather it into a mass. Do not overwork the dough. Gently pat the dough into a disk or rectangle, as needed.

MAKE IT AHEAD

The dough can be made ahead, wrapped tightly, and refrigerated for up to two hours.

STRAWBERRY SHORTCAKE

This shortcake is the real thing, made with biscuits, not cake.

4 SERVINGS

1 pint strawberries, hulled and thinly sliced lengthwise

2 tablespoons plus 3 teaspoons granulated sugar

1½ cups flour

2¼ teaspoons nonaluminum baking powder

⅜ teaspoon salt

2 cups heavy cream

⅛ teaspoon vanilla extract

Confectioners' sugar, for dusting

1. In a medium bowl, toss the strawberries with the 2 tablespoons granulated sugar. Refrigerate for 1 hour.

2. Heat the oven to 400°. Butter a large baking sheet. In a medium bowl, mix the flour, baking powder, salt, and 2 teaspoons of the granulated sugar. Stir in 1 cup less 1 tablespoon of the cream until just combined. Knead briefly.

3. Turn the dough out onto a lightly floured surface and roll out to a scant ½-inch thickness. Using a biscuit cutter or a glass, cut out eight 2½-inch rounds. Place on the prepared baking sheet and bake them until golden, 10 to 12 minutes.

4. In a large bowl, using a hand-held electric mixer, whip the remaining 1 cup plus 1 tablespoon of cream with the remaining 1 teaspoon granulated sugar and the vanilla until the mixture holds a soft shape when the beaters are lifted.

5. To serve, split the shortcakes horizontally and place two bottoms on each of four dessert plates. Spoon the strawberries and their juices on top of the biscuits. Dollop with whipped cream. Cover with the shortcake tops, set slightly askew. Lightly sift confectioners' sugar over the biscuit tops and serve.

—LINDSEY SHERE

BAKING POWDER

Many commercial baking powders contain sodium aluminum sulphate, which can leave a slightly bitter flavor in baked goods. Rumford baking powder is a brand that does not contain any aluminum compounds. It's available nationally at health food stores. You can also make your own. For ½ teaspoon baking powder, mix ¼ teaspoon cream of tartar, ⅛ teaspoon baking soda and ⅛ teaspoon cornstarch and use at once.

BLUEBERRY COBBLER

Here's a simple-as-can-be, not-too-sweet version of this homey dessert and breakfast dish. Serve with vanilla ice cream or just pour unsweetened heavy cream over each serving.

6 TO 8 SERVINGS

2   pints blueberries

1   cup plus 2 teaspoons flour

5   tablespoons plus 2 teaspoons sugar

1   teaspoon kirsch

½   teaspoon finely grated lemon zest

2   teaspoons baking powder

¼   teaspoon salt

5   tablespoons cold unsalted butter

½   cup plus 1 tablespoon milk

    Vanilla ice cream, for serving

1. Heat the oven to 375°. Toss the blueberries with the 2 teaspoons flour, 4 tablespoons of the sugar, the kirsch, and lemon zest. Pour the blueberry mixture into a 9-by-12-inch oval baking dish.

2. Mix the remaining 1 cup flour with 1 tablespoon of the sugar, the baking powder, and salt. Cut the butter into the dry ingredients until the mixture resembles coarse meal. Stir in the ½ cup of milk to make a very soft dough.

3. Drop the dough by spoonfuls on top of the blueberry mixture. Dampen your hands with half of the remaining 1 tablespoon milk and spread out the dough to cover most of the fruit. Brush the top of the dough with the remainder of the milk. Sprinkle the surface of the cobbler with the remaining 2 teaspoons sugar.

4. Bake the cobbler until it is golden brown and the berries are bubbling, about 35 minutes. Serve the cobbler warm with vanilla ice cream.

—LINDSEY SHERE

CHERRY LATTICE COBBLER

Without a doubt, the best cherries to use here are fresh sour cherries. If all you can find are sweet cherries, cut the sugar back to two-thirds cup. Don't let the cherries macerate in the sugar more than 15 minutes, or too much liquid will seep out. Out of season, you can use frozen sour cherries. Spread them in a single layer on a baking sheet and let defrost for about 30 minutes.

6 TO 8 SERVINGS

¾ cup plus 1 tablespoon sugar

1½ tablespoons cornstarch

1 tablespoon quick-cooking tapioca

1½ pounds sour cherries, pitted (about 6 cups)

1 teaspoon almond extract

Biscuit Dough, page 204, patted into a rectangle

1 tablespoon unsalted butter, melted

1. Heat the oven to 450° and line the oven floor with foil to catch any drips. In a large bowl, whisk the ¾ cup sugar with the cornstarch and tapioca. Gently fold in the cherries and almond extract with a rubber spatula.

2. Choose a 6-cup ovenproof glass or ceramic baking dish or a 10-inch glass pie plate. On a lightly floured surface, roll the biscuit dough out ⅛-inch thick and at least as large as the baking dish you are using. Lift the dough frequently as you roll and lightly reflour the surface as needed to prevent the dough from sticking. Using a fluted pastry wheel, cut the dough into 1½-inch-wide strips.

3. Gently stir the cherries. Spoon the cherries and their juice into the baking dish and spread the fruit evenly with a rubber spatula. Lay about half the strips of biscuit dough, spaced evenly apart, across the pie without stretching. Allow the extra dough to hang over the sides of the dish. Weave in the remaining strips of dough (see Weaving a Lattice Top, next page.) Using a small sharp knife and a swift downward motion, trim the overhanging dough flush with the edge of the baking dish.

4. Brush the lattice top with the melted butter (you may not need to use all of it) and sprinkle the remaining 1 tablespoon sugar on the dough. Bake the cobbler until the top is beginning to brown, about 20 minutes. Lower the oven temperature to 350° and bake 30 minutes longer. If the edge is browning too quickly, cover it with foil. Let the cobbler cool for at least 30 minutes. Serve the cobbler warm or at room temperature.

—PEGGY CULLEN

WEAVING A LATTICE TOP

It's easy to weave biscuit dough into a lattice top for a cobbler. Be sure the dough is rolled thin enough—⅛ inch is perfect. If the dough is too thick, the underside of the dough will still be raw when the fruit filling is cooked. The wider you cut the strips, the easier they are to work with.

To start, lay half the strips, spaced evenly, across the pie without stretching the dough. Fold back every other strip to its midway point. Starting at the fold, place a new strip at a 90° angle over the unfolded strips. Unfold the folded strips, crossing the new one. Now fold back the strips that alternate with the first ones you folded. Place another new strip of dough parallel to and evenly spaced from the first. Continue in this fashion until you reach the edge of the pie, half of which is now latticed.

Then repeat the process on the other half of the pie. Don't worry about overhanging dough. Just cut it off flush with a sharp paring knife in a quick downward motion.

SPICED RHUBARB RASPBERRY COBBLER

Like asparagus, rhubarb is among the harbingers of spring. And, a cobbler is a great way to show off the plant's distinctive, pleasantly astringent taste. (Be sure, though, to use only the stalks; the leaves are toxic and must be discarded.) This tart cobbler—similar to a deep-dish pie—combines rhubarb and raspberries with cinnamon, ginger, and cardamom. Add a tablespoon or two more sugar for a slightly sweeter version. You can substitute individually quick-frozen rhubarb pieces if you can't find fresh or want a taste of spring in winter. Plan to serve the cobbler with generous scoops of vanilla ice cream.

6 SERVINGS

- 1 cup plus 3 teaspoons sugar
- 2½ tablespoons cornstarch
- 1 teaspoon cinnamon
- 1 teaspoon finely grated fresh ginger
- ¼ teaspoon ground cardamom
- 1½ pounds fresh rhubarb, cut into ¾-inch pieces (about 5 cups)
- 5½ tablespoons cold unsalted butter
- 12 ounces fresh or unsweetened frozen raspberries (about 3 cups)
- 1¼ cups flour
- 1 teaspoon baking powder
- Pinch salt
- ⅔ cup buttermilk

1. Heat the oven to 375°. In a large nonreactive saucepan, stir together the 1 cup sugar, the cornstarch, cinnamon, ginger, and cardamom. Add the rhubarb, stirring until coated with the sugar mixture. Add ½ tablespoon of the butter. Bring to a simmer over moderate heat and cook, stirring occasionally, until the rhubarb exudes its juices and the mixture thickens, about 5 minutes. Immediately remove the pan from the heat. Gently stir in the raspberries. Turn the mixture into a round 9½-by-1¾-inch casserole or baking dish.

2. In a medium bowl, stir together the flour, 2 teaspoons of the remaining sugar, the baking powder, and salt. Using your fingertips, a pastry blender, or two knives, cut in the remaining 5 tablespoons butter until the mixture resembles coarse meal. Stir all but 1 tablespoon of the buttermilk into the dry ingredients, tossing with a fork just until evenly incorporated. Pat the dough gently into a ball and flatten into a disk.

3. Place the disk between two sheets of waxed paper and roll it out to a 9-inch round. Peel off the top sheet of waxed paper. If desired, using lightly buttered fingertips, flute the edges of the dough. Invert the dough over the fruit mixture. Peel off the waxed paper. ➤

4. Make five or six slashes with a knife, about 2½-inches long by ¼-inch wide, that radiate from the center of the dough. Brush the dough evenly with the reserved 1 tablespoon buttermilk and sprinkle the remaining 1 teaspoon sugar on top.

5. Bake the cobbler in the middle of the oven for 30 minutes. Lower the temperature to 350° and bake until the top is nicely browned, the fruit filling is bubbling around the edges, and a toothpick stuck in the center of the dough comes out clean, 15 to 20 minutes longer. Let the cobbler cool for 15 minutes before serving.

—NANCY BAGGETT

MAKE IT AHEAD

The cobbler can be made up to five hours ahead. Set it aside at room temperature and reheat it for 15 minutes in a warm oven before serving.

STRAWBERRY AND RHUBARB PANDOWDY

A pandowdy is a deep-dish fruit dessert, traditionally made with apples, covered with a biscuit batter. With strips of pastry covering the fruit, this is a personal interpretation of that old-fashioned dessert.

6 SERVINGS

- ¾ cup flour
- 4 tablespoons unsalted butter
- 4 tablespoons cream cheese
- 1 teaspoon vanilla extract
- 1½ pounds rhubarb, peeled, if stringy, and cut into ½-inch dice
- 1 pint strawberries, quartered
- 1 cup granulated sugar
- 1 tablespoon lemon juice
- 2 teaspoons grated lemon zest
- 1 teaspoon grated fresh ginger
- 1 tablespoon crystallized sugar or coarsely crushed sugar cubes

1. Put the flour in a bowl and add the butter, cream cheese, and vanilla. Cut or rub in the butter and cream cheese just until a dough is formed. Pat the dough into a square, wrap securely, and refrigerate for 30 minutes.

2. Heat the oven to 400°. In a shallow 2-quart baking dish, toss the rhubarb with the quartered strawberries, granulated sugar, lemon juice, lemon zest, and ginger.

3. On a lightly floured surface, roll the dough out to a rectangle about ⅛-inch thick. Cut the dough crosswise into 2-inch-wide strips. Lay the strips of dough over the rhubarb and strawberries mixture, anchoring the strips to the side of the dish. Trim the dough if necessary. Sprinkle the strips with the crystallized sugar. Set the dish on a baking sheet and bake the pandowdy until the topping is golden and the fruit is bubbling, about 45 minutes.

—BRADLEY OGDEN

APPLE PECAN CRISP

Crisps are a terrific way to use apples during the fall and winter when apples are at their best. This delicious winter fruit and nut dessert can be made just as easily in one medium baking dish as in six small ones.

6 SERVINGS

1 cup pecans

¼ cup plus 2 tablespoons flour

¼ cup plus 2 tablespoons light-brown sugar

¼ cup plus 6 tablespoons granulated sugar

6 tablespoons unsalted butter, cut into ½-inch dice

½ cup old-fashioned rolled oats

2½ pounds Cortland or other tart cooking apples (about 5), peeled, quartered, cored, and sliced crosswise ¼-inch thick

½ cup dried cranberries (about 2½ ounces)

1 pint vanilla ice cream

1. Heat the oven to 350°. Spread the pecans in one layer on a baking sheet and bake until lightly toasted, 6 to 8 minutes. Let the pecans cool and then coarsely chop them. Leave the oven on.

2. In a food processor, pulse the flour with the brown sugar and the ¼ cup of the granulated sugar until combined. Add the butter and pulse until the mixture resembles coarse meal. Transfer the crumbs to a bowl and stir in the toasted pecans and oats.

3. Generously butter six individual baking dishes, each about 6-inches wide and 1-inch deep. In a medium bowl, toss the apples with the cranberries and the remaining 6 tablespoons granulated sugar. Divide the apple mixture among the prepared baking dishes and cover with the crumb topping. Set the dishes on a large baking sheet and bake in the bottom third of the oven until the apples are tender when pierced and the topping is toasted, 45 to 50 minutes. Serve warm with the ice cream.

—JAMES HENAHAN

NECTARINE CRUMBLE

This low-fat version uses less butter in the topping than most crisps or crumbles and is accompanied with thickened honey yogurt instead of whipped or ice cream.

8 SERVINGS

- 1 cup plain low-fat yogurt
- 3 pounds nectarines, pitted and cut into ½-inch-thick slices
- 2 tablespoons kirsch, or plum or peach brandy
- ¼ cup plus 1 tablespoon mild-flavored honey, such as clover
- 1 cup old-fashioned rolled oats
- ½ cup flour
- ⅓ cup dark-brown sugar
- ¼ teaspoon freshly grated nutmeg
- ¼ teaspoon salt
- 4 tablespoons cold unsalted butter, cut into small pieces

1. Place the plain low-fat yogurt into a fine strainer set over a medium bowl. Allow the yogurt to drain overnight in the refrigerator.

2. Heat the oven to 375°. In a large bowl, toss the nectarines, kirsch, and the ¼ cup honey together. Spoon the mixture into a shallow 2-quart nonreactive baking dish.

3. In a medium bowl, combine the rolled oats, flour, brown sugar, nutmeg, and salt. Work in the butter until the mixture resembles coarse crumbs.

4. Sprinkle the topping evenly over the nectarines. Bake until lightly browned and bubbly, about 45 minutes. Let cool for at least 15 minutes.

5. In a small bowl, mix the thickened yogurt with the remaining 1 tablespoon honey. Serve with the warm crumble.

—MARTHA ROSE SHULMAN

MAKE IT AHEAD

The fruit and the topping can be prepared up to three hours ahead. Set the fruit aside, covered, at room temperature, and refrigerate the topping. Then assemble and bake the crisp when it's time to eat.

BLUEBERRY AND BANANA BROWN BETTY

Making your own bread crumbs for this dessert is easy. Cut the brioche in slices and then trim off the crusts. Tear the slices into pieces, drop them into a food processor, and pulse into fine crumbs.

6 SERVINGS

- 5 large egg yolks
- ½ cup granulated sugar
- Pinch salt
- 1 pint half-and-half
- 1 vanilla bean, split lengthwise
- 1 3-inch cinnamon stick
- 2 cups fresh brioche crumbs
- ½ cup dark-brown sugar
- 4 tablespoons unsalted butter, melted
- 1 teaspoon ground cinnamon
- 4 ripe bananas, sliced ¼-inch thick
- 1 pint blueberries

1. Heat the oven to 325°. In a bowl, whisk the egg yolks with the granulated sugar and salt. In a heavy saucepan, combine the half-and-half, vanilla bean, and cinnamon stick and cook over moderately high heat until bubbles appear around the edges. Gradually whisk the hot liquid into the yolks. Return the mixture to the saucepan and cook over low heat, stirring constantly with a wooden spoon, until the custard is thick enough to coat the back of the spoon, about 5 minutes. Do not boil, or it will curdle.

2. Spread the brioche crumbs in a baking pan and bake until lightly toasted, about 5 minutes. In a medium bowl, toss the crumbs with the brown sugar, butter, and cinnamon.

3. In a shallow 2-quart baking dish or six individual ramekins, combine the bananas and blueberries. Strain the custard over the fruit. Sprinkle the crumb topping over all. Set the baking dish or ramekins in a roasting pan and pour about an inch of hot water into the pan. Bake the dessert until it is heated through and the topping is golden, about 20 minutes.

—BRADLEY OGDEN

BLACKBERRY POLENTA BREAD PUDDING

At Nana's in Durham, North Carolina, Scott Howell serves this rich dessert with a lemon-curd sauce; he often uses blueberries in place of the blackberries.

4 TO 6 SERVINGS

POLENTA BREAD:

¾ cup flour

⅔ cup yellow cornmeal

1 tablespoon baking powder

Pinch salt

½ pound unsalted butter, at room temperature

1 cup plus 1 tablespoon sugar

4 large eggs, separated

2 large egg yolks

BLACKBERRY CUSTARD:

1 vanilla bean, split lengthwise

4 cups heavy cream

10 large egg yolks

1 cup sugar

1 pint fresh blackberries, more for garnish

1. Heat the oven to 325°. For the polenta bread, butter a 9-by-5-inch loaf pan. In a bowl, combine the flour, cornmeal, baking powder, and salt. In another bowl, cream the butter with the sugar until fluffy. Beat in the 6 egg yolks in three batches. Fold in the dry ingredients in three batches just until combined.

2. In another bowl, beat the egg whites until they hold firm peaks when the beaters are lifted. Stir one-third of the egg whites into the batter, then fold in the remaining whites. Spread the batter in the prepared pan and bake until a toothpick stuck in the center comes out clean, about 50 minutes. Let cool in the pan. Leave the oven on.

3. For the blackberry custard, in a medium saucepan, scrape the seeds from the vanilla bean into the cream and add the pod of the bean. Bring just to a simmer over moderately high heat. Meanwhile, in a bowl, whisk the egg yolks with the sugar. Gradually whisk in the hot cream. Strain the mixture into a medium bowl and let cool. Stir in the fresh blackberries.

4. Butter a 9-by-13-inch baking dish. Cut the polenta bread into ½-inch-thick slices and spread them on a baking sheet. Toast the slices in the oven until the polenta is lightly browned, about 7 minutes. Let cool. Leave the oven on.

5. Tear the slices of toasted polenta bread into ¾-inch-thick strips and spread

them in the prepared baking dish. Pour the blackberry custard over the polenta bread, evenly distributing the blackberries. Set the baking dish in a larger pan and add enough hot water to the pan to reach halfway up the sides of the baking dish. Cover the blackberry polenta bread pudding with foil and bake until the blackberry custard is set, about 2 hours. Let cool slightly. Serve the bread pudding garnished with fresh blackberries.

—Scott Howell

Make It Ahead

The polenta bread can be made ahead. Cover and let it stand at room temperature for up to one day before making the bread pudding.

STRAWBERRY SPIRAL PIE

This makes a great breakfast dish as well as a wonderful summer dessert served warm with vanilla ice cream.

6 TO 8 SERVINGS

1½ pounds strawberries, hulled, washed, and drained (about 4½ cups)

⅔ cup strawberry jam

1 tablespoon unsalted butter

1 tablespoon cornstarch

1 tablespoon quick-cooking tapioca

½ teaspoon ground ginger

¼ teaspoon cinnamon

⅛ teaspoon nutmeg

⅓ to ½ cup sugar, according to the sweetness of the berries

Biscuit Dough, page 204, patted into a rectangle

1. Heat the oven to 450° and line the oven floor with foil to catch any drips.

2. Spread the strawberries on paper towels to dry. In a small bowl, stir the jam to loosen it. In a saucepan, melt the butter and keep warm.

3. In a large bowl, whisk together the cornstarch, tapioca, ginger, cinnamon, nutmeg, and sugar. Halve any very large berries. Gently toss the berries with the dry ingredients.

4. On a lightly floured surface, roll the biscuit dough out to a 10-by-18-inch rectangle. Square off the corners. Brush the dough lightly with about half of the melted butter. Using an icing spatula, spread the strawberry jam over the rectangle, leaving a ½-inch border on one long side. Starting at the opposite long side, roll up the dough jelly-roll fashion and pinch the seam closed. Roll the log so that it is an even diameter, exactly 18-inches long. Turn the log seam-side down.

5. Using a large sharp knife, quarter the log, then cut each quarter into three equal pieces so that there will be twelve spiraled biscuits in all.

6. Using a rubber spatula, fold the strawberry filling once to remix. Spoon the filling into a 9-inch glass pie plate and smooth the top. Arrange eight biscuits around the perimeter of the pie and the remaining four biscuits in the center. Don't push the biscuits down into the strawberries.

7. Bake the pie until the top is golden brown and the strawberry filling is bubbling, about 20 minutes. Lower the oven temperature to 350°, loosely cover the pie with foil, and bake for 15 minutes longer. Let the pie cool on a rack for 30 minutes before serving.

—PEGGY CULLEN

218

PLUM POT PIES

You can make these individual pies with any fruit. If you have only one-cup dishes, that's fine. You'll be able to make eight portions instead of six.

6 SERVINGS

¾ cup plus 2 tablespoons sugar

2 tablespoons cornstarch

1 tablespoon quick-cooking tapioca

1   teaspoon ground ginger

¼ teaspoon cinnamon

2 pounds red or black plums, pitted and sliced ⅜-inch thick (about 6 cups)

Biscuit Dough, page 204, patted into any shape

1 tablespoon unsalted butter, melted

Vanilla ice cream or Ginger Whipped Cream, next page

1. Heat the oven to 450°. In a large bowl, whisk together the ¾ cup sugar, the cornstarch, tapioca, ¼ teaspoon of the ginger, and the cinnamon. Add the plum slices and toss gently to coat.

2. Butter the inside rim of six 1½-cup ovenproof ramekins or baking cups. In a small bowl, combine the remaining 2 tablespoons sugar and the remaining ¾ teaspoon ginger.

3. On a lightly floured surface, roll out the biscuit dough ⅛-inch thick. Using a round cutter that is ½ inch larger than the ramekins, cut out six rounds of dough. Cut small decorative shapes from the dough scraps for appliqués if you like.

4. Stir the plum slices and spoon them and their juice evenly into the ramekins. The ramekins should be about three-quarters full. Place a round of dough over each ramekin, tucking the excess inside the rim. Press the dough gently to adhere to the rim.

5. Brush the top of the dough round with the melted butter. If using, affix the appliqués on the top of the pot pies and brush each of the appliqués with butter. Sprinkle the top of each pot pie with about 1 teaspoon of the ginger-sugar. Using the tip of a sharp knife, slice a few vents in the dough rounds.

6. Place the ramekins on a baking sheet, making sure they don't touch one another. Bake the pot pies for 20 minutes, then lower the temperature to 350° and bake until the tops are nicely browned and the plum filling is bubbling, about 15 minutes longer. Let cool for 30 minutes. Serve the pot pies warm with ice cream or ginger whipped cream.

—PEGGY CULLEN

GINGER WHIPPED CREAM

MAKES ABOUT 3 CUPS

1   cup heavy cream

3   tablespoons confectioners' sugar

1   teaspoon ground ginger

In a medium bowl, combine all the ingredients and beat until soft peaks form. Refrigerate until ready to use.

MAKE IT AHEAD

The ginger whipped cream can be made a day ahead. Keep it in the refrigerator, tightly covered, and rewhip briefly before using.

SUMMER PUDDING

This classic English dessert consists of layers of cooked berries and bread, which absorbs the sweet berry juice as the pudding sits overnight. To decorate the top of the pudding, crystallize red currants: Dip them in beaten egg white, sprinkle with sugar and then let dry on parchment paper at room temperature.

9 SERVINGS

18 very thin slices of white bread, such as Pepperidge Farm sandwich bread (about 10 ounces)

1½ pints red or black raspberries (about 4 cups)

½ pint blackberries or boysenberries (about 2 cups)

½ pint red currants (about 1 cup), stems removed

1 cup sugar

1 tablespoon kirsch or brandy

Lightly sweetened whipped cream, for serving

1. Line a 9-inch-square glass baking dish with plastic wrap, leaving enough overhang on all four sides to cover the finished pudding.

2. Trim the crusts from the bread. Place six slices in a tight overlapping layer in the bottom of the prepared dish. Place the raspberries, blackberries, and currants in a heavy medium nonreactive frying pan. Add the sugar and cook over moderate heat, stirring occasionally, until the berries yield some of their juices, about 5 minutes.

Sprinkle the kirsch over the berries and remove from the heat.

3. Using a slotted spoon, spread a third of the berries over the bread in the dish. Cover with another layer of bread. Repeat the layering with the remaining berries and bread. Spoon half of the berry juice over the pudding. Refrigerate the remaining juice. Cover the pudding with the overhanging plastic wrap. Place another dish or pan on top of the pudding and weigh it down with some cans. Refrigerate the pudding overnight.

4. To serve, unwrap the top of the pudding and invert onto a platter. Cut into squares. Serve with the whipped cream and the reserved berry juice.

—LINDSEY SHERE

SUMMER FRUIT "PIZZA"

Any fruit can be used for this very colorful free-form tart. Alternatively, you can make small individual pizzas. Roll the dough into a log and slice crosswise into equal pieces. Then roll each piece into a round and top with the fruit as described here.

MAKES ONE 9-INCH PIZZA

½ recipe of Biscuit Dough, page 204

2 tablespoons unsalted butter, melted

1 small plum, pitted and sliced ¼-inch thick

½ peach, pitted and sliced ¼-inch thick

½ cup raspberries

½ cup small strawberries, halved

1½ cup blackberries or blueberries

3½ tablespoons sugar

Ginger Whipped Cream, page 220

1. Heat the oven to 450°. On a lightly floured surface, roll the biscuit dough out to a 9-inch round. (Do not roll it any larger.) Fold the round of dough in half and place it on a heavy ungreased baking sheet. Unfold the dough and smooth the edges.

2. Using a pastry brush, lightly coat the dough round with some of the melted butter. Arrange the plum and peach slices, raspberries, strawberries, and blackberries in a decorative overlapping pattern all the way to the edge of the dough, fanning the plum and peach slices and clustering the berries. Dab the fruit with the remaining melted butter. Sprinkle 2½ tablespoons of the sugar over the fruit.

3. Bake the fruit "pizza" until the bottom is golden brown, about 20 minutes. Remove the pizza from the oven and turn on the broiler. Sprinkle the remaining 1 tablespoon of sugar over the fruit. Broil the pizza, watching carefully, until the fruit begins to bubble and brown, about 1 minute. Slide the pizza onto a rack to cool slightly. Serve the pizza warm with the ginger whipped cream.

—PEGGY CULLEN

BERRY REHAB

If you must use berries that haven't fully ripened, try one or more of the following to improve their flavor.

• Spread the berries out in one layer on a baking sheet covered with a cloth towel; pick over and discard any bad ones. Leave uncovered at room temperature overnight or as long as their taste and texture continue to improve.

• Place berries on a baking sheet and put them in a 350° oven for five minutes. The heat releases their perfume; the effect lasts even after the berries have cooled.

• Intensify the flavor of bland berries by adding a bit of sugar and either lemon juice or balsamic vinegar.

• Mix several different berries to complement each other's flavors. Strawberries, blueberries, and black raspberries add sweetness; currants and blackberries, tartness.

SUMMER PEACH CLAFOUTIS

To peel peaches easily, blanch them first in boiling water for one minute. A 1994 Arrowood Preston Ranch Late Harvest White Riesling, rich in honeysuckle and apricot aromas, is a natural with this custardy peach dessert.

6 SERVINGS

4 large eggs

½ cup heavy cream

½ cup milk

3 tablespoons flour

¾ cup sugar

4 tablespoons unsalted butter

6 peaches, peeled and quartered

1. Heat the oven to 350°. In a blender, combine the eggs with the cream, milk, and flour. Add ½ cup of the sugar and blend until smooth.

2. In a large heavy frying pan, melt the butter over moderate heat. Add the peaches, sprinkle with the remaining ¼ cup of sugar and cook, stirring occasionally, until tender, about 4 minutes.

3. Butter a 10-inch round glass pie plate and pour in one-quarter of the batter. Spoon the peaches with their liquid into the dish and pour the remaining batter on top. Set the pie plate on a baking sheet and bake the clafoutis until it is golden and just set, about 1 hour. Cool to room temperature before serving.

—JOACHIM SPLICHAL

MAKE IT AHEAD

The clafoutis can be made a day ahead and refrigerated overnight. Reheat the clafoutis in a 300° oven until just warmed through before serving.

Individual Warm Berry Gratins

Sweetened berries, flavored with cherry brandy, are covered with a sabayon and browned under the broiler. This recipe uses strawberries, boysenberries, and raspberries but you can use any assortment of berries you like in these gratins.

6 SERVINGS

¾ pint strawberries

½ pint boysenberries or blackberries

½ pint raspberries

1 teaspoon kirsch or brandy

10 tablespoons sugar, more to taste

4 large egg yolks

½ cup dry champagne

¼ cup heavy cream

1. Hull the strawberries and slice lengthwise ¼-inch thick. In a large bowl, toss the strawberries, boysenberries, raspberries, kirsch, and 2 tablespoons of the sugar. If you like, add a little more sugar depending on the berries' sweetness (remember the topping will also add sweetness).

2. In a large bowl, whisk the egg yolks with the champagne and 4 tablespoons of the sugar. Set the bowl over a large saucepan filled with about an inch of simmering water. Whisk the egg mixture until it holds its shape when the whisk is raised, about 6 minutes. Remove the bowl of sabayon from the heat and place it in a bowl of ice water to cool, whisking occasionally.

3. In a medium bowl, whip the cream to soft peaks. Fold it into the sabayon.

4. Heat the broiler. Divide the berries among six 5-inch gratin dishes and set the dishes on a baking sheet. Spread 2 tablespoons of the sabayon over each serving. Sprinkle the remaining 4 tablespoons sugar over the gratins. Slide the baking sheet under the broiler and cook just until the tops turn golden brown, 3 to 4 minutes. Watch carefully and turn the baking sheet if necessary. Serve at once.

—Lindsey Shere

Kirsch

Kirsch, an eau-de-vie made from the fermented mash of small black wild cherries and their stones, heightens the flavor of many berries and other fresh summer fruits, such as cherries, apricots, peaches, and nectarines. A touch is all that's needed to enhance the natural goodness of fruit.

ORANGE GRATIN WITH SABAYON

A rich yet airy sauce accented with amaretto envelops juicy citrus segments. If you're short on time, you can cut the peeled oranges crosswise into half-inch-thick rounds rather than sectioning them.

8 SERVINGS

- 5   navel oranges
- 6   large egg yolks
- ½   cup sugar
- ½   cup dry white wine
- ¼   cup amaretto liqueur

MAKE IT AHEAD

The sabayon can be made ahead and refrigerated for up to one hour. The orange sections may stand for one hour at room temperature.

1. Using a sharp knife, peel the navel oranges, removing any bitter white pith. Cut in between the membranes to release the orange sections. Arrange the orange sections in a 10-inch gratin dish or quiche pan.

2. In a large bowl, using a hand-held mixer or a whisk, beat together the egg yolks, white wine, and amaretto. Set the bowl over a large saucepan filled with about an inch of simmering water. Beat the egg mixture until it mounds when the beaters are lifted, about 5 minutes.

3. Heat the broiler. Put an oven rack about 6 inches from the heat. Spoon the sabayon over the orange sections and broil until browned on top, about 1 minute.

—PEGGY RYAN

Muscat Zabaglione with Winter Fruits

Cool winter fruits are covered with a warm cloud of sweet, Muscat-flavored sabayon. If Bonny Doon Muscat Vin de Glacière isn't available, use another California Muscat or a Muscat de Beaumes-de-Venise.

6 SERVINGS

- 1 navel orange
- 3 kiwis, peeled and thinly sliced
- 1 banana, peeled and thinly sliced
- ½ cup seedless red grapes, halved
- 3 large egg yolks
- ½ cup Bonny Doon Muscat Vin de Glacière
- ½ cup granulated sugar
- 1½ teaspoons confectioners' sugar

1. Using a paring knife, peel the navel orange, removing all of the bitter white pith. Working over a bowl, cut in between the membranes to release the orange sections. Add the kiwis, banana, and grapes.

2. Heat the broiler. In a large bowl, using a hand-held mixer or a whisk, beat together the egg yolks and the Muscat and the granulated sugar. Set the bowl over a large saucepan filled with about an inch of simmering water. Beat the egg mixture until it mounds when the beaters are lifted, about 10 minutes. Set the bowl in ice water and continue beating the zabaglione until cool, 2 to 3 minutes.

3. Arrange the fruit mixture on six heatproof dessert plates and dollop the zabaglione on top. Set one dessert plate on a baking sheet and broil three inches from the heat until the zabaglione is browned, 5 to 10 seconds. Repeat with the remaining plates. Sift the confectioners' sugar lightly over the plates and serve immediately.

—JIM DENEVAN

DRIED CHERRY AND PEACH STEAMED PUDDING

To make the chopping of the dried peaches a little easier, rub your knife with vegetable oil so that the fruit doesn't stick to it. You'll need to start the cherry and peach pudding at least one day before you plan to serve it to allow time for the fruit to macerate in the beer and bourbon.

8 SERVINGS

½ pound dried sour cherries

½ pound dried peaches, chopped

½ cup dark beer

⅓ cup plus 2 teaspoons bourbon

14 tablespoons (7 ounces) unsalted butter, at room temperature

1 cup dark-brown sugar

2 large eggs, at room temperature

1 tablespoon finely grated orange zest

2 teaspoons finely grated lemon zest

1 cup flour

½ teaspoon baking powder

1 teaspoon cinnamon

½ teaspoon ground cardamom

½ teaspoon ground cloves

½ teaspoon ground nutmeg

2½ cups fine brioche bread crumbs (about 4 ounces)

2 tablespoons confectioners' sugar

Fresh mint sprigs, for garnish (optional)

Lightly sweetened whipped cream, for serving

1. In a medium bowl, combine the cherries, peaches, beer, and the ⅓ cup bourbon. Cover the mixture and let macerate overnight.

2. Butter a 1½-quart steamed pudding mold or soufflé dish. Using a standing mixer fitted with a paddle or a hand-held electric mixer, beat the butter and brown sugar on moderate speed until fluffy. Add the eggs one at a time, beating well after each addition. On low speed, add the grated orange and lemon zest. Sift in the flour, baking powder, cinnamon, cardamom, cloves, and nutmeg, and blend just until smooth. Add the brioche crumbs and macerated dried fruit and its liquid and mix just until combined.

3. Bring 2 inches of water to a boil in a large enameled cast-iron casserole. Scrape the batter into the prepared mold. Cover with foil and tie with string to hold the foil in place. Set the pudding in the casserole, cover with a lid, and steam over moderate heat until the pudding is set and a toothpick stuck in the center comes out clean, about 1¼ hours. Let cool for 30 minutes.

4. Run a knife around the sides of the mold to loosen the pudding, then invert

the pudding onto a large serving plate. In a small bowl, whisk the confectioners' sugar with the remaining 2 teaspoons bourbon until smooth. Spoon the icing into a small sturdy plastic bag and cut off a very small corner of the bag. Drizzle the icing in a crisscross pattern over the top of the pudding. Garnish the pudding with mint sprigs, if using, and serve warm with whipped cream.

—SANFORD D'AMATO

MAKE IT AHEAD

The pudding can be steamed up to eight hours ahead. Set it aside at room temperature and then reheat it in the water bath in the casserole for about 20 minutes before serving.

LEMON FLANS WITH LEMON SAUCE AND CANDIED ZEST

Jamie Shannon, of Commander's Palace in New Orleans, likes to serve these luxurious, tangy, and sweet lemon flans at room temperature so that they resemble cheesecake. Alternatively, you can chill the flans for a denser, creamier texture that's more like that of custard. Clarifying the butter for the phyllo helps the pastry crisps brown evenly during baking.

8 SERVINGS

FLANS:

- 1 pound cream cheese, at room temperature
- 1 cup sugar
- 5 large eggs
- ¾ cup lemon juice
- ¼ cup white rum

LEMON SAUCE:

- 5 large egg yolks
- ⅔ cup sugar
- ⅓ cup lemon juice
- 3 tablespoons white rum
- 2 to 3 tablespoons cold water

CANDIED LEMON ZEST:

- 6 lemons
- 1½ cups sugar
- ¼ cup water

  Fresh mint leaves, for garnish (optional)

  Pastry Crisps, next page

1. Heat the oven to 250°. For the flans, butter eight 4-ounce ramekins and sprinkle them with sugar. In a large bowl, beat the cream cheese with the sugar until smooth. In a medium bowl, beat the eggs with the lemon juice and rum. Gradually beat the eggs into the cream cheese. Strain into a large measuring cup.

2. Pour the flan mixture into the prepared ramekins. Set the ramekins in a baking dish and add enough hot water to the dish to reach halfway up the sides of the ramekins. Bake until the flans are set, about 1 hour. Let the flans cool in the water bath for about 2½ hours.

3. For the lemon sauce, in a heavy medium nonreactive saucepan, combine the egg yolks, sugar, and lemon juice. Whisk over low heat until slightly thickened, about 5 minutes. Do not boil, or it will curdle. Remove from the heat and stir in the rum. Pour the sauce into a medium bowl, set it in a larger bowl of ice water and let cool, stirring occasionally. As the mixture cools, gradually stir in the cold water

until the sauce has a pourable consistency.

4. For the candied lemon zest, using a lemon zester, strip the zest from the lemons. In a small saucepan of boiling water, blanch the zest for 1 minute and then drain. Repeat the blanching process two more times to remove the bitterness. Pat dry with paper towels.

5. In a heavy medium saucepan, combine 1 cup of the sugar with the water. Stir over moderate heat to dissolve the sugar, then boil the syrup until it reaches 238° on a candy thermometer, about 7 minutes. Remove from the heat and stir in the lemon zest. Drain the zest and put it in a bowl. Toss the zest with the remaining ½ cup sugar until coated.

6. To serve, run a knife around the inside of each ramekin and invert the lemon flans onto plates. Top each of the lemon flans with a pastry crisp, sugared side up. Spoon the lemon sauce around the lemon flans and garnish each flan with the candied lemon zest and fresh mint leaves, if using.

—JAMIE SHANNON

MAKE IT AHEAD

The flans, the sauce, and the zest can be made up to a day ahead. Cover and refrigerate the flans and the sauce separately. The zest can stand, covered, at room temperature.

PASTRY CRISPS

MAKES 8 PASTRY CRISPS

4 tablespoons unsalted butter
4 sheets phyllo dough
2½ tablespoons sugar
¼ teaspoon cinnamon

1. Heat the oven to 350°. Line a small baking sheet with parchment paper. In a small saucepan, melt the butter over low heat. Pour the butter into a small bowl, leaving the milky residue behind.

2. Spread one sheet of the phyllo dough on a work surface. Keep the remaining sheets covered with a damp towel. Lightly brush the phyllo with the melted butter. Lay another sheet of phyllo on top and brush with butter. Repeat the process with the remaining phyllo and butter.

3. In a small bowl, combine the sugar and cinnamon. Using a 3-inch round pastry cutter, cut out eight circles from the phyllo and put them on the prepared baking sheet. Sprinkle the circles with the cinnamon sugar and cover them with another sheet of parchment paper. Bake the phyllo until crisp and golden, about 25 minutes. Remove the top layer of parchment paper and let the circles cool on the baking sheet for up to 2 hours.

LEMON SOUFFLÉ

This is an impressive and surprisingly easy dessert to make for entertaining. You can prepare the molds and make the lemon curd base of the soufflé ahead of time so that when it's time for dessert, all you have to do is beat and fold the egg whites into the base mixture, and bake. The lemon curd can be made up to four hours ahead of time. Press plastic wrap directly on the surface of the curd and set it aside at room temperature.

4 TO 6 SERVINGS

½ cup granulated sugar

4 tablespoons unsalted butter

⅓ cup lemon juice

4 large egg yolks

1 tablespoon finely grated lemon zest

5 large egg whites, at room temperature
   Confectioners' sugar, for dusting

1. In a medium nonreactive saucepan, combine ¼ cup of the granulated sugar, the butter, and lemon juice, and cook over moderate heat, stirring, until the sugar and butter are melted. Remove from the heat and stir in the egg yolks one at a time, mixing well after each addition. Add the lemon zest and cook over moderately low heat, stirring, until the curd is slightly thickened, about 2 minutes. Do not boil, or it will curdle.

2. Heat the oven to 425°. Butter a 5-cup soufflé dish and freeze until set. Butter the dish again and coat with granulated sugar. Rewarm the lemon curd over moder-ately low heat, stirring, until the curd is just hot to the touch.

3. Meanwhile, in a medium bowl, beat the egg whites until soft peaks form. Continue beating the egg whites, adding the remaining ¼ cup granulated sugar, until the whites are glossy and hold firm peaks when the beaters are lifted, about 1 more minute. Stir one quarter of the egg whites into the lemon curd, then fold the mixture into the remaining whites just until combined.

4. Spoon the soufflé mixture into the prepared dish and smooth the surface. Run your thumb around the inside edge of the dish. Bake the soufflé in the lower third of the oven until puffed, nicely browned on top, and set around the edges, about 13 minutes. Dust with confectioners' sugar and serve immediately.

—ANNE WILLAN

Three-Citrus Custard with Fresh Figs

Figs are a delicious complement to this custard flavored with lemon, orange, and grapefruit juice and zests. Serve the custard with store-bought butter cookies, or make your own Butter Cookies, page 115.

8 SERVINGS

1 cup lemon juice

½ cup grapefruit juice

½ cup orange juice

6 large eggs

1 cup sugar

¼ pound unsalted butter, cut into small pieces

1 tablespoon finely grated lemon zest

1 tablespoon finely grated grapefruit zest

1 tablespoon finely grated orange zest

8 figs, preferably green and purple, cut into thick wedges

Butter cookies, for serving

1. In a double boiler or a large heat-proof bowl set over a saucepan filled with about an inch of simmering water, whisk the citrus juices with the eggs and sugar until combined. Cook, stirring constantly with a wooden spoon, until the custard is smooth and thick, 10 to 12 minutes. Do not boil, or it will curdle. Remove the custard from the heat and stir in the butter.

2. Strain the custard into a bowl and stir in the grated citrus zests. Stir for 1 minute to cool slightly, then cover with waxed paper or plastic wrap and refrigerate overnight.

3. Spoon the custard into shallow bowls or stemmed glasses and garnish with the figs.

—Rori Spinelli

PEACHES IN MUSCAT WITH HONEY

Use your hands to crush the fresh basil leaves lightly and release their fragrance into this elegant dessert of peaches and wine.

3 TO 4 SERVINGS

½ cup dessert wine, such as Muscat de Beaumes-de-Venise or California Muscat

½ cup crushed fresh basil leaves

2 tablespoons honey

3 large ripe peaches, preferably white, sliced ⅓-inch thick

In a large glass bowl, combine the wine, crushed basil, and honey. Add the peaches and let macerate at room temperature for 1 hour. Refrigerate for at least 1 hour or up to 4 hours before serving.

—MARCIA KIESEL

HOW TO BUY AND STORE PRODUCE

• PEARS Summer pears turn yellow or crimson as they mature; most varieties you'll find in winter remain brown or green. To tell if a pear is ready to eat, see if it gives slightly near the stem when pressed. If the base is soft, the pear is probably overripe.

• GRAPES Refrigerate in pierced plastic bags. Don't wash them first—the dusty residue provides protection.

• PEACHES, NECTARINES, PLUMS The flesh should give a bit near the stem when pressed. If the fruit is hard, put it in a loosely closed paper bag at room temperature for several days; the fruit will emit ethylene gas, which speeds ripening.

—JULIA CALIFANO

GINGER-SPICED MELONS WITH SPARKLING WINE

Casaba melons make a fragrant alternative to Crenshaws and provide the same colorful contrast to the honeydew cubes. When shopping, choose melons that are heavy and yield only slightly when pressed at the stem end. The fragrance at the stem end should be strong and pleasant and nothing should rattle when you shake the melon: If you sense seeds or juices moving, the melon is over-ripe.

6 SERVINGS

- 1   vanilla bean, split lengthwise
- 2   tablespoons finely chopped fresh ginger
- 3   tablespoons honey
- 2   cups water
- ½   medium Crenshaw melon
- ½   medium honeydew melon
- 1   bottle (750 ml) sparkling wine or brut champagne

1. In a small saucepan, combine the vanilla bean, ginger, and water, and bring to a boil over high heat. Cover, remove from the heat, and let steep for 15 minutes. Strain the liquid into a small bowl and stir in the honey until it is dissolved. Let the syrup cool to room temperature.

2. Peel the Crenshaw melon and cut it into ½-inch slices. Cut the slices into ½-inch dice. (You should have about 3 cups dice). Repeat the process with the honeydew. In a large bowl, combine the diced melons, pour in the syrup, and let macerate in the refrigerator for 10 to 20 minutes.

3. To serve, spoon the melon cubes and syrup into six long-stemmed glasses. Fill the glasses with the sparkling wine and serve.

—MARCIA KIESEL

MAKE IT AHEAD

The sugar syrup can be refrigerated, covered, for up to three days.

BANANAS IN ORANGE-CARAMEL SAUCE

Banana slices in an orange-caramel sauce garnished with yogurt are a luscious and surprisingly low-fat finish. If you are not concerned about calories, serve the bananas with full-fat yogurt or even vanilla ice cream.

4 SERVINGS

½ cup sugar

3 tablespoons water

½ cup orange juice

2 teaspoons thinly sliced orange zest

4 ripe bananas, thinly sliced

1 cup plain low-fat yogurt

1. In a heavy medium saucepan, combine the sugar and the water. Bring the mixture to a boil over moderately high heat and boil (brushing the inside of the saucepan occasionally with a pastry brush dipped in water to dissolve any sugar crystals) until the sugar turns a rich, tea-like brown, about 5 minutes. Immediately remove from the heat. Add the orange juice, pouring it down the side of the pan so that the caramel does not boil over. Stir in the orange zest and cook the caramel over low heat, stirring, until smooth and melted, about 2 minutes. Let cool, then cover the caramel and refrigerate.

2. Just before serving, gently combine the banana slices and chilled caramel sauce in a medium bowl. Spoon the sliced bananas into bowls and top each serving with ¼ cup of yogurt.

—MICHELE SCICOLONE

239

BAKED PEARS

Candied ginger and toasted pecans turn this simple fall dessert into something out of the ordinary.

4 SERVINGS

4 firm but ripe Bartlett pears

3 tablespoons light-brown sugar

2 tablespoons chopped candied ginger (optional)

1 tablespoon unsalted butter

¼ cup pecan pieces

Vanilla ice cream or frozen yogurt, for serving

Heat the oven to 350°. Peel and halve the pears. With a small spoon or melon baller, scoop out the seeds from the pear halves. Butter a 9-by-13-inch baking dish and put in the pear halves, cut sides up. Sprinkle the pears with the brown sugar and the candied ginger, if using. Dot with the butter and scatter the pecan pieces on top. Bake the pears on the top shelf of the oven until hot and bubbling, about 20 minutes. Serve immediately with vanilla ice cream.

—SARAH FRITSCHNER

MELON BALLERS

Ask any cook to name a useless cooking gadget, and you are likely to hear more than a few unkind words about the humble melon baller. Okay, it's not as versatile as, say, a chef's knife. But in the spirit of fair play, FOOD & WINE would like to sing its praises. Besides coring pears for this and the following recipe, melon ballers are perfect for:

• Neatly coring halved apples.

• Stripping seeds from cucumbers and zucchini.

• Making tiny, elegant balls of ice cream.

• Scooping the seeds from cherry tomatoes in order to stuff them.

PEARS POACHED IN WHITE WINE WITH STAR ANISE

Choose pears with a pretty shape that are ripe but still firm. Bartlett, Bosc, Comice, and Winter Nellis are good choices for poaching in this recipe.

6 SERVINGS

- 6 pears with stems
- 3 cups riesling or gewürztraminer
- ¼ cup sugar
- Zest of 1 lemon
- 2 star anise pods, broken up
- ¼ cup mascarpone cheese
- 2 ounces semisweet or bittersweet chocolate, melted

1. Cut a thin slice from the base end of the pears so that they will stand upright. Peel the pears.

2. In a nonreactive saucepan just large enough to hold the pears, combine the wine and sugar and cook over low heat until the sugar dissolves. Stand the pears upright in the pan and add the lemon zest, star anise, and enough water to just cover the fruit. Simmer over moderate heat, partially covered, until the pears are tender when pierced with a knife, about 30 minutes.

3. Transfer the pears to a plate. Boil the poaching liquid over moderately high heat until it has been reduced to ½ cup, about 30 minutes. Strain.

4. Using a melon baller, scoop out the core from the underside of each poached pear. Fill the cavities with the mascarpone. Stand the pears on six plates and spoon the syrup over them. Drizzle the melted chocolate on the plates and serve.

—BRIGIT LEGERE BINNS

MAKE IT AHEAD

The pears can be poached ahead and the syrup reduced. Refrigerate the pears in the syrup for up to one day, then return them to room temperature before finishing the recipe.

CARAMELIZED PINEAPPLE WITH GRILLED BANANAS AND TAHITIAN VANILLA SAUCE

For this dessert, use firm, slightly under-ripe bananas that will hold their shape during cooking. If you'd like to serve a wine with dessert, a Muscat de Beaumes-de-Venise from the Rhône Valley in France is a good choice, as is a 1990 Chapoutier or nonvintage Prosper Maufoux.

8 SERVINGS

1 vanilla bean, split lengthwise

1 cup low-fat (1%) milk

One 1-inch strip of lemon zest

2 large egg yolks

About ½ cup sugar

⅛ teaspoon salt

1 pineapple (about 2¼ pounds)

4 slightly under-ripe bananas

2 tablespoons sugar-free pineapple jam or honey

2 tablespoons lemon juice

2 tablespoons safflower oil

Fresh mint sprigs, for garnish

1. Scrape the seeds from the vanilla bean into a small heavy saucepan and add the pod of the bean. Add the milk and lemon zest and cook over moderate heat until small bubbles form around the edge of the pan. Cover, remove from the heat, and let steep for 15 minutes.

2. Meanwhile, in a small bowl, beat the egg yolks and 3 tablespoons of the sugar until thick and pale, about 5 minutes. Reheat the milk to a simmer, then whisk the hot milk into the egg yolks. Return the mixture to the saucepan and cook over moderate heat, stirring constantly, until the custard just starts to thicken and reaches 160° on a candy thermometer, 3 to 4 minutes. Do not boil, or it will curdle. Immediately strain the custard into a medium bowl and stir in the salt.

3. Trim off the top and bottom of the pineapple and slice off the skin. Using the tip of a vegetable peeler, remove the eyes. Cut the pineapple crosswise into eight ½-inch-thick slices and cut out the core with a pineapple or apple corer or a sharp knife.

4. Heat a large nonstick frying pan. Sprinkle two pineapple rings with 1 teaspoon of sugar each. Place the rings in the pan, sugared side down, and cook over high heat until the edges begin to caramelize,

244

about 2 to 3 minutes. Sprinkle each ring with 1 teaspoon sugar, turn them over, and cook until the other side is caramelized, about 2 minutes. Transfer to a large plate. Repeat with the remaining pineapple rings and sugar. Spoon the caramelized juices from the frying pan over the pineapple and set aside at room temperature for up to 2 hours.

5. Light a grill or heat a large heavy frying pan. Cut the bananas in half lengthwise and then in half crosswise. In a small bowl, combine the jam and lemon juice. Brush the grill or frying pan lightly with the oil (if using a frying pan, you won't need as much oil). Add the bananas, cut side down (if grilling, arrange the bananas diagonally across the grill). Brush the banana tops lightly with the jam and grill or sauté until lightly browned, 2 to 3 minutes. Turn the banana quarters over and cook for 2 minutes longer.

6. To serve, arrange two banana quarters on each dessert plate and top with a caramelized pineapple ring, spooning any exuded juices over the pineapple. Spoon 1½ tablespoons of the vanilla custard sauce in a zigzag pattern over each serving and garnish the desserts with fresh mint sprigs.

—ANN CHANTAL ALTMAN

MAKE IT AHEAD

You can make the custard sauce one day ahead. Press a piece of plastic wrap directly onto the surface of the sauce and refrigerate.

ORANGES IN CARAMEL SYRUP

This simple yet elegant fruit dessert contains no fat. The caramel chips may be made ahead and stored in an airtight container for up to one week. If the chips stick together, just shake the container to break them up.

8 SERVINGS

⅔ cup plus ½ cup sugar

¼ cup plus 3 tablespoons water

8 large or 10 medium seedless oranges
  Fresh mint sprigs, for garnish

1. Lightly oil a baking sheet. In a small, deep heavy saucepan, combine the ½ cup sugar with the 3 tablespoons water. Bring the mixture to a boil over moderately high heat and boil (brushing the inside of the saucepan occasionally with a pastry brush dipped in water to dissolve any sugar crystals) until the caramel turns a rich, tea-like brown, about 5 minutes. Immediately pour the caramel onto the oiled baking sheet and tilt the baking sheet to spread it as thin as possible. (Use a pot holder because the caramel will heat the baking sheet very quickly.) Let cool thoroughly.

2. Using any handy utensil, break up the cooled caramel into 1- to 2-inch pieces. (Be careful, the shards will be sharp.) In a food processor, pulse the caramel shards until they are finely chopped. Do not overprocess.

3. Using a small sharp knife, peel the oranges, removing all of the bitter white pith. Working over a heatproof bowl, cut between the membranes to release the orange sections. Squeeze the remaining membrane into the bowl to collect the juice. Measure out ½ cup of the orange juice and reserve.

4. In a small deep heavy saucepan, combine the remaining ⅔ cup sugar and ¼ cup of water. Bring the mixture to a boil over moderately high heat and boil (brushing the inside of the saucepan occasionally with a pastry brush dipped in water to dissolve any sugar crystals) until the caramel turns a rich, tea-like brown, 5 to 7 minutes.

5. Remove the caramel from the heat and add the reserved ½ cup orange juice. Stand back to avoid spatters. Stir the mixture with a wooden spoon, then cook over low heat, stirring, until smooth. Remove from the heat and let cool slightly. Pour the caramel sauce over the orange sections, cover, and refrigerate for at least 2 hours or overnight, stirring occasionally.

6. To serve, arrange the orange slices in dessert bowls. Spoon some of the juices over the oranges and sprinkle the caramel chips on top. Garnish with mint sprigs.

—JUDITH SUTTON

GREEN APPLE SORBET WITH CALVADOS

Champagne is a perfect stand-in for the apple brandy called for in this recipe, if you prefer. The apple sorbet can be prepared up to two days ahead and frozen, tightly covered. Let the sorbet soften slightly before serving.

8 SERVINGS

2¼ pounds Granny Smith apples (about 5)

¼ cup lemon juice

1 cup plus 2 tablespoons sugar

1⅓ cups water

Calvados, for serving

Fresh mint sprigs (optional)

1. Peel and core the Granny Smith apples, then cut them into ¼-inch dice. Place the diced apples in a bowl and toss with the lemon juice.

2. In a medium nonreactive saucepan, combine the sugar and water. Bring the mixture to a boil over high heat, stirring occasionally. Add the diced apples and cook for 1½ minutes. Remove from the heat.

3. Transfer the apples and liquid to a blender and puree until completely smooth, scraping down the sides as necessary. Pour the puree into a 9-by-13-by-2-inch glass baking pan and freeze until thoroughly chilled.

4. Transfer the chilled apple puree to an ice cream maker and freeze according to the manufacturer's instructions. Alternatively, freeze the apple puree until it becomes icy around the edges, then stir well and refreeze. Repeat this procedure every 30 minutes for 4 to 5 hours (see How to Stir Granitas, page 253), until the apple puree is frozen evenly. When it is ready, you should not have any icy lumps.

5. To serve, scoop the apple sorbet into glass bowls, pour a splash of Calvados on top and garnish with a mint sprig, if using.

—BOB CHAMBERS

APPLE SORBET WITH CARAMELIZED APPLES

This delicious dessert contrasts two apples; Golden Delicious make a sweet apple sorbet while raw and oven-caramelized slices of Granny Smith apples are refreshingly tart. You will need a juice extractor to make this dessert.

6 SERVINGS

7 Golden Delicious apples or 10 medium McIntosh apples (about 3 pounds)

¼ cup lemon juice (from 1 large lemon)

½ cup plus 1 tablespoon granulated sugar

1½ cups water

3 Granny Smith apples (about 1½ pounds)

1 tablespoon confectioners' sugar

1. Peel, halve, and core the Golden Delicious apples. Toss them with 2 tablespoons of the lemon juice to coat. Crush the apples in a juice extractor, reserving the juice and pulp separately.

2. Stir 5 tablespoons of the granulated sugar into the apple juice. Pour the syrup into an ice cream maker and freeze according to the manufacturer's instructions until the sorbet is firm but not grainy, about 20 minutes. Transfer the sorbet to a freezer container and freeze while you proceed, or for up to 4 hours.

3. Meanwhile, in a medium nonreactive saucepan, combine the reserved apple pulp and the remaining 2 tablespoons lemon juice and 4 tablespoons granulated sugar with the water. Bring to a boil over moderately high heat and cook, stirring, until smooth, about 2 minutes. Strain the liquid into a medium heatproof bowl and let cool.

4. Peel, quarter, and core two of the Granny Smith apples and cut them lengthwise into very thin slices. Add them to the strained liquid.

5. Heat the oven to 325°. Peel and core the remaining Granny Smith apple. Slice it crosswise into ⅛-inch-thick rings. Place the rings on a nonstick baking sheet or a baking sheet lined with parchment paper and bake until lightly browned, about 8 minutes. Sprinkle the rings with the confectioners' sugar, place under the broiler, and broil until the sugar melts, about 30 seconds. Cool the caramelized apples completely, then transfer to the freezer while you proceed.

6. To serve, scoop some of the thinly sliced Granny Smith apples with their liquid into chilled dessert bowls. Dollop the sorbet on top. Garnish with the caramelized apple rings.

—JACQUES TORRES

STRAWBERRY RHUBARB SORBET

The stalks of early spring rhubarb are not the deep, rich red of summer's established crop, but they are tender and delicious all the same. Be sure to discard the leaves of the rhubarb because they are toxic.

6 SERVINGS

1¼ pounds rhubarb stalks, sliced ¾-inch thick (about 4 cups)

1¼ cups sugar

½ cup water

1 pint ripe strawberries, hulled and halved

¾ cup orange juice

1. Combine the rhubarb with the sugar and water in a nonreactive medium saucepan and bring to a boil over high heat. Reduce the heat to moderately low and simmer gently until the rhubarb is very tender, about 20 minutes.

2. Transfer the rhubarb to a food processor and puree until smooth. Scrape the puree into a large bowl.

3. Add the strawberries and orange juice to the processor and puree. Stir the strawberry puree into the rhubarb. Let the puree cool to room temperature.

4. Transfer the puree to an ice cream maker and freeze according to the manufacturer's instructions. Firmly pack the sorbet into a container. Cover tightly and freeze for at least 3 hours or up to one day.

—SHEILA LUKINS

BERRY ABC'S

• Use local fresh fruits in season for the most flavor.

• Choose the ripest, most fragrant berries with no soft spots or mold and no smell of fermentation.

• Buy organic berries so that you won't have to wash them (unless they're sandy or dirty). Washing will leach out the juice—and with it the flavor. The only berries that will survive washing with their taste more or less intact are the firmer ones, such as blueberries and strawberries. Raspberries and other delicate berries won't make it.

• If you must wash berries to remove dirt or pesticide residue, don't hull them first; a berry without its stem collects water. Rinse a few berries at a time in a colander, using lukewarm water. Gently pat dry with a soft cloth towel.

• Try to use the berries right away. Although most can be refrigerated for up to three days in a bowl or a basket lined with a paper towel, they'll lose some fragrance and taste.

PEACH AND RED WINE GRANITA

The classic Italian summer dessert of peaches in red wine inspires a zesty granita made with both these ingredients.

6 SERVINGS

1½ pounds large fresh peaches (about 4), peeled and thickly sliced

¾ cup sugar

2 cups water

⅓ cup dry red wine

1 tablespoon lemon juice

1. Chill a 13-by-9-inch baking dish, preferably metal, in the freezer. In a medium saucepan, combine the peaches with the sugar and water. Bring to a simmer over moderate heat. Lower the heat and cook, stirring occasionally, until the peaches are very tender when pierced with a fork, about 5 minutes. Let the peaches cool completely in the syrup.

2. In a blender or food processor, working in two batches, combine the peaches and their cooking liquid with the wine and lemon juice. Process until smooth.

3. Pour the peach mixture into the chilled baking dish. Freeze until ice crystals form around the edges, about 40 minutes. Stir well to incorporate the ice. Continue freezing, stirring every 30 minutes (see How to Stir Granitas, page 253), until all the liquid freezes completely, about 3 hours. Spoon the granita into bowls and serve.

—MICHELE SCICOLONE

LIME GRANITA

Made with fresh lime juice and flecks of grated peel, this frozen dessert is especially invigorating when topped with a splash of grappa, vodka, or tequila.

8 SERVINGS

¾ cup sugar

3 cups water

½ cup lime juice

1 teaspoon finely grated lime zest

1. Chill a 13-by-9-inch baking dish, preferably metal, in the freezer. In a medium saucepan, combine the sugar and the water. Bring to a simmer over moderate heat and cook, swirling occasionally, until the sugar dissolves, about 3 minutes. Let cool completely, then stir in the lime juice and zest.

2. Pour the lime mixture into the chilled baking dish. Freeze until ice crystals form around the edges, about 30 minutes. Stir well to incorporate the ice. Continue freezing, stirring every 30 minutes, (see How to Stir Granitas, opposite page) until all the liquid freezes completely, about 2 hours. Spoon the granita into bowls and serve.

—MICHELE SCICOLONE

FRUIT JUICE GRANITA

Many store-bought fruit juices make great granitas. Keep a batch of sugar syrup in a covered container in the refrigerator ready to add to the fruit juice. Using the following recipe as a guideline, add sugar syrup to taste and balance it with an extra squeeze or two of fresh lemon juice, depending on the sweetness of the fruit juice:

Boil ½ cup sugar with 1 cup water until the sugar dissolves. Let cool, then stir into 3 cups bottled fruit juice; add about 2 teaspoons of fresh lemon juice. Pour into a chilled 13-by-9-inch baking dish and freeze, stirring every 30 minutes, until all the liquid freezes completely. This will serve 8.

HONEYDEW GRANITA

This delicious icy treat is full of intense melon flavor. Try it with others of the so-called winter melons: Crenshaws and Casabas.

6 SERVINGS

½ cup sugar

1 cup water

1 very ripe honeydew melon (about 4 pounds), peeled and cut into 1-inch chunks

3 tablespoons lemon juice

1. Chill a 13-by-9-inch baking dish, preferably metal, in the freezer. In a small saucepan, combine the sugar and water. Bring to a simmer over moderate heat and cook, swirling occasionally, until the sugar dissolves, about 5 minutes. Let cool completely. In a food processor or blender, working in two batches, combine the melon with the sugar syrup and lemon juice. Process until smooth.

2. Pour the melon mixture into the chilled baking dish. Freeze until ice crystals form around the edges, about 30 minutes. Stir well to incorporate the ice. Continue freezing, stirring every 30 minutes, until all the liquid freezes completely, about 3 hours. Spoon into bowls and serve.

—MICHELE SCICOLONE

HOW TO STIR GRANITAS

Stir the granita every 30 minutes during freezing to incorporate the ice crystals that have formed on the bottom and sides of the pan into the mixture; if it is not stirred regularly, it will freeze solid. A fork is the best utensil to use for stirring because the tips of the tines can be used to break up larger ice crystals.

chapter 5
OTHER DESSERTS

Bread Pudding with Whiskey Sauce

BREAD PUDDING WITH WHISKEY SAUCE

This Southern classic can be served hot or warm from the oven, or it can be made early in the day and served at room temperature. The whiskey sauce, however, must be warm.

12 SERVINGS

BREAD PUDDING:

½ cup raisins

¼ cup bourbon

8 cups torn bite-sized pieces of French bread (from 1 or 2 baguettes with a total weight of 1 pound)

5 cups milk

1 cinnamon stick

1 teaspoon vanilla extract

6 large eggs

1 cup sugar

WHISKEY SAUCE:

1 large egg

½ cup sugar

¼ pound unsalted butter, melted

Reserved bourbon from soaking the raisins, more if needed

1. For the bread pudding, soak the raisins in the bourbon for at least 30 minutes or overnight if possible.

2. Heat the oven to 350°. Butter a 3-quart baking dish, such as a 9-by-13-inch rectangular glass dish. Place the torn, bite-size pieces of French bread in a large bowl. Drain the raisins and add them to the bowl with the bread. Reserve the bourbon

soaking liquid for making the whiskey sauce.

3. In a medium saucepan, combine the milk, the cinnamon stick, and vanilla, and cook over moderate heat until bubbles just begin to break the surface.

4. Beat the eggs with the sugar until well blended, then gradually stir in the scalded milk. Pour the hot mixture over the bread pieces and the raisins, and discard the cinnamon stick. Let the bread soak for 10 minutes.

5. Fill the baking dish with the soaked bread pieces, patting them even. Set the baking dish inside a larger roasting pan and pour enough hot water into the pan to reach about an inch up the sides of the baking dish. Bake the pudding until a knife stuck in the center of the pudding comes out clean, about 45 minutes.

6. Meanwhile, for the whiskey sauce, in a medium heatproof bowl, using a hand-held mixer or a whisk, beat together the egg and the sugar. Set the bowl over a large saucepan containing about an inch of simmering water. Beat the egg mixture until very light and nearly doubled in volume,

about 3 minutes. Beat in the melted butter, a little at a time, then beat in the reserved bourbon (if you don't have ¼ cup, add enough to make up for what was absorbed by the raisins). Remove the pan from the heat but keep the sauce warm over the water.

7. To serve, bring the water in the saucepan under the whiskey sauce back to a simmer to rewarm the sauce if necessary. Cut the bread pudding into twelve pieces and transfer the pudding pieces to dessert plates. Drizzle the warm whiskey sauce on top.

—JOHN MARTIN TAYLOR

BITTERSWEET CHOCOLATE BREAD PUDDING

In this unusual bread pudding, cubes of brioche are frozen, then barely moistened with a bitter chocolate custard and used to line individual ramekins. The truffle-like mixture in the center melts into a sauce as it cooks. Ground star anise can be found in specialty-food shops, but omit it if you can't find it.

6 SERVINGS

4 ounces bittersweet chocolate, chopped

¼ cup boiling water

1 tablespoon unsalted butter, melted

2 extra-large eggs

6 tablespoons sugar, more for the ramekins

3 tablespoons unsweetened cocoa powder, preferably Dutch-process

3 tablespoons flour

⅛ teaspoon finely ground star anise (optional)

½ cup half-and-half

1½ tablespoons dark rum

1 ¾-pound brioche or challah, crusts removed, bread cut into ½-inch cubes and frozen

Vanilla or coffee ice cream, for serving

1. In a medium heatproof bowl, combine the chocolate and boiling water and stir until completely melted and smooth. Refrigerate the filling until firm, for at least 1 hour and as long as overnight.

2. Heat the oven to 350°. Brush six 4-ounce ramekins with the melted butter. Line the bottoms with rounds of waxed paper, butter the paper and sprinkle the paper with sugar.

3. In a large bowl, beat the eggs and the 6 tablespoons sugar with an electric mixer until pale and thick. Sift the cocoa powder, flour, and star anise, if using, into a bowl. Whisk in the half-and-half and rum just until smooth. Lightly whisk in the beaten egg mixture.

4. Working in batches, moisten 1 cup of frozen brioche cubes at a time in the chocolate custard until slightly saturated, about 30 seconds. Using a slotted spoon, drain the brioche cubes and use them to fill the ramekins halfway. Place 1½ tablespoons of the chocolate filling in the center of each ramekin. Moisten the remaining frozen brioche cubes in batches and fill the ramekins, mounding them slightly in the center. Discard any remaining chocolate custard. ➤

5. Set the ramekins in a roasting pan and pour enough hot water into the pan to reach about an inch up the sides. Cover the pan with aluminum foil and bake until the puddings are puffed and set, about 25 minutes. Remove the ramekins from the water bath and let cool for 10 minutes before unmolding.

6. Invert the bread puddings onto small dessert plates. Remove the waxed paper and serve warm with the ice cream.

—Heidi Steele

Why Does Chocolate Bloom?

Ever had the experience of opening up a package of chocolate that's been on the shelf for a while and finding that it has taken on a funny gray-white color? That coloring is called "bloom" (technically it's the cocoa butter in the chocolate that has risen to the surface) and it happens when the temperature at which your chocolate is being stored exceeds or drops below an optimal range of 60° to 70°F. The good news is that bloom doesn't effect the flavor of the chocolate and will disappear once the chocolate is melted.

BITTERSWEET CHOCOLATE PUDDING

To make this soft, rich pudding, use the best-quality chocolate you can find. Serve it with whipped cream, beaten just long enough to hold a soft shape. See photo on page 262.

6 SERVINGS

1 cup whole milk

½ cup heavy cream, preferably not ultrapasteurized

4 ounces imported bittersweet chocolate, such as Callebaut, chopped

1 teaspoon vanilla extract

½ teaspoon instant espresso granules

4 large egg yolks

¼ cup sugar

Softly whipped cream, for serving

1. In a medium saucepan, warm the milk with the cream over moderately high heat until steaming, about 2 minutes. Remove from the heat and stir in the chocolate, vanilla, and instant espresso granules until smooth.

2. In a medium bowl, whisk the egg yolks and the sugar until combined. Gently whisk in the chocolate mixture without creating a foam. Set the bowl over a saucepan filled with about an inch of simmering water. Cook the pudding, stirring and scraping the bottom and sides of the pan constantly with a wooden spoon, until the pudding thickens slightly and reaches a temperature of 165° to 170°, 8 to 12 minutes. Do not overcook.

3. Strain the pudding into a medium heatproof bowl and stir constantly with a wooden spoon for 2 minutes to prevent a skin from forming. Transfer to 4- to 6-ounce ramekins (the larger ramekins will be about half full) and let cool to room temperature. Cover and refrigerate overnight or for up to two days. Serve chilled, topped with a generous dollop of whipped cream.

—SHELLEY BORIS

BASQUE-FLAVORED PUDDING WITH ALMOND PRALINE

Toasted almond praline provides a crunchy foil to this silky pudding made with an infusion of orange-flower water and spirits. Both almonds and orange-flower water are typical Basque ingredients.

There is enough topping for two batches of pudding. Store the remainder in an airtight container in a cool, dry place; it will keep for up to one month. The photo on the facing page pictures this pudding (left) next to Butterscotch Pudding (center), page 265, and Bittersweet Chocolate Pudding (right), page 261.

4 SERVINGS

⅓ cup blanched, sliced, or slivered almonds

½ cup sugar

¼ cup water

1 teaspoon anise-flavored liqueur

1 teaspoon orange-flower water*

½ teaspoon dark rum

½ teaspoon Armagnac or cognac

1½ cups heavy cream, preferably not ultrapasteurized

2 vanilla beans, split lengthwise

2 2-by-¼-inch strips of lemon zest

6 large egg yolks

*Available at specialty food shops

1. In a dry medium frying pan, toast the almonds over moderate heat, stirring, until fragrant, 4 to 5 minutes. Let cool.

2. Lightly grease a small baking sheet. Place ¼ cup of the sugar in a small nonreactive frying pan. Slowly and evenly drizzle the water all over of the sugar. Cook over moderately high heat until the caramel turns a rich, tea-like brown, about 6 minutes; swirl the pan when the caramel begins to brown but do not stir. Remove the pan from the heat and stir in the almonds. Immediately pour the hot caramel onto the prepared pan. Let it cool until firm, about 30 minutes.

3. Crack the praline into 1-inch pieces and place in a food processor. Pulse until it resembles coarse salt. Do not overprocess. Set the praline aside.

4. In a small bowl, combine the anise liqueur, orange-flower water, rum, and the Armagnac.

5. In a nonreactive saucepan, scald the cream with the vanilla beans and lemon zest over moderate heat.

6. In a medium bowl, whisk the egg yolks with the remaining ¼ cup sugar. Slowly whisk in the hot cream. Set the

bowl over a saucepan filled with about an inch of simmering water and cook over moderate heat, stirring constantly, until the mixture reaches 165° to 170°. Immediately pass the custard through a fine strainer into a glass measure.

7. Pour the custard into the 4-ounce ramekins or custard cups. Cover the custards with plastic wrap and refrigerate until chilled, at least 6 hours or up to two days. To serve, sprinkle each custard with 1 tablespoon of the praline.

—Shelley Boris

Three Stages of Caramel

• Light Caramel, about 320°F, has just a hint of color and little flavor; it is used for coating nuts or fruit and for making spun sugar and caramel cages.

• Medium Caramel, about 345°F, is cooked until a golden amber; it has a strong, sweet taste and is used in sauces, candies such as the almond praline in this recipe, and many caramel-based desserts.

• Dark Caramel, about 375°F, is a deep amber-mahogany in color; less sweet than medium caramel, it is used in many sauces, to line crème caramel molds, and for flavoring other desserts.

—Judith Sutton

BUTTERSCOTCH PUDDING

This recipe makes a rich, creamy, and not-too-sweet pudding with a wallop of butterscotch flavor. If you like, top each serving with a spoonful of lightly sweetened, softly whipped cream. See photo on page 262.

4 SERVINGS

- 6 large egg yolks
- 1 cup heavy cream, preferably not ultrapasteurized
- ⅓ cup dark-brown sugar
- 3 tablespoons unsalted butter, cut into tablespoons
- ¼ cup whole milk
- ½ teaspoon vanilla extract

1. In medium bowl, lightly whisk the egg yolks. In a small saucepan, warm the cream over moderate heat until steaming; keep hot.

2. In a heavy medium frying pan, cook the brown sugar and butter over moderately high heat, stirring with a wooden spoon, until melted and bubbling, about 2 minutes. Remove from the heat and stir in the hot cream until blended. Let cool for 2 minutes, then stir in the milk.

3. Gently whisk the butterscotch mixture into the egg yolks. Stir in the vanilla. Set the bowl over a large saucepan filled with about an inch of simmering water and cook over moderate heat, stirring, until the pudding thickens slightly and reaches 165° to 170°, about 6 minutes. Do not overcook.

4. Strain into a heatproof bowl and stir for 2 minutes to prevent a skin from forming. Transfer to 4-ounce ramekins and let cool to room temperature. Cover and refrigerate for at least 2 hours or up to two days.

—SHELLEY BORIS

MAPLE INDIAN PUDDING

Indian pudding is a classic New England dessert. The delicate flavor, color, and texture of this maple-syrup-sweetened version are lighter and more refined-tasting than those of the traditional dessert made with molasses.

6 TO 8 SERVINGS

1 cup stone-ground yellow cornmeal

1 quart whole milk

½ cup maple sugar granules or light-brown sugar

1 cup heavy cream, preferably not ultrapasteurized

½ cup pure maple syrup

⅛ teaspoon freshly grated nutmeg

1. Heat the oven to 275°. Lightly butter a 1½-quart soufflé dish. In a heavy-bottomed medium saucepan, whisk the cornmeal into the milk over moderately high heat until thickened slightly, about 5 minutes.

2. Remove from the heat and stir in the maple sugar granules. Stir in the cream, syrup, and nutmeg. Pour into the prepared dish. Bake in the middle of the oven until bubbling and brown on top, about 4 hours. Let rest 30 minutes before serving.

—SHELLEY BORIS

MAPLE SYRUP SWEETENERS

Maple syrup, maple honey, maple cream or butter, and maple sugar are all products made from maple-tree sap. Maple trees are tapped during midwinter and then the sap is boiled down to evaporate some of the water; the amount of evaporation determines the end product. *Maple syrup*, the most familiar and most liquid of this family of sweeteners, is sap that has been boiled just until it becomes thick and syrupy. If the sap is boiled longer, it thickens further to a more viscous liquid sold as *maple honey*. With further evaporation we get *maple cream* or *butter*, which is thick enough to spread. And if almost all of the water is evaporated out of the sap, we get *maple sugar*, a sweetener that is significantly sweeter than granulated sugar.

INDIAN PUDDING WITH PEARS AND GINGER

This unusual indian pudding is made with corn-bread crumbs, rather than with the traditional cornmeal, and diced pears, cooked into the pudding. It's served topped with a creamy butterscotch sauce.

12 SERVINGS

- ¾ cup buttermilk
- ¾ cup cornmeal
- 1 cup flour
- ½ cup sugar
- 1½ teaspoons baking powder
- 1 teaspoon cinnamon
- ½ teaspoon ground ginger
- ½ teaspoon salt
- ¼ pound unsalted butter, melted and cooled
- ½ cup sour cream
- 9 extra-large eggs, 1 lightly beaten
- 6 cups milk
- ¼ cup plus 2 tablespoons thinly sliced fresh ginger
- 12 extra-large egg yolks
- 1 cup unsulphured molasses
- 2 ripe large pears, such as Anjou or Comice, peeled, cored, and cut into ½-inch dice

Butterscotch Sauce, next page

1. Heat the oven to 375°. Butter an 8-inch square baking pan. In a large bowl, combine the buttermilk and the cornmeal and allow the mixture to stand for 5 minutes. In another bowl, sift together the flour, sugar, baking powder, cinnamon, ground ginger, and salt.

2. In a small bowl, whisk the melted butter with the sour cream and the lightly beaten egg and stir into the cornmeal mixture. Stir in the sifted dry ingredients. Pour the corn-bread batter into the prepared pan and bake until a toothpick stuck in the center of the corn bread comes out clean, about 30 minutes. Let cool slightly, then unmold the corn bread to cool completely. Cut three-quarters of the corn bread into 1-inch dice and let dry. (You can snack on the rest.) Put the diced corn bread in a food processor and pulse until fine.

3. Turn the oven heat down to 325°. Generously butter twelve 1-cup ramekins and set them in a large roasting pan.

4. In a medium saucepan, combine the milk and the sliced fresh ginger and bring the milk to a boil. Remove the pan from the heat and let the milk steep, covered, for 10 minutes.

5. Put the corn-bread crumbs in a large bowl. In a medium bowl, whisk the remaining 8 whole eggs with the egg yolks and the unsulphured molasses. Bring the milk back to a boil and slowly whisk it into the egg mixture. Strain the custard over the corn-bread crumbs and stir well. Add the diced pears to the ramekins and spoon the custard mixture on top. Pour enough hot water into the pan to reach about one-third of the way up the sides of the ramekins.

6. Cover the roasting pan tightly with foil and bake in the middle of the oven until the puddings are set, about 1 hour.

7. Run a thin knife around the puddings and invert each one onto a plate. Spoon the butterscotch sauce on top of the puddings and serve.

—WALDY MALOUF

BUTTERSCOTCH SAUCE

MAKES ABOUT 3 CUPS

1½ cups light-brown sugar
⅔   cup light corn syrup
¼   pound unsalted butter, cut into tablespoons
1   cup heavy cream
¼   cup brandy

In a heavy medium saucepan, bring the brown sugar, corn syrup, and butter to a boil over high heat. Add the cream and return to a boil. Reduce the heat to moderate and simmer the sauce, stirring, until the temperature registers 240° on a candy thermometer and the sauce is thick when a spoonful is cooled on a plate, about 10 minutes. Stir in the brandy. Serve warm.

MAKE IT AHEAD

The corn-bread crumbs can be made up to three days ahead and the butterscotch sauce can be refrigerated for up to a week. Once baked, the puddings can be refrigerated for up to a day. Just bring the puddings to room temperature and then rewarm in a water bath, covered with foil, in a 300° oven for 20 minutes.

OVERNIGHT CHEESECAKE

Because it bakes slowly at a low temperature, this cheesecake never cracks, it never dries out, and it requires no water bath. In short, it comes out just about perfect everytime.

16 SERVINGS

½ cup graham cracker crumbs

2 pounds cream cheese, at room temperature

1 cup sugar

5 large eggs

¼ cup brandy

2 tablespoons vanilla extract

1. Heat the oven to 200°. Coat a 2-quart soufflé dish or 9-inch springform pan with vegetable-oil cooking spray and dust with the graham cracker crumbs (if necessary, spray and dust again to coat well).

2. In a large bowl, using a wooden spoon, mix the cream cheese with the sugar until smooth, scraping as necessary. Mix in the eggs, brandy, and vanilla until blended.

3. Pour the batter into the prepared pan and bake until the cake just barely wiggles in the center, 6 to 8 hours. (The cake will firm up as it cools.) Cool the cake in the pan for 1 hour.

4. Cover the cake with waxed paper, invert onto a plate, remove the pan, and refrigerate upside down for at least 1 and up to 24 hours. Invert onto a platter. Cut the cake with a long sharp knife; dip it in warm water to prevent sticking.

—ANDREW SCHLOSS

MAKE IT AHEAD

The cheesecake can be made ahead, wrapped, and refrigerated for up to four days.

Pumpkin Cheesecake

Here's a spin on the classic pumpkin pie: This is a luxurious pumpkin-flavored cheesecake. Don't be afraid to use unseasoned, unsweetened canned pumpkin here; the smooth texture and distinct but mellow flavor work just as well as fresh pumpkin puree.

MAKES ONE 9½-INCH CHEESECAKE

- 2 cups gingersnap crumbs (from about ½ pound cookies)
- ⅓ cup unsalted butter, melted
- 3 8-ounce packages cream cheese, at room temperature
- 1 cup granulated sugar
- ½ cup light-brown sugar
- 3 large eggs, lightly beaten
- 1 15-ounce can pumpkin puree
- ¼ cup heavy cream
- 1 tablespoon vanilla extract
- 1 teaspoon cinnamon
- 1 teaspoon ground ginger
- ½ teaspoon freshly grated nutmeg
- 2 cups sour cream, at room temperature

1. Heat the oven to 350°. Butter a 9½- or 10-inch springform pan and coat lightly with flour. In a medium bowl, toss the gingersnap crumbs with the melted butter until evenly moistened. Press the crumbs into the bottom and about an inch up the side of the prepared pan. Bake until the crust begins to color, about 12 minutes. Let the crust cool. Reduce the oven temperature to 325°.

2. In a large bowl, using an electric mixer, beat the cream cheese until smooth. Beat in ¾ cup of the granulated sugar and the brown sugar, then beat in the eggs in three additions until the mixture is thoroughly combined, scraping down the side of the bowl occasionally.

3. In a medium bowl, combine the pumpkin puree and the cream with 1 teaspoon of the vanilla and the cinnamon, ginger, and nutmeg. Add the pumpkin mixture to the cream-cheese mixture. Beat until thoroughly combined, scraping the bowl a few times.

4. Wrap aluminum foil loosely around the bottom and up the side of the springform pan. Pour the cheesecake batter into the prepared pan and set it in a large baking dish or roasting pan. Place in the middle of the oven and pour about an inch of hot water into the baking dish. Bake the cheesecake until the edges are firm and the center of the cheesecake is still slightly shaky, about 70 minutes.

5. In a small bowl, combine the sour cream with the remaining ¼ cup granulated sugar and 2 teaspoons of the vanilla.

Remove the pumpkin cheesecake from the water bath and pour on the sour-cream mixture. Gently tap the pan to spread the sour-cream topping, and continue baking the cheesecake for 10 minutes more.

6. Let the cheesecake cool for 1 hour. Remove the foil and the side of the pan and refrigerate the cheesecake for at least 4 hours or overnight. If you like, remove the cheesecake from the bottom of the pan by sliding a metal spatula under the crust to loosen it completely, then use two large metal spatulas to transfer the cheesecake to a serving plate. Alternatively, you can serve the cheesecake on the pan bottom.

—Peggy Cullen

Make It Ahead

The pumpkin cheesecake can be made ahead and refrigerated for up to two days before serving.

CHOCOLATE CRÈME CARAMEL

Since this dessert must be refrigerated overnight, you'll have to make it the day before serving. Be sure to scrape the delicious caramel sauce from the bottom of the ramekins when you unmold these custards.

8 SERVINGS

- 1 cup plus 2 tablespoons sugar
- 3 tablespoons water
- 6 ounces bittersweet chocolate, chopped
- 2 cups milk
- ½ vanilla bean, split lengthwise
- 3 large eggs, at room temperature
- 3 large egg yolks, at room temperature

1. Heat the oven to 325°. In a small, deep heavy saucepan, combine ½ cup plus 2 tablespoons of the sugar with the water. Bring the mixture to a boil over moderately high heat and boil (brushing down the sides of the saucepan occasionally with a pastry brush dipped in water to dissolve any sugar crystals) until the sugar turns a rich, tea-like brown, 6 to 8 minutes.

2. Immediately pour the hot caramel into eight 6-ounce ramekins and swirl to coat the bottoms of the dishes evenly. Place the ramekins in a baking pan large enough to hold them without touching.

3. Put the chocolate in a medium heatproof bowl. Pour the milk into a medium saucepan. Scrape the seeds from the vanilla bean into the milk, add the pod of the bean, and whisk to combine. Bring the milk just to a boil over moderate heat. Remove the vanilla bean pod and reserve for another use. Pour the hot milk over the chocolate and let sit for 30 seconds. Whisk until smooth.

4. In a large bowl, whisk the whole eggs and egg yolks with the remaining ½ cup sugar until well blended. Gradually whisk in the chocolate-milk mixture. Strain the custard into a large measuring cup, then pour the custard into the caramel-lined ramekins.

5. Set the baking pan in the lower third of the oven and pour enough hot water into the pan to reach about halfway up the sides of the ramekins. Bake until the custards are just set and the centers still wiggle slightly when the ramekins are jiggled, 30 to 35 minutes. Cool, then cover with plastic wrap and refrigerate overnight.

6. To serve, fill a heatproof bowl with hot water. Run a thin knife around each custard and dip the bottom of each ramekin in the hot water. Invert the custards onto plates. Scrape any caramel remaining in the ramekins over the custards.

—JUDITH SUTTON

INDIVIDUAL CHOCOLATE SOUFFLÉS

If you're using a copper bowl and balloon whisk, you can make up to eight soufflés. You'll incorporate less air with an electric beater and stainless bowl and therefore get fewer servings.

6 TO 8 SERVINGS

  4 ounces good-quality bittersweet chocolate, chopped

  ½ cup heavy cream

  3 large egg yolks

  ½ teaspoon vanilla extract

  5 large egg whites, at room temperature

  ¼ cup granulated sugar

     Confectioners' sugar, for dusting

1. In a medium saucepan, melt the chocolate in the cream over moderately low heat, stirring, until perfectly smooth, about 3 minutes. Remove from the heat and whisk in the egg yolks, one at a time, mixing well after each addition. Stir in the vanilla.

2. Heat the oven to 425°. Butter six to eight ⅔-cup ramekins. Put them in the freezer for a few minutes to set the butter quickly. Butter the ramekins again. Rewarm the chocolate mixture over moderately low heat, stirring, just until hot to the touch.

3. Meanwhile, in a medium bowl, beat the egg whites until they hold soft peaks. Add the granulated sugar and continue beating until the egg whites are glossy and hold stiff peaks when the beaters are lifted, about 1 minute longer. Stir one quarter of the egg whites into the chocolate mixture to lighten it. The chocolate mixture and the egg whites should be very close to the same density. Then fold the chocolate mixture into the remaining whites just until combined.

4. Scrape the soufflé mixture into the prepared ramekins, smooth the surfaces, and run your thumb around the inside rim of each ramekin. Set the ramekins on a baking sheet and bake the soufflés in the middle of the oven until puffed and set around the edges, about 8 minutes. Dust the soufflés with confectioners' sugar and serve at once.

—ANNE WILLAN

MAKE IT AHEAD

The chocolate soufflé base (without the beaten whites) can be made up to four hours ahead. Press plastic wrap directly on the surface of the mixture to prevent the formation of a skin and let stand at room temperature. Then whip and fold in the egg whites and bake when you're ready.

Coffee Crème Caramel

In this recipe, the caramel used to line the custard molds is made without water; the sugar is simply cooked on its own until it melts and then caramelizes. Once the melted sugar begins to change color, watch it carefully so that it doesn't burn.

4 SERVINGS

1 cup sugar

2 large eggs

3 large egg whites

1 12-ounce can evaporated skim milk

¼ cup coarsely ground coffee beans

¼ cup heavy cream

½ teaspoon vanilla extract

1. Heat the oven to 350°. Line a baking sheet with parchment paper.

2. In a small heavy saucepan, cook ⅔ cup of the sugar over moderately low heat without stirring until it is melted and turns a rich, tea-like brown, about 12 minutes. Working quickly, pour about 1 tablespoon of the caramel into each of four ⅔-cup ramekins. Drizzle the remaining caramel over the parchment paper on the baking sheet and let the caramel stand at room temperature to harden.

3. In a bowl, whisk the eggs with the egg whites and the remaining ⅓ cup sugar until combined. In a small saucepan, warm the evaporated skim milk and the ground coffee beans over moderate heat until the milk steams, about 3 minutes. Let stand for 1 minute. Whisk the hot milk into the egg mixture, then whisk in the heavy cream and the vanilla.

4. Strain the coffee custard, then pour it into the ramekins and set them in a baking dish. Add enough cold water to the dish to reach three-quarters of the way up the sides of the ramekins. Bake until the custards are almost set, about 35 minutes. Let the custards cool in the water bath. Cover and refrigerate the coffee crème caramels until they are chilled, for at least 2 hours or overnight.

5. To serve, dip the bottom of each ramekin in hot water, then run a knife around each of the coffee crème caramels and invert them onto individual plates. Break the hardened caramel into large pieces and arrange the pieces decoratively around the custards.

—Diana Sturgis

Make It Ahead

The hardened caramel pieces can stand at room temperature, covered, overnight.

CRÈME BRÛLÉE

Air-dried brown sugar gives this crème brûlée a particularly thin and even crust: Sift the sugar onto a plate and leave it out, uncovered, for one day. Alternatively, if the weather is humid, the sifted brown sugar can also be dried in the oven. Set the oven temperature at 250° and bake the sugar on a cookie sheet for 20 minutes.

4 SERVINGS

- 4 large egg yolks
- 6 tablespoons plus 1 teaspoon granulated sugar
- 2 cups heavy cream
- 1 vanilla bean, split lengthwise
- ¼ cup air-dried, light-brown sugar (see above)

1. Heat the oven to 275°. In a medium bowl, whisk the egg yolks with half (3 tablespoons plus ½ teaspoon) of the granulated sugar. Combine the cream and the remaining granulated sugar in a small saucepan and scrape in the seeds from the vanilla bean. Warm the mixture over moderate heat until steaming. Gradually whisk the hot cream into the egg-yolk mixture until blended. Strain the custard and pour it into four 5-ounce ramekins or shallow gratin dishes.

2. Set the ramekins in a small baking dish and add enough hot tap water to the dish to reach halfway up the sides of the ramekins. Bake until the custards are just set, about 1 hour and 15 minutes. Let the custards cool in the water bath for 10 minutes, then remove from the baking dish and allow them to cool completely. Cover and refrigerate for at least 4 hours or overnight.

3. Heat the broiler. Sift a thin, even layer of the air-dried brown sugar over each of the custards. Broil one ramekin at a time as close as possible to the heat source until the brown sugar melts, forming a caramelized crust on top of the custard. Serve immediately.

—PAUL BOCUSE

Cinnamon-Rice Crème Brûlée

The easiest way to caramelize crème brûlée is to use a household propane torch (Julia Child swears by hers), which is available at hardware stores.

8 SERVINGS

¼ cup long-grain white rice

1½ cups milk

¾ cup plus 3 tablespoons sugar

Pinch salt

½ teaspoon plus ⅛ teaspoon cinnamon

6 large egg yolks

3 cups heavy cream

1 vanilla bean, split lengthwise

1. In a small heavy saucepan, using a wooden spoon, stir together the rice, milk, ¼ cup of the sugar, and the salt. Bring the mixture to a gentle simmer over low heat, stirring occasionally, and cook until the rice is very tender and most of the liquid has been absorbed, about 30 minutes. Stir in the ⅛ teaspoon cinnamon. Let cool.

2. Heat the oven to 300°. Place eight 6-ounce ramekins or custard cups in a large baking pan. Spoon the rice mixture evenly into the ramekins, smoothing the surface with the back of the spoon.

3. In a large bowl, whisk the egg yolks with ½ cup of the remaining sugar until thick and pale.

4. In a large saucepan, bring the cream to a boil with the vanilla bean. Gradually add the hot cream to the egg yolk mixture, whisking constantly to avoid curdling the eggs, until thoroughly combined. Strain through a fine sieve into a bowl. Rinse and reserve the vanilla bean for another use. Stir in the remaining ½ teaspoon cinnamon.

5. Pour the custard into the ramekins, filling them almost to the top. Set the baking pan in the lower part of the oven and pour enough hot water into the baking pan to reach halfway up the sides of the ramekins. Bake until the custard is just set and the center wiggles very slightly, about 50 minutes. (The center will firm up as the custard cools.) Let cool in the water bath for about 10 minutes, then remove the ramekins and let the custard cool to room temperature. Refrigerate the custard until well chilled, at least 3 hours or overnight.

6. Heat the broiler. Sprinkle the remaining 3 tablespoons sugar evenly over the custards, making sure to cover the edges. With a damp cloth, wipe the rims of the ramekins. Set the ramekins on a baking sheet and broil as close to the heat as possible, turning as necessary, until the sugar is evenly caramelized, about 1 minute. Let sit for 1 to 2 minutes to set the caramel, then serve immediately or within 1 hour.

—JUDITH SUTTON

CHOCOLATE ZABAGLIONE CREAM TRIFLE

A light zabaglione cream is layered with espresso-infused chocolate cake and covered with chocolate shavings in this elegant Italianate trifle, served at Stars restaurant in San Francisco.

10 SERVINGS

CHOCOLATE CAKE:

 1 cup flour

 ¼ cup unsweetened cocoa powder

 2½ teaspoons baking powder

   Pinch salt

 5 large eggs, at room temperature, separated

 1¼ cups granulated sugar

 ⅓ cup boiling water

 1 teaspoon vanilla extract

   Confectioners' sugar, for dusting

ZABAGLIONE CREAM:

 8 large egg yolks

 ½ cup granulated sugar

 ½ cup marsala

 ¼ cup sherry

   Pinch salt

 1½ cups heavy cream

 1½ cups brewed espresso or very strong coffee

 6 ounces semisweet chocolate

1. Heat the oven to 350°. For the cake, line a 10½-by-15½-by-¾-inch jelly-roll pan with parchment or waxed paper.

2. In a medium bowl, sift the flour twice with the cocoa, baking powder, and salt. In a large bowl, beat the egg yolks and granulated sugar at high speed until thick and pale, about 5 minutes. Gradually beat in the boiling water and vanilla at medium speed. Raise the speed to high and continue beating until the mixture is thick enough to hold a ribbon on the surface when the beaters are lifted, about 5 minutes. Fold in the dry ingredients.

3. In another medium bowl, beat the egg whites until they hold soft peaks when the beaters are lifted. Fold half of the whites into the batter, then fold in the remaining whites.

4. Spread the batter evenly in the prepared pan. Bake until the top springs back when pressed lightly in the center, about 15 minutes. Invert the cake onto a clean kitchen towel dusted with confectioners' sugar and peel off the paper. Let cool.

5. For the zabaglione cream, in a large bowl, using a hand-held mixer or whisk, beat together the egg yolks, sugar, marsala, sherry, and salt. Set the bowl over a large saucepan filled with about an inch of simmering water. Beat the egg yolk mixture

at medium speed until it triples in volume and reaches 165°. Set the bowl in a larger bowl of ice water and continue beating until the zabaglione has cooled.

6. In another large bowl, beat the cream until it holds soft peaks when the beaters are lifted. Fold the zabaglione into the whipped cream. Cover and refrigerate until chilled.

7. Pour 1¼ cups of the zabaglione into a 2½-quart glass bowl or trifle dish. Using a long serrated knife, cut the cake in half horizontally. Cut and fit cake pieces on top of the cream in a single layer, using one-third of the cake. Brush the cake generously with ½ cup of the espresso. Continue layering with the remaining ingredients so that you have three layers of cake and four layers of cream.

8. Using a vegetable peeler, shave the semisweet chocolate over the trifle. Cover with plastic wrap and refrigerate for at least 8 hours or up to two days.

—EMILY LUCHETTI

BAKING POWDER AND BAKING SODA

Baking soda and powder are chemical leavening agents. These fast-acting gas sources create a reaction between acidic and alkaline elements to produce the carbon dioxide bubbles that help all baked goods rise.

The alkaline component in the equation is sodium bicarbonate, known as *baking soda*. It can be used alone for leavening if the recipe also calls for an acidic ingredient. Buttermilk, sour cream, yogurt, brown sugar, molasses, and some chocolates are acidic ingredients often used in baking.

Baking powder is baking soda plus a mild acid. It contains cornstarch to absorb moisture and keep the soda and acid dry. Because it contains the exact amount of acid needed to neutralize the soda, baking powder is often preferred to the less precise combination of baking soda and an acidic ingredient.

Most baking powders available today are double-acting. They contain one acid (such as cream of tartar) that dissolves in liquid and produces gas immediately, and another acid that does not dissolve until the batter is baked. These baking sodas produce a small amount of leavening right after they are mixed, followed by a maximum amount of leavening in the oven.

—SHIRLEY CORRIHER

RICH CHOCOLATE MOUSSE

This mousse is quick and simple enough to make for a weeknight meal but you won't be disappointed if you make it for company either.

4 SERVINGS

4 ounces imported bittersweet chocolate, chopped

1 cup plus 2 tablespoons heavy cream

2 tablespoons Kahlúa or other coffee liqueur

1. Melt the chocolate in a small bowl set over a pan of barely simmering water, stirring until smooth. Remove the pan from the heat and let cool to tepid.

2. In a medium bowl, beat the cream with the Kahlúa just until it holds soft peaks when the beaters are lifted. Stir about 3 tablespoons of the whipped cream into the melted bittersweet chocolate, then fold in the remaining whipped cream, reserving ¼ cup for garnish. Do not over-work, or the mousse will be grainy. Cover and refrigerate the chocolate mousse and remaining whipped cream until chilled, at least 30 minutes.

3. Spoon the mousse into bowls and garnish each serving with a dollop of the reserved whipped cream.

—JUDITH SUTTON

WHIPPED CREAM

Ever wonder why heavy and light whipping creams will whip but light cream and half-and-half won't? The answer lies in the butterfat content of these creams. By law, heavy whipping cream (also sold as heavy cream) has a butterfat content of 36 to 40 percent, light whipping cream (also sold as whipping cream) contains 30 to 36 percent butterfat, light cream contains about 20 percent or less butterfat, and half-and-half, a mixture of cream and milk, contains roughly 10 to 20 percent butterfat. Below a certain percentage of butterfat, cream simply won't whip (except with an immersion blender that will whip even light cream); light cream and half-and-half weigh in under that percentage. So when buying cream for whipping, choose either heavy or light whipping cream, understanding that heavy whipping cream is slightly richer in fat.

QUICK STRAWBERRY MINT MOUSSE

Sour cream adds tang to this quick mousse of whipped cream and fresh strawberries. Make it at the beginning of summer when strawberries are in season.

4 SERVINGS

1 pint strawberries, hulled and quartered

3 tablespoons sugar

½ cup sour cream

½ cup heavy cream

1 heaping tablespoon thin-sliced fresh mint (optional)

1. In a medium bowl, sprinkle the hulled and quartered strawberries with the sugar and mash them lightly with a fork until the strawberries have exuded some juice and the sugar has started to dissolve. Let macerate for 15 minutes.

2. Strain the juice from the strawberries into a bowl. Whisk the sour cream into the strawberry juice. In a medium bowl, whip the heavy cream until it holds soft peaks. Fold in the sour cream mixture and then gently fold in the sweetened strawberries. Refrigerate the strawberry mousse until it is chilled, at least 20 minutes. Spoon into bowls and garnish the mousse with the slivered fresh mint, if you like.

—STEPHANIE LYNESS

VARIATIONS

This recipe can be varied to use any berries you find in season—raspberries, blueberries, and blackberries, for example, all make a delicious mousse. You can mix a few different kinds of berries as well.

CARAMEL MERINGUES

Make these treats on a dry day; humidity makes for sticky meringues. A sweetly floral-fragrant California Muscat, such as the 1995 Quady Essensia Orange Muscat or the 1996 Robert Pecota Moscato d'Andrea, will accompany these meringues beautifully, recalling the classic pairing of orange and caramel. You can make the meringues ahead and store them in an airtight container for up to one day.

MAKES ABOUT 4 DOZEN

- 4 large egg whites
- 2 cups sugar
- ½ teaspoon cream of tartar
- 1 teaspoon vanilla extract
- Pinch salt
- ¼ cup water

1. Heat the oven to 200°. Line four large baking sheets with parchment paper or aluminum foil. Bring a large frying pan of water to a simmer over moderately high heat. Place the egg whites in a large stainless-steel or glass bowl and swirl over the hot water to warm the whites. Remove the bowl from the water and add 1 cup of the sugar and the cream of tartar. Beat with an electric mixer at medium speed for 30 seconds. Increase the speed to high and beat until the meringue is thick and glossy and holds firm peaks when the beaters are lifted, 3 to 5 minutes. Beat in the vanilla and salt.

2. Fit a large pastry bag with a ½-inch plain tip and scoop the meringue into the bag. Pipe the meringue into tight, 3-inch-long S shapes. Bake the meringues until they are firm to the touch and lift easily off the pan, 1½ to 2 hours. Let cool on the baking sheets.

3. In a small heavy saucepan, combine the remaining 1 cup of sugar with the water. Bring the mixture to a boil over moderately high heat and boil (brushing the inside of the saucepan occasionally with a pastry brush dipped in water to dissolve any sugar crystals) until the sugar turns a rich, tea-like brown. Set the bottom of the pan in a bowl of ice water for 30 to 60 seconds and stir the caramel as it cools.

4. When the caramel falls off the spoon in a thin, steady stream, lift the pan from the water and dry the bottom with a towel so that no water falls on the meringues. Hold the spoon high and drizzle the caramel over the meringues in abstract patterns. Keep the spoon moving so you get pretty lines rather than blobs. Let the caramel set for 1 minute.

—LARRY HAYDEN

FONDUE AU CHOCOLAT

When this fabulous simple dessert was on the menu at the original Le Cirque restaurant in New York City, it was served with thin crisp cookies.

4 TO 6 SERVINGS

1 cup heavy cream

7 ounces imported bittersweet chocolate, such as Valrhona Manjari, chopped

2 tablespoons green Chartreuse

Seasonal fruits, such as pineapple, bananas, pears, kiwis, papayas, and starfruits, cut into bite-size chunks or slices

Unsweetened whipped cream

1. In a small saucepan, bring the heavy cream to a boil over moderate heat. Place the chocolate in a medium bowl and pour in the hot cream. Stir until smooth. Stir in the Chartreuse.

2. Divide the chocolate between two 1-cup ramekins. Set them on two large plates lined with doilies. Arrange the fruit around them. Garnish the fondue with a small dollop of whipped cream. Serve immediately, while the fondue is hot.

—JACQUES TORRES

WHAT IS CHARTREUSE?

Chartreuse is an herb liqueur originally developed by Carthusian monks in France; it takes its name from the Carthusian monastery of La Grande Chartreuse, near Grenoble. Today, both a green and yellow Chartreuse are made (either can be used in this recipe); the green is stronger flavored than the yellow and higher in alcohol.

CARAMELIZED FLAKY PASTRIES

This is one of Pierre Hermé's (one of France's master pastry chefs) versions of a traditional pastry from Brittany called *kouign amann* (queen-yaman), which literally means "bread and butter" in the local dialect. The rich, croissant-like dough is usually layered with sugar and baked as a large flat cake. To provide more caramelized sugar crunch, this recipe uses miffin tins to make miniature pastries. Everyone who has tasted these delicious little pastries says they're irresistible.

MAKES 24 PIECES

- 1 envelope (¼ ounce) active dry yeast
- 1½ cups warm water (115°F)
- 3½ cups bread flour
- 1 tablespoon coarse sea salt
- ¾ pound (3 sticks) cold unsalted butter plus 3½ tablespoons melted butter
- 1¾ cups sugar, more for sprinkling

1. In a small bowl, sprinkle the yeast into the warm water and stir to dissolve. In a large bowl, combine the flour and salt. Add the yeast mixture and stir rapidly to blend. Turn the dough out onto a floured work surface and knead until smooth, 2 to 3 minutes. Place the dough in a lightly oiled bowl and cover with plastic wrap. Set aside in a warm spot until the dough has risen slightly, about 30 minutes.

2. Meanwhile, on a large work surface, place the three sticks of butter side by side between two large pieces of waxed paper. Using a rolling pin, press and roll them into a solid 7-inch square block.

3. On a lightly floured surface, roll the dough out to a 14-by-7½-inch rectangle about ½-inch thick. Set the block of butter in the center. Fold the short sides of the dough over the butter to completely enclose it (as if you were folding a business letter). Cover and let rest in the refrigerator for 20 minutes.

4. Return the dough to the floured work surface, seam side down. Roll out the dough to form the same size rectangle and fold it again, as above. Wrap the dough in plastic wrap and refrigerate for 1 hour.

5. Dust the work surface with ⅔ cup of the sugar and set the dough on top, seam side down. Roll out again to a 14-by-7½-inch rectangle. Sprinkle some of the remaining sugar on top and fold the dough like a business letter, as above. Repeat the rolling and folding operation once more, sprinkling the remaining sugar over the work surface and the dough as you roll. Refrigerate the dough for a few minutes at a time if the butter becomes too soft at any

point during the process. Cover and refrigerate the dough for 30 minutes.

6. Lightly butter two 12-cup, standard-size muffin tins. On a lightly floured work surface, roll out the dough to a 12-by-10-inch rectangle about ½-inch thick. Using a sharp knife, cut the dough into twenty-four 3⅓-by-1½-inch rectangles.

7. Set each piece of dough in a muffin cup. The ends of the rectangles will reach up the sides of the muffin cups slightly. Brush lightly with the melted butter and sprinkle each rectangle with ¼ teaspoon sugar. Let the dough rise at room temperature until almost doubled in bulk, about 1½ hours.

8. Heat the oven to 350°. Bake the mini *kouign amanns* until they are golden brown, 30 to 40 minutes. Unmold them at once and let cool.

—Pierre Hermé

WALNUT BAKLAVA

Though baklava is not a typical Moroccan dessert, versions do exist. This one comes from Fatèma Hal's hometown of Oujda, where it was brought by the Turks.

MAKES ABOUT 40 PIECES

 1 pound walnuts

 ½ pound unsalted butter, melted

 ¾ cup sugar

 3 tablespoons rosewater* (optional)

 ½ teaspoon cinnamon

10 sheets phyllo dough

40 whole blanched almonds

 1 cup honey

*Available at Middle Eastern markets

1. Heat the oven to 425°. Generously butter a baking dish, about 13-by-10½-inches. In a food processor, pulse the walnuts until coarsely chopped. Do not overprocess to a paste. Transfer to a large bowl and stir in half the melted butter, the sugar, rosewater, if using, and cinnamon.

2. Cover half of the phyllo sheets with a damp towel. Generously brush the remaining five phyllo sheets with melted butter and layer them in the prepared baking dish. Spread the walnut mixture on top. Butter the remaining phyllo sheets and layer them over the walnut filling. Fold any overhanging phyllo over the top. Brush the top with any remaining melted butter.

3. Using a serrated knife and a gentle sawing motion, slice the baklava on the diagonal into 1½-inch-wide strips. Then slice on the diagonal in the opposite direction to form diamond shapes. You should have forty diamonds. Top each of the diamonds with a whole almond. Bake the baklava in the center of the oven until the phyllo dough is crisp and golden brown, about 25 minutes.

4. Meanwhile, in a small saucepan, warm the honey gently over low heat. As soon as the baklava comes out of the oven, drizzle the warm honey all over the top and let the baklava cool to room temperature.

—FATÈMA HAL

MAKE IT AHEAD

The baklava will keep in an airtight container for up to two weeks.

ICE CREAM SANDWICHES

Chocolate ice cream and a pair of sauces dress up the humble ice cream sandwich. The coffee sauce is a delicious alternative to the usual caramel.

8 SERVINGS

¼ pound unsalted butter

3 ounces bittersweet chocolate, chopped

½ cup sugar

1 large egg

1½ tablespoons strong brewed coffee, at room temperature

1¼ teaspoons vanilla extract

¾ cup flour

2 tablespoons unsweetened cocoa powder

½ teaspoon baking powder

⅛ teaspoon cinnamon

⅛ teaspoon salt

2 pints good-quality coffee ice cream

Chocolate Sauce, next page

Coffee Sauce, next page

1. Heat the oven to 325°. Butter a 10-by-15-inch rimmed baking sheet and line it with parchment paper. Butter the parchment paper and refrigerate the baking sheet until the butter is firm, about 15 minutes.

2. In a small saucepan, melt the butter and the bittersweet chocolate over low heat, stirring occasionally. Remove from the heat and let cool.

3. In a medium bowl, beat the sugar and the egg until blended. Beat in the brewed coffee, vanilla, and melted chocolate. Sift together the flour, cocoa powder, baking powder, cinnamon, and salt. Stir the dry ingredients into the chocolate mixture until combined. Spread the chocolate batter out to the edges of the prepared baking sheet in an even layer and smooth the top. Bake the chocolate wafer until the center is just set but not dry, about 15 minutes. Allow the wafer to cool in the baking sheet for 15 minutes.

4. Run a knife around the edge of the chocolate wafer. Cover the baking sheet with a cutting board and invert. Peel off the parchment paper and allow the wafer to cool completely.

5. Cut the chocolate wafer in half to form two 7½-by-10-inch rectangles. Spread the coffee ice cream evenly on one of the rectangles and cover it with the other rectangle. Poke a few holes in the top of the ice cream sandwich with a fork or a toothpick for decoration. Wrap the ice cream sandwich in plastic wrap and freeze it until firm, at least 2 hours.

6. To serve, cut the ice cream sandwich into eight triangles. Drizzle the coffee sauce in a spiral onto each of eight dessert plates. Set one ice cream sandwich triangle in the center of each of the plates and spoon some of the warm chocolate sauce over the top of each triangle.

—ALI SEEDSMAN

CHOCOLATE SAUCE

MAKES ENOUGH FOR 8 SANDWICHES

1   tablespoon unsalted butter
⅔   cup heavy cream
6   tablespoons milk
¼   cup brown sugar
¼   cup plus 1 tablespoon unsweetened cocoa, sifted

In a small saucepan, melt the butter in the cream and the milk over moderate heat. Stir in the brown sugar and boil, stirring occasionally, until the mixture is slightly thickened, about 3 minutes. Remove the pan from the heat and then whisk in the cocoa until the sauce is smooth.

COFFEE SAUCE

MAKES ENOUGH FOR 8 SANDWICHES

⅔   cup brewed espresso
1⅓   cups plus 2 tablespoons sugar

In a small saucepan, combine the espresso and the sugar and bring the mixture to a boil. Cook over moderately low heat until the coffee syrup is slightly thickened and coats the back of a spoon, about 18 minutes. Remove the pan from the heat. The sauce will continue to thicken as it cools.

MAKE IT AHEAD

The sandwiches can be made ahead and frozen for up to two days. You can also refrigerate the chocolate sauce for up to two days; rewarm it before serving.

FROZEN CAFFÈ LATTE

Caffè latte granita is a wonderful dessert and coffee combination. Or, imitate the Sicilians and have it with breakfast instead of hot espresso.

8 SERVINGS

½ cup sugar

3 cups freshly brewed espresso or strong coffee

1 cup whole milk

1. Chill a 13-by-9-inch baking dish, preferably metal, in the freezer. In a medium bowl, stir the sugar into the coffee until dissolved. Let the mixture cool completely. Stir in the milk.

2. Pour the coffee mixture into the chilled baking dish. Freeze until ice crystals form around the edges, about 30 minutes. Stir well to incorporate the ice. Continue freezing, stirring every 30 minutes (see How to Stir Granitas, page 253), until all the liquid freezes completely, about 3 hours. Spoon the granita into bowls and serve.

—MICHELE SCICOLONE

MEXICAN CHOCOLATE SUNDAES

This rich sauce, made with almond- and cinnamon-flavored sweet Mexican chocolate, can be combined instead with vanilla ice cream and soda water to make an ice cream soda.

4 SERVINGS

6 ounces Mexican chocolate,* such as Ibarra, chopped

2 tablespoons unsalted butter

¾ cup heavy cream

Vanilla, coffee, or chocolate ice cream, for serving

*Available at specialty food stores and many supermarkets

In a medium bowl set over a saucepan of simmering water, melt the chocolate and the butter in the cream, stirring occasionally, until smooth. Do not let the sauce boil. Serve the sauce warm or at room temperature, with the ice cream.

—TRACEY SEAMAN

WALNUT CARAMEL SUNDAES

Heat the cream while the caramel cooks so that it can be added as soon as the caramel is removed from the heat, otherwise the sauce may burn.

4 SERVINGS

⅔ cup walnut halves

½ cup sugar

¼ cup water

½ cup heavy cream

   Pinch salt

1 pint vanilla ice cream

1. Heat the oven to 400°. Toast the walnut halves until fragrant, about 5 minutes. Coarsely chop the toasted walnuts.

2. In a medium heavy saucepan, combine the sugar with the water. Bring the mixture to a boil over moderately high heat and boil (brushing down the sides of the saucepan occasionally with a pastry brush dipped in water to dissolve any sugar crystals) until the sugar turns a rich, tea-like brown, about 7 minutes.

3. Meanwhile, in a small saucepan, bring the cream and the salt just to a boil over moderate heat. Slowly pour the hot cream into the caramel and stir gently until combined. Be careful because the caramel may spatter. Stir in the chopped toasted walnuts and let cool.

4. Scoop the vanilla ice cream into four tall glasses or small bowls. Spoon the walnut caramel sauce on top.

—BOB CHAMBERS

CANDIED GINGER CANNOLI SANDWICHES

At Mesa Grill in New York City, Wayne Harley Brachman uses the unlikely combination of flour tortillas, mascarpone cheese, and candied ginger to create a deliciously rich and surprisingly easy dessert. If you don't have a four-inch round pastry cutter, use a large can or a wide glass.

4 SERVINGS

4   8- or 9-inch flour tortillas

2   tablespoons granulated sugar

1   teaspoon cinnamon
    Vegetable oil, for frying

1   cup mascarpone cheese (½ pound), at room temperature

⅓   cup plus 1 teaspoon confectioners' sugar

2   ounces candied ginger, chopped

½   teaspoon vanilla extract

1. Using a 4-inch round pastry cutter, cut out two circles from each tortilla. In a small bowl, combine the granulated sugar and cinnamon.

2. In a medium frying pan, heat ¾ inch of vegetable oil over moderate heat until very hot but not smoking. Add two or three tortilla rounds and fry, pressing them down in the oil with a slotted spoon, for 20 seconds. Let the rounds rise to the surface and cook until lightly golden on the bottom, about 1 minute. Turn the rounds over and cook until golden, about 30 seconds longer. Transfer to paper towels and generously sprinkle the tops with some of the cinnamon sugar. Repeat with the remaining tortilla rounds and cinnamon sugar.

3. In a medium bowl, combine the mascarpone cheese, the ⅓ cup confectioners' sugar, the candied ginger, and vanilla.

4. Arrange four tortilla rounds, sugared sides down, on a work surface. Spoon one-quarter of the filling on each round and top with the remaining rounds, sugared sides up. Sift the remaining 1 teaspoon confectioners' sugar on top and transfer to individual plates.

—WAYNE HARLEY BRACHMAN

MAKE IT AHEAD

The fried tortillas and the mascarpone filling can be made up to four hours ahead and the sandwiches assembled at the last minute. The mascarpone filling must be covered and refrigerated but the tortilla rounds are fine at room temperature.

WHITE CHOCOLATE ICE CREAM IN PECAN LACE COOKIE CUPS

White chocolate lovers beware: This rich, sweet, silky smooth ice cream from The Trellis in Williamsburg, Virginia, is addictive. It's served in shaped cookie cups, and garnished with rolled cookie "cigars". Tangy blood oranges make a striking substitute for the navels used here.

8 SERVINGS

¾ pound white chocolate, chopped

3¼ cups milk

¾ cup sugar

3 large eggs

Pecan Lace Cookies, opposite page

4 medium navel oranges

4 ounces semisweet chocolate, chopped

Fresh mint sprigs, for garnish

1. In a medium bowl, combine the white chocolate with ¼ cup of the milk and cover tightly with plastic wrap. Set the bowl over a large saucepan filled with about an inch of simmering water and let stand until the chocolate melts, about 10 minutes. Remove the bowl from the heat and stir until smooth.

2. In a medium nonreactive saucepan, bring the remaining 3 cups milk and ¼ cup of the sugar to a boil over moderately high heat, whisking occasionally.

3. In a large bowl, beat the eggs with the remaining ½ cup sugar at high speed until thick, about 3 minutes. Gradually whisk in the boiling milk. Return the custard to the saucepan and cook over moderate heat, stirring constantly, until it reaches 185°, about 3 minutes. Strain into a bowl set in a larger bowl of ice water. Whisk in the melted white chocolate. Let stand, whisking occasionally, until chilled, about 45 minutes.

4. Freeze the custard in an ice cream maker according to the manufacturer's instructions. Scrape the ice cream into a chilled container and freeze until firm, about 4 hours.

5. Using a zester, strip the zest from two of the oranges. Alternatively, use a vegetable peeler to remove the zest in long strips, then cut the strips into thin matchsticks. Using a sharp knife, peel the four oranges, removing all the bitter white pith. Slice the oranges crosswise ⅜-inch thick.

6. To assemble, place each cookie cup on a dessert plate and arrange four or five overlapping orange slices alongside.

Spoon three scoops of ice cream into each cookie cup and sprinkle the orange zest and chopped semisweet chocolate on top. Garnish with a cigar cookie and mint sprig.

—MARCEL DESAULNIERS

PECAN LACE COOKIES

MAKES 8 COOKIE CUPS AND 8 COOKIE CIGARS

⅔ cup light-brown sugar

½ cup light corn syrup

¼ pound unsalted butter

1 cup pecans, chopped

⅔ cup cake flour

1. Heat the oven to 325°. In a medium saucepan, bring the brown sugar, corn syrup, and butter to a boil over moderate heat. Remove from the heat and stir in the pecans and flour.

2. Make the cookie cups two at a time: Drop 2 tablespoons of the batter onto a nonstick cookie sheet, allowing room for it to spread to 5 inches. Bake in the middle of the oven until golden brown, about 12 minutes. Let cool for 30 seconds. Carefully remove the cookies with a wide metal spatula and invert each one on a 19-ounce can. (If the cookies harden, rewarm them in the oven for 30 seconds.) Working quickly, loosely mold the cookies around the cans. Repeat until you have eight cookie cups.

3. For the cigar cookies, drop teaspoons of the remaining batter about 3 inches apart on the cookie sheet. Bake until golden brown, about 8 minutes. Let cool 15 seconds. One by one, scrape up the cookies and roll them around a chopstick. Repeat until you have eight cigars.

PRUNE ICE CREAM WITH ARMAGNAC

Andre Daguin is the chef-hotelier of the Hotel de France in Auch, in south-west France. One of Daguin's signature dishes, this dessert of prune ice cream flavored with Armagnac elevates stewed prunes to cult status. This recipe has been adapted from Daguin's book, *Foie Gras, Magret, and Other Good Food from Gascony* (Random House).

MAKES ABOUT 4 CUPS

1¼ cups pitted prunes (about 7 ounces)

½ cup Armagnac

2 cups milk

½ cup sugar

4 large egg yolks

1. In a small saucepan, combine the prunes with the Armagnac, cover and simmer over low heat until the prunes are soft, about 5 minutes. Remove the pan from the heat and set aside, covered, until cool. Transfer the prunes and Armagnac to a food processor and puree.

2. In a heavy medium saucepan, combine the milk with ¼ cup of the sugar. Cook over moderate heat, stirring, until bubbles appear around the edge. Remove from the heat.

3. In a heatproof bowl, whisk the egg yolks with the remaining ¼ cup of sugar until the eggs are pale and thick. Gradually whisk in the hot milk. Pour the mixture back into the saucepan and cook over moderate heat, whisking constantly, until the custard reaches 175° on a candy thermome-

ter, about 5 minutes. Do not boil, or it will curdle. Immediately pour the custard into a heatproof bowl and stir often until cooled to room temperature. Cover and refrigerate until well chilled.

4. Add the prune puree to the custard, transfer to an ice cream maker, and freeze according to the manufacturer's instructions. Pack the ice cream into a chilled container and freeze for up to three days.

—ANDRE DAGUIN

SPICY PECAN ICE CREAM

A hint of cayenne pepper spices up caramelized pecans in this unusual and delicious ice cream. Serve the ice cream on its own or with plain pound cake.

MAKES ABOUT 3 CUPS

1½ cups heavy cream

½ cup half-and-half

½ vanilla bean, split lengthwise

5 large egg yolks

¾ cup sugar

2 tablespoons dark rum

4 tablespoons unsalted butter

½ cup pecan halves

¼ teaspoon cayenne pepper

Pinch salt

1. In a medium saucepan, combine the cream and half-and-half. Scrape the seeds from the vanilla bean into the pan and add the pod of the bean. Bring just to a simmer over moderately high heat. Meanwhile, in a bowl, whisk the egg yolks with ½ cup of the sugar. Gradually whisk in the hot cream. Pour the mixture back into the saucepan and cook over moderately high heat, stirring constantly, until the custard thickens and coats the back of a spoon, about 5 minutes. Strain into a bowl and let cool. Stir in the rum.

2. In a small frying pan, melt the remaining ¼ cup sugar over moderately high heat until golden brown, about 5 minutes. Stir in the butter and the pecan halves and cook, stirring constantly, until the pecans are thoroughly coated. Spread the nuts on a plate and let cool. Sprinkle with the cayenne and salt.

3. Break the spiced pecans into small pieces and stir them into the custard. Transfer to an ice cream maker and freeze according to the manufacturer's instructions. Pack the ice cream into a chilled container and freeze for up to three days.

—SCOTT HOWELL

CREAMY CARAMELS

Use this recipe as a base and vary it as you like according to our suggestions on the next page for walnut-, coffee- and spice-flavored caramel candies. Don't refrigerate caramels or they get soggy.

MAKES 64 CARAMELS

1 tablespoon canola or other flavorless vegetable oil

1½ cups heavy cream

1 cup light corn syrup

¾ cup sugar

3 tablespoons unsalted butter, at room temperature

2 teaspoons vanilla extract

1. Line an 8-inch-square metal baking pan with aluminum foil, extending the foil over the sides of the pan. Thoroughly coat the aluminum foil with the canola oil.

2. In a heavy 3-quart saucepan, combine the cream, corn syrup, and sugar. Stir continuously over moderate heat with a long-handled wooden spoon (brushing the inside of the saucepan occasionally with a pastry brush dipped in water to dissolve any sugar crystals) until the sugar is dissolved, about 5 minutes.

3. Raise the heat to moderately high and place a candy thermometer in the pan. Continue to cook the syrup, stirring constantly, until the temperature registers 250°, about 30 minutes.

4. Remove the saucepan from the heat and quickly stir in the butter and the vanilla. Pour the caramel into the prepared baking pan and let it cool to room temperature, at least 2 hours.

5. Use the ends of the foil to lift the caramel from the pan. Peel the foil off the back of the caramel. Coat the blade of a large chef's knife with oil. Cut the caramel into eight equal strips, and then cut each strip into eight pieces. Arrange the caramels, without touching one another, between sheets of waxed paper, or wrap the caramels individually in waxed paper.

—CAROLE BLOOM

VARIATIONS

• When stirring in the butter and the vanilla in Step 4, add 1½ cups toasted and coarsely chopped walnuts or unskinned almonds.

• Dissolve 1 tablespoon plus 1 teaspoon of instant espresso powder in 1 tablespoon of warm water. When stirring in the butter and vanilla in Step 4, add the espresso.

• Reduce the vanilla to ½ teaspoon. In a small bowl, mix ½ teaspoon each of cinnamon, ground ginger, and ground allspice, ¼ teaspoon freshly grated nutmeg and ¹⁄₁₆ teaspoon ground cardamom. Add when stirring in the butter and vanilla in Step 4.

MAKE IT AHEAD

The caramels can be made ahead. The candies will keep in an airtight container at room temperature for up to two weeks.

PRALINES

Orange zest adds a delicious, tangy taste of citrus to these pralines. They need your undivided attention for almost an hour, but they're worth it.

MAKES ABOUT 4 DOZEN PRALINES

4 cups heavy cream

2 cups sugar

Finely grated zest of 1 orange (about 2 teaspoons)

4 cups shelled pecans

MAKE IT AHEAD

The pralines can be stored between sheets of waxed paper in an airtight tin for up to one week.

---

1. Lightly oil four baking sheets. In a large heavy saucepan, combine the cream, sugar, and orange zest. Bring to a boil over moderately high heat, stirring constantly with a wooden spoon. Cook, stirring constantly, until the mixture is thick, bubbly, and golden brown, and registers 240° on a candy thermometer; this can take up to 50 minutes. Add the pecans and cook, stirring, for 3 minutes.

2. Meanwhile, place a large bowl of cold water in the sink. Remove the saucepan from the heat and place the bottom in the cold water for 5 seconds to stop the cooking. With two spoons, drop tablespoon-size pralines 1 inch apart on the oiled baking sheets.

—JAMIE SHANNON

COGNAC ALMOND TRUFFLES

After enjoying these chocolate truffles at our house, our guests are always delighted to receive a small box of them to take home. This is based on a recipe that appears in *Jacques Pépin's The Art of Cooking*.

MAKES ABOUT 3 DOZEN

½ pound bittersweet chocolate, chopped

4 tablespoons unsalted butter

2 large egg yolks

1 tablespoon cognac

¾ cup toasted sliced almonds

1. Melt the chocolate in a bowl over a saucepan filled with about an inch of simmering water. Stir in the butter until melted. Off the heat, whisk in the egg yolks until glossy. Add the cognac and refrigerate until solid.

2. Using a teaspoon, scoop small balls of the truffle mixture onto a baking sheet lined with waxed paper. Roll the truffles between your hands, then roll the truffles in the almonds.

—JACQUES PÉPIN

MAKE IT AHEAD

The truffles can be made ahead and refrigerated for up to four days

Index

Page numbers in **boldface** indicate photographs

Contributors

Joe Abuso is the chef/owner of Abuso Catering Company in Houston, Texas.

Jody Adams is a chef, food writer, cooking teacher, and cookbook author.

Ann Chantal Altman is the executive chef for the Joseph E. Seagram Company in New York City and teaches at Peter Kump's School of Culinary Arts in New York City.

Nancy Baggett, cookbook author and food writer, is the author of *The International Cookie Cookbook* and *The International Chocolate Cookbook* (both from Stewart, Tabori & Chang).

Karen Barker is a pastry chef and co-owner of Magnolia Grill in Durham, North Carolina.

Brigit Legere Binns is a cookbook author, food writer and editor, and menu consultant. She is the author of *Polenta* (Chronical) and the forthcoming *The Complete Idiot's Guide to Low-Fat Cooking* (Macmillan).

Carole Bloom, pastry chef, cookbook author, food writer, is the author of *All About Chocolate* and the forthcoming *The Complete Idiot's Guide to Cookies* (both from Macmillan), due out in 1999.

Shelley Boris is a chef, caterer, and food writer in Garrison, New York.

Michelle Bracken is a pastry chef and chef/owner of The Ultimate Cake and **Bill Bracken** is the executive chef at The Peninsula in Beverly Hills.

Wayne Harley Brachman, pastry chef at Mesa Grill/Bolo in New York City, is the author of *Cakes & Cowpokes*, whose forthcoming book on desserts (both from William Morrow) is due out in 2000.

Bob Chambers is the executive chef for J. & W. Seligman Investment in New York City.

Julia Child, well-known cookbook author, food writer, and cooking teacher, is the host of her own television series.

Shirley Corriher, cookbook author, food writer, teacher, and consultant, is the author of *CookWise* and the forthcoming *BakeWise* (both from William Morrow), due out in 2001.

Peggy Cullen is a New York-based baker, candymaker, and food writer.

Sanford D'Amato is a chef/owner at The Sanford Restaurant in Milwaukee, Wisconsin.

Andre Daguin is the author of *Foie Gras, Magrets, and Other Good Foods from Gascony* (Random House). He is working on a new book.

James Denevan, a chef and artist, is now working on a cookbook using his illustrations.

Marcel Desaulniers is a chef and author of many cookbooks, including *Salad Days, Desserts to Die For, The Trellis Cookbook* (all from Simon & Schuster), and *Death by Chocolate* (Rizzoli). His two forthcoming books on chocolate desserts (both from William Morrow) will be published in 2000 and 2001.

Jonathan Eismann is a chef and restaurateur. He is the chef/owner of Pacific Time and Pacific Time Cafe in Miami Beach and is working on a cookbook.

Jim Fobel is a food writer, cooking teacher, and author of eight books, including *Jim Fobel's Big Flavors*, 1996 winner of the James Beard Award for Best General Cookbook, and *Jim Fobel's Casseroles* (Clarkson Potter).

Sarah Fritschner is a food writer and author of *Express Lane Cookbook* and *Vegetarian Express Lane Cookbook* (both from Chapters).

Fran Gage owned the critically acclaimed Pâtisserie Française in San Francisco. She is teaching, consulting, and writing. Her essays on food with recipes will be published in 1999 (Sasquatch Books).

Dorie Greenspan is a cookbook author and food writer. She has written five books including *Baking with Julia* (William Morrow), the cookbook that accompanies Julia Child's PBS series, *Desserts by Pierre Hermé*, and in 2000, *Chocolate Desserts by Pierre Hermé* (both from Little Brown).

Ken Haedrich is a freelance writer and author of six cookbooks (all from Bantam) including *Home For The Holidays*, for which he won the Julia Child Cookbook Award. His most recent book is *Feeding the Healthy Vegetarian Family*.

Fatèma Hal is a food writer and chef based in Paris, France.

Gordon Hamersley, a chef and cooking teacher, is at work on a cookbook.

Marcella Hazan is the owner of the cooking school Master Class with Marcella Hazan in Venice, Italy, and a renowned cookbook author, most recently of *Marcella Cucina* (HarperCollins).

Larry Hayden is a food writer and pastry chef at Barefoot Contessa Fine Foods in East Hampton, New York. His forthcoming book on desserts (Scribner) is due out in the spring of 1999.

Maida Heatter is the acclaimed author of seven dessert books. *Maida Heatter's Book of Great Desserts* was inducted into the James Beard Cookbook Hall of Fame in 1998. *Maida Heatter's Book of Great Chocolate Desserts* and *Maida Heatter's Great Cookies* were both James Beard Award winners. She is working on the revised 25th anniversary edition of her first book due in 1999 (Andrews and McMeel Publishing).

Peter Hoffman is chef and owner of Savoy restaurant in New York City.

Joseph Keller is a cooking teacher and part owner/executive chef of Woodbox Inn in Nantucket, Massachusettes and Bouchon in Napa Valley, California.

Melissa Kelly is a chef who is working on a book with recipes of the Old Chatham Sheepherding Company.

Marcia Kiesel is the associate test-kitchen director at FOOD & WINE magazine and the author of *Simple Art of Vietnamese Cooking* (Prentice Hall Press).

Susan Lantzius is a pastry chef and food writer.

Emily Luchetti, former pastry chef at Stars in San Francisco, is now the pastry chef at Farallon. She is the author of *Four-Star Desserts* (HarperCollins).

Sheila Lukins is the author of *One USA Cookbook, Sheila Lukins Around the World*, and co-author of *The Silver Palate Cookbook, The New Basics*, and *The Silver Palate Good Times Cookbook* (all from Workman).

Stephanie Lyness is a food writer, cookbook author, and cooking teacher. Her most recent book is *Cooking with Steam* (Hearst Books).

Waldy Malouf is a restaurateur, chef, and cookbook author of the forthcoming book, *Magnificent Meats* (Harvard Common Press), due out in Fall 1998.

Lydie Marshall is a cookbook author, food writer, and owner and cooking teacher at A la Bonne Cocotte en Provence in Nyons, France. She is the author of *Chez Nous* and *A Passion for Potatoes* (both from HarperCollins).

Alice Medrich is a cookbook author, cooking teacher, consultant, and dessert chef. Her cookbooks include the James Beard Award-winning *Chocolate and the Art of Low Fat Dessert* and *Cocolat* (both from Warner Books). She is working on a book of cookie recipes.

Pamela Morgan is the owner of Flavors Catering & Carryout in New York City, and the author of *Pamela Morgan's Flavors* (Viking).

Jan Newberry is a cookbook editor, author, food writer, and FOOD & WINE columnist.

Bradley Ogden is the chef/owner of Lark Creek Inn in Larkspur, California and One Market Restaurant in San Francisco. He wrote *Breakfast, Lunch and Dinner* (Random House), and is working on his next cookbook.

Grace Parisi, test-kitchen associate at FOOD & WINE magazine, is the author of *Summer/Winter Pasta* (Quill).

Jacques Pépin is the celebrated host of award-winning cooking shows on national public television, master chef, food columnist, cooking teacher, and author of 16 cookbooks.

Colette Peters, owner of Colette's Cakes in New York City, is a cookbook author, cake designer, and teacher. She is the author of *Colette's Wedding Cakes, Colette's Cakes, Colette's Christmas,* and the forthcoming *Colette's Birthday Cakes* (all from Little Brown), due out in 1999.

Joanna Pruess is a food writer and author of the forthcoming *D'Artagnan's Glorious Game Cookbook* in 1999 (Little Brown).

Anne Quatrano and **Clifford Harrison** are chef/owners of Bacchanalia in Atlanta, Georgia.

Ruth Rogers and **Rose Gray** are chefs and the authors of *Rogers Gray Italian Country Cookbook* (Random House) and *The Cafe Cookbook* (Broadway Books).

Maury Rubin is the chef/owner of The City Bakery in New York City and author of *The Book of Tarts* (William Morrow). He is launching a new retail business "Drink City" and "Maury's Cookie Doughs," a packaged line.

Peggy Ryan is the chef/owner of Va Pensiero Restaurant in Evanston, Illinois.

Andrew Schloss is a cooking teacher, food writer, and author of *Fifty Ways to Cook Most Everything* (Simon & Schuster), *One-Pot Chocolate Desserts,* and *One-Pot Cookies* (both from Broadway Books).

Michele Scicolone, cookbook author, food writer, and cooking teacher, is the author of *A Fresh Taste of Italy* (Broadway Books), *La Dolce Vita* (Morrow), and *The Antipasto Table* (Ecco Press). Her latest book is *Pizza—Anyway You Slice It!* (Broadway Books).

Mary Seaman is a grandmother and home baker who makes at least 1 million brownies a year.

Tracey Seaman is a food writer and food editor for Great American Home Cooking magazine. The author

of *Tunafish Gourmet* (Villard), she is working on a cookie cookbook.

Jamie Shannon is the executive chef at Commander's Palace in New Orleans, Louisiana.

Lindsey Shere was the pastry chef of Chez Panisse in Berkeley, California for twenty-six years. She is the author of *Chez Panisse Desserts* (Random House) and is part-owner of the Downtown Bakery and Creamery in Healdsburg, California.

Lydia Shire is the chef/owner of Biba and Pignoli Restaurants in Boston, Massachusetts.

Martha Rose Shulman, cookbook author and cooking teacher, is the author of *Mediterranean Light, Provençal Light* (both from Bantam), and *The Vegetarian Feast* (HarperCollins). She is working on her next book, *Light Basics,* due out in January 1999.

Kristine M. Smith is a pastry chef and cooking teacher at Blackberry Farm Hotel in Walland, Tennessee.

Rori Spinelli is a professional cook, food writer, and food stylist who is based in New York City.

Joachim Splichal is chef/owner of Patina restaurant in Los Angeles, and author of *Joachim Splichal's Patina Cookbook* (Collins).

Diane Sturgis is the test-kitchen director of FOOD & WINE magazine.

Judith Sutton is a food writer and consultant, cookbook editor, and author of *Champagne & Caviar & Other Delicacies* (Black Dog & Leventhal).

John Martin Taylor, owner of Hoppin' John's, a culinary bookstore and cooking school in Charleston, South Carolina, is a food writer and the author of *The Fearless Frying Cookbook* (Workman).

Jacques Torres is the pastry chef at Le Cirque 2000, cookbook author, teacher, and consultant. His books include *Dessert Circus* and *Dessert Circus at Home* (both from William Morrow). He is the host of the TV series *Dessert Circus with Jacques Torres.*

Patricia Wells is a food writer, cookbook author, and

cooking teacher. Her books include *Patricia Wells At Home in Provence* (Scribner), and the forthcoming updated edition of *The Food Lover's Guide to Paris* in 1999 and *The Paris Cookbook* in 2000.

Anne Willan, cookbook author and teacher, is the President and Founder of Ecole de Cuicine La Varenne. The author of *Cook it Right* (Reader's Digest), her forthcoming book, *Anne Willan's Burgundy* (Clarkson Potter), is due out in 1999.

We would also like to thank the following individuals and restaurants for their contributions to this cookbook:

Anne Americk, Paul Bocuse, Julia Califano, Jessie Cromwell, Marilyn Descours, Florence Fabricant, James Henahan, Pierre Hermé, Scott Howell, Richard Sax, Ali Seedsman, Heidi Stelle, Evan Kleiman, and The French Loaf, in Columbus, Ohio.

PHOTO CREDITS

William Abranowicz/A+C Anthology: 262; **Melanie Acevedo:** 130, 132; **Edward Addeo:** 304; **Bill Bettencourt:** 140, 152, 158; **Beatriz Da Costa:** 18; **Reed Davis:** 104; **Mark Ferri:** 300; **John Reed Forsman:** 254, 256; **Matthew Hranek:** 24, 52; **Maura McEvoy:** 40; **Michael McLaughlin:** 200; **Victoria Pearson:** 8, 242; **Alan Richardson:** 6, 10, 12 78; **Carin and David Riley:** 6, 82, 90, 230, 294; **Ellen Silverman:** 118, 124; **Jerry Simpson:** 34; **Laurie Smith:** 214; **Bill Steele/A+C Anthology:** 240; **Ann Stratton:** 36, 46, 66, 98, 108, 168, 198, 234, 236, 246, 272; **Mark Thomas:** 2, 54, 174, 182, 186; **Lisa Charles Watson:** 170; **Elizabeth Watt:** 5, 278, 284